THE WEST BANK HANDBOOK

A Political Lexicon

Meron Benvenisti

with Ziad Abu-Zayed and Danny Rubinstein

WESTVIEW PRESS
Boulder, Colorado

The Jerusalem Post

WESTVIEW PRESS
Frederick A. Praeger, Publisher
5500 Central Avenue
Boulder, Colorado 80301

ISBN 0-8133-0473-3
LC 86-50979

THE WEST BANK HANDBOOK

Copyright © 1986

Meron Benvenisti

Distributed by The Jerusalem Post, POB 81, Jerusalem 91000, Israel.

The views expressed in this publication are those of the authors and do not necessarily reflect the views of the staff or editors of The Jerusalem Post.

Printed in Israel.

ISBN 965-310-001-7

Alphabetic Table of Contents

E.

FOREWORD

Our intention in compiling this glossary of social, economic, institutional, legal, cultural and political topics relating to the West Bank is to demystify the treatment of this highly contentious subject. Our long association with the area, and especially with Israeli-Palestinian interaction, has taught us that it is almost invariably perceived in ideological, political, indeed in conflictual terms. These perceptions tend to blur the multi-dimensional nature of the interactions and to neglect the fast-changing realities on the ground. It seems to us appropriate to take stock of these realities in the form of an alphabetical listing of entries, covering such diverse topics as curfews and soccer games, national accounts and extra-parliamentary groups, deportations and student unions.

We embarked on this venture mainly to acquaint those directly involved, namely Jews and Arabs living in the Holy Land, with the facts as well as with the institutions and agencies affecting their daily lives. This is because we have come to realize how little they know or, indeed, wish to know, about them. Ignorance of the facts, exclusionary perceptions and a view of the other side as a menacing monolith, characterize Israeli and Palestinian attitudes. Israelis are surprised to discover that Palestinians possess welfare, cultural and sports organizations. Many Israelis are totally unaware of the ramifications and implications of the dual system by which Israel governs the territories. Palestinians themselves are unfamiliar with the bureaucracy that governs them, and the departmental in-fighting that forms the backdrop to many of the developments affecting their day-to-day existence. They also lack reliable data concerning their own community.

This handbook is a translation of the Hebrew-Arabic original work, now being edited for publication. The choice of entries is in no way random. It is carefully selected, based on our experience of what people want to know when they approach the West Bank Data Project for information. The material is drawn from the data accumulated in the Project's retrieval system. Our analysis and conclusions are, we believe, fully supported by the sources at our disposal. We intend however to revise, and update the information on a continuing basis.

Ziad Abu Zayad, Danny Rubinstein and I served as the editorial board of the Handbook. In addition Mr. Abu Zayad contributed entries on Palestinian institutions and Mr. Rubinstein, on Israeli political groups. Other contributors include Moshe Negbi, Amir Oren, Avner Halperin, Erela Brilliant-Levi, and Usamah Halabi. The English translation was done by Jeffrey Green and Haim Weizmann. Marcia Kretzmer edited the Handbook and made additional contributions to the text. David Horowitz prepared the manuscript for publication. Word processing was done by Hannah Orgel. The final version of this collective undertaking was written by the undersigned who takes full responsibility for all value judgments and errors.

Meron Benvenisti
Jerusalem, March 1986

AGRICULTURE (ARAB)

Until 1981/82 agriculture was the most important and stable sector in the West Bank economy. It's share of the Gross National Product (GNP) varied between 22–34 percent and its contribution to the Gross Domestic Product (GDP) was 33–40 percent. This stability was attained despite the decline in the number of those employed in the sector – 42% of Palestinians employed in the West Bank to about 30% at the beginning of the 1980's. The average rate of increase in value of agricultural production between 1968–1981 amounted to 9.6 percent. Since 1983, however, the share of agriculture in the West Bank GDP shows a continuous decline. The value of agricultural production in 1984 was about $250 million, compared with about $300 million in 1983 and $320 million in 1982.

The production-employment ratio and the constant increase in the value of production between 1968–1981 points to an appreciable rise in productivity. Productivity has risen due to changes in methods of cultivation, increased mechanization, technological innovations, investments in expertise and capital, a decrease in disguised unemployment in agriculture, phasing out of marginal cultivated areas, and replacement of low-value by high-value cash crops. There was growth in the value of purchased inputs: the use of fertilizer quadrupled, the number of tractors more than quadrupled. As a result, there was a dramatic increase in rural family income. Income per rural family head was $133 in 1966, $666 in 1974, and $950 in 1979 (See STANDARD OF LIVING).

All these developments came about without any radical change in the resource base of Palestinian agriculture. Arable areas did not increase, and irrigated areas also remained at the 1967 level of 100,000 dunams (See WATER). Private and public investment in agriculture remained low (See PUBLIC INVESTMENT). From the middle of the 1970s there was a marked decrease in government assistance. Total loans available to farmers shrank, and were eventually completely eliminated; the number of agricultural advisers went into steady decline; no aid has been given to the regional cooperatives; marketing has remained in the hands of local wholesalers in the large cities. Employment in Israel did not affect agriculture until the middle of the 1970s, and even increased its productivity by eliminating disguised unemployment. Towards the end of the decade, however, the shortage of workers slowed growth in agricultural production.

The minimal changes in the agricultural sector's resource base reflect intentional Israeli strategy. This is characterized by Israeli efforts to improve conditions as far as possible within the framework of existing resources, without any essential changes. The aim is to develop Palestinian agriculture without introducing structural changes such as investments in physical infrastructure, agrarian reform, or support systems like marketing or credit. Palestinian agriculture developed successfully within the constraints of the existing system. It is possible to argue, however, that actual growth, measured against a low base point (primitive conditions under Jordan), is not that significant. It would be more significant to measure the development achieved by the "improvement" policy with the probable results of an alternative strategy, i.e. structural and fundamental change in the resource base, re-allocation of land and water resources, capital investment, regional support systems, marketing and improvements in terms of external trade. Israeli strategy did not make this possible, as the resources available to the agricultural sector were frozen and all growth potential was transferred to the Israeli economy and the Jewish settlers in the West Bank.

Palestinian agriculture was allowed to develop only insofar as it would not affect Israeli agriculture, and on condition that its development would not involve a fiscal or economic drain on the Israeli economy or government. West Bank agriculture has been made to fit into the Israeli system and adjust itself to the demands of the "common market" created after the occupation. Naturally, the stronger and more developed economy gained the advantage over the weak and undeveloped one.

West Bank agriculture was thus forced into unequal competition with Israeli agriculture, capital intensive, subsidized and protected by administrative orders. The total dependence of West Bank agriculture on the Israeli economy is reflected in the fluctuations of growth rates during the occupation years, which always followed fluctuations in the growth rates in the Israeli economy. When the latter burgeoned, so did production on the West Bank, and when there was a halt in Israeli growth, agricultural growth rates in the West Bank also slowed.

Export to Jordan, the alternative outlet for West Bank production, is dependent on the policies of the neighboring state. While this export is of considerable importance to the West Bank, it does not encourage growth. The volume of export has remained at nearly the same absolute level as it was in 1966. With the development of a flourishing agricultural region in the eastern Jordan Valley, import quotas from the West Bank were set, creating added difficulties for the development of Palestinian agricultural export.

It seems that in the mid 80's Palestinian farming could not function properly any longer within the constraints imposed by Israel and its productivity declined. Due to the centrality of cultivation in the Palestinian economy, this is bound to have a long term impact on the viability of the entire Palestinian sector and on Palestinian society at large.

AGRICULTURAL LAND USE (ARAB)

In 1983, the area under Palestinian cultivation in the West Bank totalled 1,722 millions dunams, comprising over a million dunams of orchards (including 750,000 dunams of olives), about 550,000 dunams of field crops, 100,000 dunams of vegetables, and 50,000 dunams of watermelons. In 1984 the cultivated area was 584 million dunams, a decline of 8.0 percent from 1983. The decline resulted mostly from a reduction in field crops following a drought year.

It should be noted that since 1967 there has been no substantial change in the extent of the cultivated area. In 1968 the cultivated area came to 1,683 million dunams and in 1975 to 1,626 million dunams. From 1966 to 1983 the irrigated area too, stayed between 80,000 and 100,000 dunams. This relative stability refutes the contention that there has been a drastic decline in cultivation as a result of land confiscation and closure. However, this stability, and in particular the lack of growth in irrigated areas, indicates that the agricultural resource base has been frozen at 1967 levels (see above). Beside agricultural cultivation, a million-and-a-half dunams were used in 1983 as natural pasture.

AGRICULTURE (JEWISH)

Only a small portion of the Israeli West Bank settlements is engaged in agriculture. These settlements are concentrated in the Jordan Valley and in the Etzion bloc. According to the World Zionist Organization development plan, a total of 55,000 dunams is planned for agricultural cultivation, and 145,000 dunams of marginal lands for pasturage. In 1984 approximately 50,000 dunams were under cultivation.

This limited agricultural land use indicates that most settlements are planned on urban or suburban lines (See DEMOGRAPHY, (ISRAELI) BUILT-UP AREAS).

ALIGNMENT (PARTY)

A union of parties established in 1969 before the elections to the seventh Knesset, composed of the Israeli Labor Party (Mapai, Ahdut Ha'Avoda, and Rafi) and MAPAM. In 1977 the Alignment failed to gain a majority, and for the first time in 44 years it was relegated to the opposition. After

3

the elections to the eleventh Knesset, the Alignment returned to power in the framework of the National Unity Government.

The Alignment's Position On The West Bank (according to the 1984 party platform):

1. The Alignment is in favor of territorial compromise in Judea, Samaria, and the Gaza Strip in return for true peace and Arab recognition of Israel's permanent borders.

2. The Arabs must take Israel's security needs into consideration and allow it to maintain military and settlement presence on the Golan and in the Jordan Valley and a settlement buffer zone in the Katif region between Sinai and the Gaza Strip.

3. Jerusalem will remain united and remain the capital of Israel.

4. The Alignment opposes the establishment of an additional Palestinian state in the region controlled by the governments of Israel and Jordan. A solution of the Palestinian problem will be achieved within the framework of a Jordanian-Palestinian state.

ALLON PLAN

The peace proposal conceived by the late government minister Yigael Allon was submitted to several Israel cabinets for approval. It was presented in its initial version in July 1967, while amended versions were submitted in June 1968, December 1968, January 1969, and September 1970. The plan was never officially approved, but served until 1977 as a guideline for the deployment of Jewish settlements in the West Bank.

The guiding assumptions were: Israel must have defensible borders. These must be based on the Jordan River and the rift valley, and the Judean Desert. Defensible borders also require a chain of Jewish settlements which themselves must be under Israeli sovereignty, though without the annexation of a large Arab population (See DEFENSE STRATEGY).

According to the latest version of the plan (1970), the area annexed by Israel was to be a 20-kilometer-wide belt from the Jordan to the border of the Arab settlements on the mountain ridge, running southwards from Nablus to Hebron. The Greater Jerusalem area, from Nebi Samwil to Bethlehem, the Etzion bloc, the Judean Desert up to Hebron (including Kiryat Arba) and the Sam'u-Yata line were also to be included.

The densely populated Arab areas on the mountain ridge are intended as part of a Jordanian-Palestinian state based on Jordan's East Bank.

The northern part of the Gaza Strip, from the northern border to the Gaza River, is also to be handed over to this state. The areas to be returned to Jordanian sovereignty are not contiguous, but made up of three sections: 1) Samaria with a corridor (the "Jericho corridor") connecting it with the East Bank; 2) Judea, including the watershed line and the western slopes of Mt. Hebron, connected to Samaria by a "Jerusalem by-pass" (not under Jordanian sovereignty); and 3) Gaza, connected by a road (also not under Jordanian sovereignty) to Judea. The total area of these Jordanian cantons, according to the Allon Plan, is about 2.5 million dunams. In other words, under the Allon Plan, half of the total area of the West Bank and three quarters of the Gaza Strip are to be annexed to Israel.

The Allon Plan served as a basis for the Alignment platforms of 1974, 1977, and 1981, but unclear language such as "Jerusalem and its satellites" effectively allowed the expansion of settlement regions beyond it. The "thickening Jerusalem" plan of Minister of Housing Avraham Ofer (1974-75), broadened the areas of settlement on the highlands, beyond those detailed in the Allon Plan. According to the Ofer Plan, there were to be Jewish settlements north of Ramallah and south of Bethlehem. In 1976, Minister without Portfolio Israel Galili approved a number of settlements in western Samaria. King Hussein of Jordan, to whom the plan was presented by Yigal Allon himself, rejected every version of it. Nonetheless, the plan, with various amendments and additions, still serves as the basis of the "territorial compromise" plan of the Labour Party, and the plans of its associated settlement movements (See UNITED KIBBUTZ MOVEMENT, MOSHAVIM).

In 1971, there were 10 settlements within the borders sketched out in the Allon Plan. By 1981 there were 22, including 14 moshavim, 6 kibbutzim, and two NAHAL outposts. A further six settlements have been planned for the region. Total investment in the region by 1984 reached $150-200 million. There were 1,800 settlers in the area in 1975 and approximately the same number in 1981. In September 1985, within the area demarcated by the original Allon Plan (the Jordan and Dead Sea Valleys), there were 2,950 people and another 1,000 in the township of Ma'aleh Ephraim (See JORDAN VALLEY REGIONAL COUNCIL). The Allon Plan settlements suffer from a chronic shortage of settlers and a high turnover. The need to supply production resources and to develop water, land reclamation and marketing networks - all of which require tremendous capital investments - has delayed the development of an economic infrastructure. Most of the settlements have suffered economic crises, causing settlers to leave. The attention given by the settlement division under Likud leadership (See DROBLESS PLAN) to the mountain ridge running southwards from Nablus to Hebron effectively froze the development of the Allon Plan settlements. Their population growth potential has been put at 4,500-5,000 by 1992. Some 32,000 Palestinians live within the boundaries of the Allon Plan. The demographic balance is therefore 9:1 in favor of the Palestinians.

AMANA

The settlement movement of GUSH EMUNIM. It was founded in 1976 when Gush Emunim switched its priorities from protest activity to the establishment of settlements according to the Likud plan.

Amana created new forms of settlement - the COMMUNITY SETTLEMENT and the COMMUNITY VILLAGE, which, unlike the kibbutz or moshav, have no agricultural characteristics or objectives.

Since 1977, Amana has become a central factor in the settlement of the West Bank and Gaza Strip. Its activists, drawn from the leadership of Gush Emunim, have become leading economic and administrative personnel in the settlements and ISRAELI REGIONAL COUNCILS.

With the multiplication of West Bank settlements, they united in the Council of Judea, Samaria and Gaza (See YESHA).

Amana sees the settlement of the entire Land of Israel as its primary goal. It places particular emphasis on the founding of settlements on the highlands running from Nablus southwards to Hebron, and around and within areas densely populated by Palestinians. Because of the similarity between its views and those of the Likud, it won support from the Likud during that party's entire period in government. This backing was expressed in generous allocation of resources, both from the budget of the World Zionist Organization (See DROBLESS PLAN) and from government budgets.

For number of Amana settlements and settlers, see COMMUNITY SETTLEMENTS, COMMUNITY VILLAGES.

ARAB CHILDREN'S HOUSE (Dar al-Tifel al-Arabi)

A charitable organization founded in 1948 to absorb children orphaned in the war. The organization was established by 16 Jerusalem women whose goal was to set up schools and clubs for young people in general and for orphans in particular.

Today, the organization owns a large building in East Jerusalem, next to the American Colony Hotel. The building houses:
1. A girls' school whose pupils include orphans boarding there.
2. A college for the social sciences, established some years ago, which it is intended to upgrade to university level.
3. A Palestinian folklore museum.

The driving force behind the organization is the elderly Hind al-Husseini, who has made it her life's work.

ARAB STUDIES SOCIETY, JERUSALEM

Established in 1980 by Faisal Husseini. The founding committee includes six other members. The center has the following goals:

1. Studying Arab culture and conducting research in education, science, politics and sociology.

2. Cataloguing documents and newspapers and administering an archive of press clippings organized by subject.

3. Translating books and scholarly articles from English and Hebrew into Arabic.

By October 1984, the center had published 30 studies in various areas.

ARAB THOUGHT FORUM (Al Multaka al-Fiqri al-Arabi)

Founded in East Jerusalem in 1977 as an independent cultural center. Its stated objectives are:

1. Mobilization of scientific and ideological forces within Palestinian society.

2. Encouragement of study, research, composition, writing and discussion of the present and future social reality.

3. Development of the possibility of dialogue among various social elements.

4. Participation in the formulation of solutions to social problems.

The forum has held a number of conferences and ideological symposia, Palestinian literary festivals, and art expositions, and has published about 30 research papers in various areas touching on Arab society under occupation.

ASSOCIATION FOR CIVIL RIGHTS IN ISRAEL

Founded in 1972 as a non-partisan body with the goal of defending human rights and civil liberties in Israel, including freedom of expression, freedom of organization, the right to protest, freedom of thought, religion and religious practice, and freedom of movement. The society defends citizens from arbitrary acts or discrimination on the part of government agencies. Particular attention is given to the protection of vulnerable groups such as national minorities, women, children, the sick, the mentally ill, detainees and suspects. The association works to defend citizens' rights without taking any political position. In 1979, it was accepted as a member of the International League for the Rights of Man, whose headquarters are in New York. The association works in several areas: approaching the authorities concerning violations of human rights; offering legal assistance and defense where violations of rights involve fundamental principles; sponsoring legislation to prevent violations of civil rights and following up on changes in the law dealing with those subjects; holding public symposia and disseminating information.

Within the framework of this organization, a special team was established to locate and solve problems of human rights violations in the occupied territories. The team mainly provides legal assistance to citizens and mediates between the citizen and the appropriate authorities.

The association has branches in Israel's main cities, and its president is former Supreme Court Justice Haim Cohn.

ASSOCIATION FOR FAMILY PLANNING AND PROTECTION

Founded in Jerusalem in 1963 with branches in all the major cities of the West Bank. It maintains close contacts with the International Organization for Family Planning and Improvement. The goal of the association is to help mothers plan their families: it supplies contraceptives to married mothers at a token price, provides treatment for mother and child up to the age of one year and guidance to mothers on infant care and planning family size according to economic circumstances and state of health. Mother and infant are under the regular care of the association's doctor.

ASSOCIATIONS FOR ELECTRIC LIGHTING

Many of the villages on the West Bank are not linked to the national or local electric grid (See ELECTRICITY). In recent years, it has become common to establish associations to provide electric lighting. Those organizations used to receive loans from Jordan or from the JOINT COMMITTEE (PLO-JORDAN). Associations of this kind include: The 'Atil Organization for Electric Lighting and the Si'ir Organization in the Hebron Hills and in Burqin, in the Jenin area. Other organization failed to come up with the necessary funds from Amman to purchase generators and were forced to join the Israeli national electric grid by the military government.

AUTONOMY PLAN (EGYPTIAN)

Because of differences of opinion between Israel and Egypt over interpretations of the CAMP DAVID ACCORDS on substantive issues, in January 1980, Egypt published its own position on the following subjects: a) the military government and civilian administration during the transition period; b) the transfer of authority; and c) the organs of the Self Governing Authority (SGA), which will take over from and replace the military government and the civilian administration. The main points in its position were as follows:

1. When the Camp David framework promises the Palestinians full autonomy, it can only mean that under the SGA they will be able to make independent decisions and formulate their own policies. The full autonomy for which the Camp David framework provides cannot amount to a reorganization of what the Palestinians on the West Bank and in the Gaza Strip already possess: carrying out decisions made for them and implementing policies formulated over their heads, which was already the case prior to the Camp David agreements.

2. A distinction is made in both the Camp David framework and the joint letter between two kinds of withdrawal: (a) withdrawal of the military government and its civilian administration, which is to be total and unqualified; and (b) partial withdrawal of Israeli armed forces and redeployment of the remaining forces into specified security locations. The withdrawal of the military government and its civilian administration is the first step towards the assumption by the SGA of its powers and responsibilities.

3. The jurisdiction of the SGA will encompass all Palestinian territories occupied after June 5, 1967, including East Jerusalem, which shall be regarded under the autonomy as a unified territorial entity.

4. The authority of the SGA extends to the inhabitants as well as the land on the West Bank and in the Gaza Strip. All changes in geographic character, demographic composition and legal status of the West Bank and Gaza Strip or any part thereof are null and void and must be rescinded. This applies in particular to the annexation of East Jerusalem and the settlements. There should be a ban on the establishment of new settlements. After the inauguration of the SGA all settlers on the West Bank and in Gaza will come under the authority of the SGA.

5. The authorities of the SGA include promulgation of laws and regulations, issuance of identity and travel documents, control of entry and exit of persons and goods, and the assumption of responsibility for the public domain and natural resources.

6. The SGA will be composed of an assembly of 80-100 members freely elected from the West Bank and Gaza, and a council composed of 10-15 members to be elected from among the membership of the assembly. The assembly will take over from and replace the authority of the military government in enacting laws and regulations and, levying taxes.

7. The council will assume the direct administration of the West Bank and Gaza in every area.

8. The judicial authority will be manifested in a system of courts of law, courts of appeal and a supreme court enjoying full guarantees of independence.

9. The SGA will have a representative, alongside the representatives of Israel, Egypt (and Jordan) on the continuing committee in accordance with Article 3 of the Camp David framework.

10. The seat of the SGA will be East Jerusalem.

It is evident that this program conflicts with that of Israel (See AUTONOMY PLAN (ISRAELI)) and the reason why the autonomy talks were deadlocked.

AUTONOMY PLAN (ISRAELI)

The plan for a permanent solution to the problem of the territories was presented to the Knesset by Menachem Begin for the first time in late December 1977. After the signing of the CAMP DAVID ACCORDS, Begin tailored the original plan to fit the framework agreement (May 1979), although it was not essentially altered. The ministerial autonomy committee, appointed by the government to negotiate with Egypt, produced a detailed plan. A committee of directors-general added certain administrative, economic, and legal aspects to it (1979-1981). The Israeli autonomy plan, including its appendices, rather than serving as a basis for negotiations, was used as a program of action guiding the government of Israel and the military government in steps taken towards annexation, settlement, seizure of land, and deployment of the IDF in the territories (1979-1984) (See CREEPING ANNEXATION, MILITARY GOVERNMENT, MINISTERIAL RESPONSIBILITY).

The main points of the Israeli autonomy plan are:

For the sake of the peace agreement Israel agrees to leave open the problem of sovereignty over the territories, although it insists on its right to claim sovereignty over Judea, Samaria and the Gaza Strip. The administration of the military government will be abolished, but its status as a legislative, executive, and judicial body will be retained (according to the principles of international law regarding occupied territories) and it will be the source of the constitutional authority of the autonomy, which will be administrative autonomy of the residents of the area, headed by an elected administrative council. The council will deal with municipal affairs, education, welfare, industry and trade.

The security arrangements will be in Israeli hands; the residents of the area will be entitled to receive Israeli citizenship if they so wish, or else retain Jordanian citizenship. Israeli residents would be permitted to buy land and settle on the West Bank and in the Gaza Strip. The IDF will remain in the territories permanently. State lands and lands declared as such will be in Israeli possession. Israel will control water sources. The autonomous region will not have geographical borders, for it will be personal-communal autonomy, not territorial.

The conceptual world in which Begin constructed the autonomy plan derives from ideas which emerged in central Europe on the eve of World War I and from the treaties regarding minorities signed after the war in eastern and central Europe (Poland, Czechoslovakia, Yugoslavia). Those treaties were intended to guarantee the cultural and ethnic rights of the large national minorities which came under the rule of the new national states after the dissolution of the Russian and Austro-Hungarian empires. At the same time the Israeli autonomy plan was being formulated, the residents of the territories still enjoyed considerable municipal autonomy, in that the cities were administered by elected Palestinian mayors. Since then and in direct relation to the Israeli attempts to implement its conceptions (See CIVILIAN ADMINISTRATION), most of the elected mayors have been suspended and the Palestinian municipal structure has been destroyed. Paradoxically, in view of that development, the autonomy plan appears liberal, although it grants even less authority to local residents than South Africa gives the self-governing black regions (Bantustans).

BANKING AND CREDIT

On the eve of the occupation, eight banks with 30 branches operated throughout the West Bank. Among them were six local banks with 24 branches and two foreign (British) banks operating six branches. Residents of the West Bank (including East Jerusalem) held about a third of the total cash assets in the Kingdom of Jordan, including some $60 million in bank deposits. The total credit available to West Bank residents was about a quarter of the total private credit in Jordan. Immediately after the war, the banks were not permitted to reopen, as the cash at their disposal covered only six percent of the public's deposits.

All Jordanian and foreign banks still maintain their offices in Jerusalem and other West Bank towns, though their activity is limited to administrative matters. However, checks drawn on bank branches in Amman are in common use throughout the West Bank. From 1971-1978, there were some attempts to renew the operations of Jordanian and foreign banks, but they failed for political reasons, due to both Jordanian and Israeli government opposition. The main problem was whether supervision of the banks' activities should be carried out by the Royal Bank of Jordan or by the Bank of Israel. In May 1968, the authorities permitted the two British banks in the region to reopen, but they refused to do so unless the Jordanian banks reopened as well.

In July 1967, a decision was made to open West Bank branches of Israeli banks. By mid-1984 there were 20 branches, including those in Israeli settlements. Arab residents make infrequent use of Israeli banks.

An analysis of banking data shows that the public holds limited deposits and credit facilities available to local residents are very low.

In 1976, total credit available to the public amounted to 22 percent of total assets. In 1984 this stood at 8.0 percent. The steep decline in credit available to the public was caused mainly by the decline in credit from government deposits. In 1978 government credit was 43 percent of total credit. By 1982 this had fallen to 4.3 percent.

The shortage of credit and the absence of a capital market is a decisive factor contributing to the stagnation of the Palestinian economic sector on the West Bank. However, alongside the formal system, an unofficial credit network exists. Cooperative associations and public organizations grant credit which comes from the JOINT COMMITTEE of Jordan and the PLO, the funds being transferred through Jordanian financial houses.

Most monetary activity is carried out through moneychangers who operate a popular banking network alongside the Israeli one. In the West Bank there are 68 moneychangers (14 in Jerusalem). The authorities have no special interest in curtailing their activities and leave them room for maneuver so as not to force the Israeli banking system into alleviating the monetary shortage.

At the close of 1984 restrictions were imposed on moneychangers' activity and they were prevented from trading in foreign currency except Jordanian dinars, and that only by Jordanian passport-holders. These restrictions, however, were not enforced.

In 1984 an application to open an Arab bank under local ownership in Nablus was submitted. The Israeli government agreed in principle, but Jordan refused to approve the application as the bank would have had to operate under Bank of Israel supervision.

BEARERS OF ARMS AND PROCEDURES FOR OPENING FIRE

On the West Bank, various security forces act for the Israeli government: the IDF, the General Security Service (Shin Bet), and the Border Police (which belongs to the Israeli police but which is, in fact, subordinate to the military commanders of the various districts of the West Bank). The distinction among the various bodies is not significant with regard to the duties and authorities of those who serve in them and bear arms on the West Bank; they are in fact called upon to act in accordance with the standing orders of those bodies and only within the framework of those functions as defined by law. That obligation also applies to other public servants whose authority is similar to the police force, such as customs officers and members of the "Green Patrol" of the Ministry of Agriculture.

There is a legal distinction between, on the one hand, a soldier, policeman or any other person bearing arms and carrying out a legal function and, on the other hand, civilians. The defined duties of a soldier or policeman on the West Bank are to preserve public order and to apprehend violators of that order. This function applies to specific territory, according to the determination of the commander, and under limitations established by military orders (or those of the police and the like). The instructions for the conduct of soldiers promulgated by the commander of Judea and Samaria empower them to arrest and investigate only "if the matter is under your authority or in the course of carrying out your duties, and only when that arrest is for the purpose of preventing a crime or violation of the law, or when the man arrested has committed a violation" (See DETENTION AND INTERROGA-TION). Use of fire "must be limited and carefully controlled, both because of the need to preserve human life and because of the political consequences of the actions of the IDF in these areas."

According to the IDF orders regarding opening fire:

"In principle fire may be opened only against hostile terror activity and to prevent injury to our forces and it is forbidden for the purpose of imposing public order or quelling riots. As a general rule, in no case may fire be opened on women and children.

"Fire may be opened only when the lives of soldiers, security forces, or citizens are in danger, when our forces are under attack, when isolated soldiers or civilians with no means of escape are in danger of their lives because of physical attack or the use of stones, bottles, iron rods, or the like.

"The stages for opening fire are:
1. A shouted warning that one intends to fire.
2. Fire in the air at an 80-degree angle upwards, with the person shooting certain that his shot will not injure anyone.
3. Fire with intent to injure but only at the legs.
Fire will be opened by the highest-ranking soldier on the spot."

These strict orders are not always enforced, especially the order forbidding the opening of fire to disperse demonstrations and the prohibition against firing on children. Most of the exceptions occur when a small group of soldiers, without a senior commander, encounters a violent demonstration, and inexperienced soldiers fear for their lives or panic. Opening fire in violation of regulations is also common among armed Israeli citizens who encounter a demonstration.

There have also been some cases of settlers opening fire on Palestinians for revenge. Fifty-five Palestinians have been killed or injured as a result of opening fire to disperse demonstrations (1979-1984).

A citizen of Israel bearing arms and present on the West Bank is only permitted to defend himself against attack. His legal obligation is to attempt to escape or at the most, to make use of force sufficient for self-defense. His task is not to arrest his attackers. From that point of view there is no difference between an Israeli living in Kiryat Arba and an Israeli visitor from Tel Aviv. A similar status is also held by licensed bearers of arms among the Arab residents of the West Bank (such as active members of the VILLAGE LEAGUES). The distinction between civilians and soldiers seems clear. However, in reality, there are situations in which the borderline between "citizen" and "soldier" (or "member of the security forces") is ambiguous. All the settlements, on the West Bank are defined as "border settlements", in which (according to the Order on Guard Duty), guards are authorized to use force and, among other things, to open fire, although only at certain times and places, i.e., when they are on guard duty and in reaction to a well-defined cause. Many residents of the West Bank are, in fact, regular soldiers on leave (students at the Hesder yeshivot, combining military service with rabbinical studies), whose weapons remain in their possession. In every settlement there is also a "security officer", who receives a salary from the Ministry of Defense or from the Israeli police. The settlers interpret their security role quite broadly (See TERRITORIAL DEFENSE).

BREZHNEV PLAN

Soviet Chairman Leonid Brezhnev's statement regarding the USSR's position on peace, February 23, 1981:

The Soviet Union is prepared to participate in such work [of achieving a Middle East settlement] in a constructive spirit with goodwill. We are prepared to do so jointly with the other interested parties – the Arabs (naturally including the Palestine Liberation Organization) and Israel. We are prepared for such a search jointly with the United States...with the European countries and with all those who show a sincere striving to secure a just and durable peace in the Middle East... As for the substance of the matter, we are still convinced that if there is to be real peace in the

14

Middle East, the Israeli occupation of all Arab territories captured in 1967 must be ended. The inalienable rights of the Arab people of Palestine must be secured, up to and including the establishment of their own state. It is essential to ensure the security and sovereignty of all the states in the region, including those of Israel.

This statement is referred to by Arab sources (including the PLO) as the Brezhnev Plan and they support its principles. This position enables them to claim that they indirectly recognize Israel.

BROOKINGS REPORT

A report drafted by a panel of diplomats and academics under the auspices of the Brookings Institute in Washington D.C., endorsed by presidential candidate Jimmy Carter in December 1975.
Excerpts:

A fair and enduring settlement should contain at least these elements as an integrated package: security, sovereignty and territorial integrity, peaceful relations, withdrawal of Israel to the June 4 boundaries, Palestinian self-determination, subject to Palestinian acceptance of the sovereignty of Israel, UN Security Council endorsement of peace agreements.

The report was rejected by Israel as unfair and hostile.

BUILD YOUR OWN HOME

A building scheme run by the MINISTRY OF HOUSING AND CONSTRUCTION. It allocates plots of land for residents to build their own detached houses. The scheme operates in all types of settlements on the West Bank (TOSHAVA, KIRIYA and COMMUNITY SETTLE-MENTS). The aid given for house construction in the West Bank is exceptional: the ministry funds the infrastructure and development (excluding development in the immediate vicinity of the lot), and the houses are individually built and do not have to meet strict criteria of maximum size and investment required elsewhere. In addition, low interest loans are allocated by the ministry for building cooperatives which in turn constitute an additional subsidy. These special incentives have increased the percentage of West Bank construction done under the build your own home scheme. Some 20 percent of the permanent building in the West Bank falls into this category.

Build your own home is particularly common in the metropolitan areas of Jerusalem and Tel Aviv. Two- and three-story houses, in varying styles and congested clusters, give the new settlements on the West Bank their particular urban character.

BUILT-UP AREAS (ARAB)

The additions to Arab construction in the years 1973-1984 were considerable (See CONSTRUCTION (ARAB)) and, as a result, the "sphere of influence" of Arab built-up areas (defined as the outer limit of Arab settlements, even if they have only scattered construction) is spread over 260,000 dunams, i.e., 8.1 percent of the territory in Palestinian hands (See LAND USE). The extent of the built-up area (within the "sphere of influence") is estimated at 140,000 dunams. Average building density is estimated at 0.8 family units per dunam, less than half that of the projected Jewish settlements.

Interestingly enough, the density of rural built-up area on the West Bank is not very different from urban density. This is because outside the inner cities there is sparse building, mostly detached, one-story structures in areas used for orchards and other cultivation. The Palestinian population will be able to double the number without expanding outside areas defined as the "sphere of influence" of the areas they inhabit. This is calculated according to a gross density of one family per dunam, taking into account the allocation of land for public use.

BUILT-UP AREAS (JEWISH)

At the beginning of 1985, there were 42,000 dunams of built-up area in the Jewish settlements (areas ready for immediate construction). Some 100,000 dunams more are planned (in primary planning stages) for the addition of new settlements and expansion of existing ones. The total Jewish built-up area (existing and planned) comes to 6.6 percent of the total area under Israeli control (2.26 million dunams). This low percentage reflects the new (1980) Israeli settlement strategy which is to construct towns and suburbs with a relatively high building density (See ALLON PLAN, DROBLESS PLAN). According to Israeli building standards, average density is computed as two family units per dunam. The town of Ariel, for instance, is planned for 35,000 families on an area of 16,000 dunams. Kedumim and Beit-El are planned for 10,000 families on 5,000 dunams each. TOSHAVOT AND COMMUNITY SETTLEMENTS are planned for lower density, but their total built-up area is not large owing to the small number of residents planned for them. The 132 small Jewish settlements planned for the West Bank will cover a total area of 60,000 dunams, to be inhabited by no more than 17.5 percent of the Jewish population.

The projected built-up area, approximately 140,000 dunams, of which the vast majority is already under Israeli control, will house 600,000–800,000 people.

CAMP DAVID ACCORDS

Agreements laying down the principles of the peace treaty between Israel and Egypt and of the future of the West Bank and Gaza Strip. They were concluded at Camp David, Maryland and signed in Washington on September 17, 1978, by Anwar Sadat, President of Egypt, and Menachem Begin, Prime Minister of Israel, and witnessed by Jimmy Carter, President of the United States. Documents dealing with the West Bank and Gaza Strip are "A Framework for Peace in the Middle East" and an exchange of letters on the commitment of Egypt to conduct peace negotiations on the future of the West Bank – even without Jordanian participation – and on East Jerusalem. Another letter dealing with the timetable for negotiations on the implementation of the Camp David accords was signed along with the peace treaty between Israel and Egypt on March 26, 1979.

The principal topics are as follows: there will be transitional arrangements for a period of not more than five years. In the framework of these arrangements, full autonomy will be established for the residents, under a Self Governing Authority (SGA). The Israeli military government and its civil administration will withdraw and be replaced by the SGA. The parties will negotiate an agreement specifying the powers and responsibilities of the SGA, which will be elected in general elections. The SGA will begin its term one month after free elections are held, at which time the transitional period will begin. A strong local police force will be established. Israeli forces will be redeployed in designated security areas. A permanent committee made up of representatives of Israel, Jordan, Egypt and the SGA will decide, by agreement, on the return of refugees, security matters and other matters of mutual concern. No later than the third year after the beginning of the transitional period, there will be discussions on the permanent disposition for the West Bank and Gaza Strip and the relations between them and their neighbors. The solution must be acceptable to all sides. Concurrently, peace talks will be held between Israel and Jordan, with elected representatives of the residents of the West Bank and Gaza Strip among the Jordanian delegation. These negotiations will take into account the agreement reached on the permanent status of the territories (as agreed upon by the four-party committee mentioned above).

After numerous delays, Egypt and Israel began, with American participation, negotiations on the implementation of the above agreement. However, the discussions soon reached a dead end. Each party had opposing interpretations of the agreement and their positions were polarized. Egypt (See AUTONOMY PLAN (EGYPTIAN)) saw the transition period as the first stage in the achievement of Palestinian self-determination and total Israeli withdrawal from the territories. Since they knew there was no chance of establishing autonomy – self governing authority – without the agreement of the residents of the territories (since it would only come into existence after free elections were held), Egypt asked Israel to assist in persuading local residents to participate by creating a more favorable political climate in the territories and taking "confidence-building measures" such as permitting the return of deportees, halting establishment of new settlements, releasing political prisoners and permitting economic development. The United States position was similar to that of Egypt, but its representatives preferred to suggest compromise formulas in order to create momentum for a step-by-step agreement.

The Israeli position, based on the Israeli autonomy plan (See AUTONOMY PLAN (ISRAELI)), saw the transitional period as a permanent arrangement (on the assumption that no agreement would ever be reached on the eventual status of the West Bank and Gaza Strip). Moreover, Israeli government policy was directed to implementing its own political objectives regarding IDF deployment, settlements, land seizure, administrative arrangements (See CIVILIAN ADMINISTRATION) and the status of Jewish residents (See ISRAELI REGIONAL COUNCILS, CREEPING ANNEXATION). These steps were in direct contradiction to Egyptian and American demands to initiate confidence-building measures. These steps, which amounted to *de facto* annexation, increased the opposition of the residents of the territories to the Camp David accords.

The Israeli government did everything in its power to frustrate the possibility of finding any group in the territories prepared to join the peace process. The Jordanian government refused to join the Camp David process and has not changed its position. Starting in 1981, the Camp David process went into deep freeze and all parties have basically given up on it. The national unity government (July 1984) announced that it does not see the Camp David process as the only framework for peace negotiations with Jordan and the Palestinians. The American government (See REAGAN INITIATIVE) has declared that it will continue to pursue the Camp David process but has hinted that it will not necessarily be bound by the provisions of the framework agreement. Egypt has once again suggested that a peace conference be convened with the participation of the superpowers, as an alternative to Camp David. Jordan and the Palestinians have declared their adherence to the Fez Plan (See FEZ SUMMIT RESOLUTIONS). In February 1985, Jordan and Egypt (with the qualified agreement of the PLO) launched a new peace initiative (See HUSSEIN-ARAFAT AGREEMENT), termed "the last chance" by King Hussein. Its major proposal concerns talks between the United States and a joint Jordanian-Palestinian delegation, as a step towards convening an international conference.

CENSORSHIP

Censorship of newspapers, books, publications, and public performances is based on the Mandatory defense regulations of 1945 (Chapter 8, regulations 86-101). Censorship is imposed on all newspapers published in Israel (paragraphs 94-100 in the above-mentioned regulations). According to an agreement between the Committee of Editors of Hebrew Newspapers and the censor, however, the papers carry out self-censorship. Only items relating to security matters (as determined by the foreign affairs and security committee of the Knesset) are submitted to the censor for vetting.

The Arabic newspapers published in East Jerusalem (See PRESS (ARAB)) are not party to this gentlemen's agreement. The entire contents of these newspapers undergo examination by the censor. All material intended for publication must be submitted. The newspapers' representatives are required to appear at the censor's office twice daily to receive the approved, banned or corrected material. Leaving blank space in a newspaper, in place of a banned article, is not permitted. The censor may also outlaw items copied from the Hebrew press. Items on disturbances of public order, demonstrations, and land expropriation in the West Bank are censored, as are death notices for PLO activists. The censor is authorized to close newspapers (prohibition on the operation of a printing press, paragraph 100). In addition, the district commissioner may revoke newspaper publication licenses. Although censorship of books and publications, based on the defense regulations (paragraph 88) also remains on the books in Israel itself, it is not enforced.

In spite of the difficulties piled on the Arabic press by the censor, all the Arabic newspapers prefer to publish in Jerusalem, Israeli law being immeasurably more lenient than the censorship laws in force in the West Bank.

Order 50 (1967) forbids the import and distribution of newspapers in the West Bank without a permit, and every publication (even if approved by the censor in Jerusalem) must be presented for examination by the military government's censor. A permit remains valid for three months. Order 379 (1970) authorizes the official in charge to confiscate any publication. Defense regulation 88 prohibits the import of books without a permit. In 1985 more than 1,000 titles were removed from a list of 1,600 books banned in the West Bank, the possession of which is a criminal offense (see below). Orders 101 (1967), 718 (1977) and in particular 938 (1981), widen the scope of regulation 88 and forbid the printing of a publication, notice, declaration, picture or any other document containing anything of political significance. Printing, for this purpose, includes drawing, copying, photographing, and so on. It also includes word of mouth. Order 862 (1980) states that a publication's absence from the list of forbidden publications does not mean that it may be brought into the West Bank; everything requires specific and separate approval. The censorship of publications and performances is strictly enforced. The security forces confiscate publications from private houses, from public libraries and social clubs, and newspapers' editors are placed under town arrest (See ENFORCEMENT AND PUNISHMENT).

In the eyes of the Israeli censor (both in Israel and in the West Bank), every expression of Palestinian nationalism constitutes a call for the destruction of Israel, incitement to revolt and a covert call for armed struggle. Every publication of events in the West Bank is seen as provocation, one-sided reporting, a call for violence against the authorities and non-recognition of the State of Israel. This conception is reinforced by the self-image and practice of the Palestinian press. It views itself as an "enlisted press," with no interest in the dissemination of information for its own sake, whose purpose is fighting for the abolition of Israeli occupation and for the fulfillment of the national aspirations of the Palestinian people. The adversaries are not engaged in an equal struggle. All the coercive power of a sovereign state is available to the censor, who enjoys fairly wide public support in Israel as well as understanding from the judicial system. The efforts of the censor to control freedom of speech are doomed, however, since he is powerless against electronic communications operated by the Arab countries, or the development of new, vital, intellectual centers in the West Bank.

Book Censorship
The authority to censor books and other publications is based on paragraph 88 (1) of the Mandatory emergency regulations (1945) and on orders 101 (1967) and 718 of the military government.

Until September 1982, there was no index of censored books and military government officers published, at random, lists of books whose distribution was forbidden. At that time, a revised list of 1,002 titles was issued and since then another 600 titles have been added. A similar list exists in the Gaza Strip. In May 1985, some 1,000 books were removed from the list.

Anyone wishing to distribute a publication on the West Bank must present it to the censor. The majority of publications are approved. In 1977, 4,624 books were approved; in 1980, 8,055 books; and in 1981, 21,342 books. Compared to this, a list of 1,500-2,000 forbidden books may seem insignificant. A quantitative approach does not, however, reflect the power of the censor. While the censored publications are only 3 or 4 percent of all imported books, they constitute 100 percent of the literature expressing Palestinian national aspirations and tradition.

A study carried out in 1983 analyzed 946 of the censored books. The publisher apparently serves as the censor's first indication of the book's content, without his needing to read it. The number of censored books published by the PLO Research Center in Beirut is noticeably high.

Six hundred and fifty-three authors have been censored. Eighty-seven percent of them appear once only on the censor's list. Seventy-seven books appear on the list without the name of their authors. Twenty-six authors have written four or more censored books and they comprise 4 percent of the total number of authors, though their books represent 20 percent (161) of the total number of censored books.

The high proportion of censored literature and poetry (25.6 percent) and the large number of literary authors and poets whose work has been censored, is an indication of the importance the censor attaches to this kind of writing. This is not surprising since literature has traditionally served as a medium of expression for national aspirations.

CENTER FOR PEACE IN THE MIDDLE EAST

An apolitical organization founded in 1982 by the monthly magazine *New Outlook*, to accommodate scholars, political figures, and businessmen in Israel and abroad who are involved in the quest for peace in the region. The goal of the center is to sponsor research and discussion leading to concrete conclusions and promoting general peace in the area, to encourage relations between Israel and the Palestinians based on mutual recognition, to free the Middle East from the arms race between the superpowers, to bring about cooperation between the Jewish and the Arab world, and to promote freedom, tolerance, and equal cultural and political rights for national minorities.

Among the members of the center are Knesset members, judges and university lecturers. The center has published a number of research papers in its fields of interest and holds conventions and symposia in Israel and abroad.

CHAMBERS OF COMMERCE

Bodies established by Jordanian law which have continued to function under Israeli occupation by order of the regional commander.

Under Jordanian rule the chambers of commerce served as clubs for the urban finance elite and naturally wielded great political and economic power. After the occupation their position became even stronger for the following reasons:

1. Regional bodies ceased functioning and community political and economic activities were taken over by local bodies such as the municipalities, chambers of commerce, and religious organizations.

2. Chamber of commerce activities were considered apolitical by the military government.

3. Economic expansion in the area increased their importance.

4. The chambers of commerce handle export of goods to Jordan and issue licenses authorizing the export of West Bank products to Jordan and the Arab world.

5. They serve as a channel of communication with the military government and represent various commercial bodies.

In the West Bank, chambers of commerce operate in all the main cities: Nablus, Ramallah, al-Bira, Bethlehem and Hebron, as well as East Jerusalem.

Although, according to Jordanian law, the chambers of commerce are subordinate to the central chamber in Amman, the West Bank chambers have shown separatist tendencies and in 1968 established a council of West Bank chambers of commerce.

During the last few years, the chambers' economic and political activities have focused on the campaign against the imposition of value added tax in the territories (See TAXATION). Their petition was rejected by the High Court of Justice.

The chambers of commerce are managed by a board of six to 12 members, elected, by law, every four years (See ELECTIONS (PALESTINIAN)).

CHARITABLE ASSOCIATION FOR THE SONS OF THE SACRED FALLEN

(Jamiyat Abna'a al Shuhadah)

A charitable institution established in 1952 to assist the children of soldiers killed in the 1948 war. The association has continued its work since then, and today it accepts orphans and children of broken homes. It runs an academic high school with some 700 students and a vocational high school with about 800 students, who learn agricultural and industrial skills. The association also runs a club for old people and a kindergarten.

CITIZENS' RIGHTS MOVEMENT (CRM)

Ratz, the Movement for Citizens' Rights and Peace, was founded in 1973. Its aims are: peace on the basis of the Camp David accords; recognition of the right of self-determination for the Palestinian people; and negotiations with any Palestinian representative on the basis of mutual recognition. The movement calls for the protection of the rights of residents of the territories while under Israeli control, according to international law; a parliamentary review of legislation in the territories and military government operations there; and the examination of all military government orders according to international law principles. The movement opposes the establishment of new settlements. In the 1984 elections it tripled its power in the Knesset, and with Yossi Sarid's move from the Labor Party to CRM, it now has four Knesset seats.

CIVILIAN ADMINISTRATION

Set up in March 1981 by Israeli government decision, its declared purpose was to prepare the ground for the implementation of the "autonomy for residents" plan (See AUTONOMY PLAN (ISRAELI)). According to the official wording, "establishment of the administration is an outgrowth of the autonomy negotiations and meant to facilitate their successful conclusion." Its assignment was "to deal with civilian matters pertaining to the local residents, with due attention to law and order." The establishment of the civilian administration totally separated the military branch of the MILITARY GOVERNMENT from the civilian branch, and was presented as a mere administrative change. In effect, however, it had far-reaching political significance. It was an attempt to implement Israel's version of the autonomy plan and create irreversible legal and administrative conditions which would impose the Israeli plan on the Egyptians and Americans.

The head of the civilian administration was appointed by the "Military Commander of Judea and Samaria," a recycled usage which replaced the title "Military Governor of Judea and Samaria." In this way, the administration's promoters wished to establish the civilian administration's subordination to "the source of authority" of the military government. The jurisdiction of the head of the administration included all the civil powers of the military government, according to both Jordanian law and the Israeli "security enactments." However, it was not granted the authority to promulgate primary legislation – to issue military orders – with the exception of secondary legislation. This was the division of powers which Israel wished to achieve between the military authority in the territories, which was to remain in place, and the Self Governing Authority (SGA).

The structure of the administration and the internal organization were also changed, in line with the structure and roles that Israel wished to grant the SGA. The civilian branch of the military government had been divided into three branches – economics, administration and services, and resources and taxes. With the establishment of the civilian administration, all the functions that, according to the Israeli plan, were not to devolve on the SGA, were transferred to the resource and taxes branch, which then became the infrastructure branch. A new branch for welfare was also created. The STAFF OFFICERS were made subordinate to the head of the civilian administration, who was provided with an assistant for Jewish settlement affairs to supervise the Jewish settlements in conjunction with the staff officer for the interior. The settlements, however, and Israeli activity in the West Bank as a whole, are not in any way subordinate to the civilian administration. Although the head of the civilian authority signs various regulations dealing with the regional and local councils, this is purely a formality.

The divisions of the civilian administration are as follows: the head; his assistant and spokesman; staff officers for finance, legal counsel, comptroller, and administration; an economic branch comprising the staff officers for agriculture, transportation, customs, mines, fuel and insurance; an administration and services branch comprising the staff officers for the interior, justice, electricity, water, religious affairs, telecommunications and mail; an infrastructure branch including public works, government and abandoned properties, surveying, auditing, nature reserves, national parks, archaeology, and land registration; and a welfare branch including education, health, welfare and housing. Since its inception, various changes have been made in the civilian administration, including the appointment of a military officer to head the administration and closer coordination between the military and civilian branches.

The failure of the autonomy talks and lack of success in eliminating Palestinian local organizations reflected in the fostering of the VILLAGE LEAGUES and dismissal of the Palestinian MUNICIPALITIES gave rise to doubts regarding the necessity of maintaining the cumbersome bureaucracy of the civil administration. There is little doubt, however, that its authority will remain as at present, because its significance goes far beyond the exigencies which brought about its establishment. It represents the passage from an *ad hoc* military government to a permanent system of rule over the local population. After 18 years of military government – by definition a stop-gap pending a political settlement – a permanent system has been established, surprisingly similar to the system by which the Israeli Arab population was governed after the 1948 war.

CLUB OF ARAB UNIVERSITY GRADUATES

Founded in 1966, with 570 members today. Its goal is to strengthen the ideological, cultural, and social connections between its members. The club holds symposia, lectures and athletic activities, organizes summer camps for members' children and all others interested. Its headquarters are in Jerusalem. The organization also deals with unemployment among UNIVERSITY GRADUATES, and pays them unemployment allowances transferred from Amman.

COMMITTEE FOR FAMILY IMPROVEMENT (Jamiyat al-anash al-usrah)

A charitable organization established in 1965 to help poor families improve their economic and social position. The committee has held courses for the last 15 years in each of the following subjects: secretarial skills, sewing, embroidery, cosmetics, knitting, and basic education. In 1982, 2,000 women completed these courses. The committee published a quarterly on the Palestinian heritage, which was closed down under pressure from the military government. It also publishes pamphlets and books on Palestinian folklore.

The committee maintains a library, a Palestinian documentary archive and a museum of the Palestinian heritage. It provides material assistance to the families of killed PLO activists and political prisoners and offers scholarships for universities. It runs kindergartens and creches to assist working mothers and owns a factory which produces food and toys.

COMMITTEE FOR THE INJURED WARRIOR (Rabitat al-munadel al-Jarih)

A Palestinian organization, established in 1953 to provide aid to invalid veterans of the 1948 war. Membership by 1983 reached 700. The organization helped its members obtain artificial limbs and found them jobs. It also established a factory for the manufacture of artificial limbs, income from which was used to assist members.

COMMITTEE OF SOLIDARITY WITH BIR-ZEIT UNIVERSITY

A body established on November 9, 1981, in response to the closure of Bir-Zeit University for two months by the military government. Its members came from "The Committee Against Settlements in Hebron" and the "Bloc Faithful to Peace." The committee is intended to counteract GUSH EMUNIM and is to the left of PEACE NOW.

The direct initiative for its establishment came from Jewish and Arab activists in "Campus" (a left-wing Arab and Jewish student organization) and from a group of radical leftists, in protest against the use of collective punishment in the territories and against the harsh policy of the military government. The organization denounces settlements and supports the establishment of a Palestinian state on the West Bank and in the Gaza Strip, alongside Israel. The group's activities are limited to demonstrations and protests in the universities in Israel and the territories. It has about 500 active members, is financed by contributions, and publishes **Daf Meyda**, (information sheet). After the outbreak of the war in Lebanon, the committee became the "Committee Against the War in Lebanon."

COMMUNIST PARTY (WEST BANK)

Officially named "The Palestinian Communist Party in the West Bank and the Gaza Strip," it is a direct extension of the communist organizations active in Mandatory Palestine and in Jordan after 1948. It took its present form in early 1982, in place of the "Communist Organization in the West Bank and the Gaza Strip," which had been established in the territories after 1967. Its activities are illegal both under Jordanian law and the security regulations of the military government, which forbid political activity.

After the Israeli occupation of 1967, members of the Jordanian Communist Party remained on the West Bank, acting underground to link up with their comrades in the Gaza Strip and severing themselves from the party headquarters in Amman. In the early 1970's Communist activists on the West Bank were at the center of the Palestinian National Front, which tried to consolidate and lead the political opposition of the Arabs in the territories occupied by Israel. At that time most of the Communist leaders were expelled from the West Bank, notably Suleiman al-Najab, Faiq Warad, and Arabi Awad.

In the territories the party is estimated to have a few thousand members, strictly organized in a hierarchy of semi-underground cells surrounded by wider circles of sympathizers. The leader of the party is thought to be Bashir al-Barghuti, from the village of Deir-Ghassana in the Ramallah district, the editor of the East Jerusalem weekly **al-Taliah**. The party has another literary and cultural publication, **al-Ktab**, edited by As'ad al-As'ad and sometimes it circulates the underground publication

al-Watan, important for the mobilization of activists for organizational activities. The party concentrates on the organization of labor unions on the West Bank and in Gaza, directed by Adel Ghanam of Nablus and in "voluntary action committees," which provide mutual assistance, social work, etc. It also organizes strikes, demonstrations, and cultural and national events such as expositions, lectures and, meetings on Palestinian subjects.

The Palestinian Communists (both in the territories and elsewhere) have no official status in the PLO, mainly because of their principled refusal to create a military arm. That issue also caused a series of disagreements and conflicts within the Communist Party and between it and the PLO leadership. At one time during the 1970's the Communists did announce the formation of a semi-military organization commanded by Arabi Awad, called "The Patriotic Front," which committed no acts of violence.

Arabi Awad later left the party and founded a separate organization ("The Temporary Headquarters") which supported armed struggle against Israel. After the war in Lebanon that small Communist splinter group joined the Palestinian organizations working under the aegis of Syria which do not recognize the PLO under Arafat's leadership.

The Communist Party was to join the PLO as a recognized group during 1984 as part of the "Aden Agreement," which was meant to prepare for the seventeenth national congress. That agreement was not put into effect, however, and the seventeenth congress was convened in Amman without Communist participation. The Communist Party was among those condemning the congress (along with the organizations of the Marxist left, members of the PLO, George Habash and Naif Hawatmah).

Although the Communist Party belongs to the REJECTION FRONT and opposes the central stream of the PLO under Arafat's leadership, the Communists are considered, from an ideological viewpoint, to be more moderate in their attitude towards Israel. They accept, in full, the position of the Soviet Union which recognizes Israel within the 1967 borders, and thus they are different from the other Marxist organizations in the PLO.

COMMUNITY SETTLEMENT (Yishuv Kehilati – Settlement Type)

Somewhat larger than the COMMUNITY VILLAGE, the main moving force behind these settlements is the World Zionist Organization, which supplies infrastructure, housing, and basic industry. The settlement is planned for 200-300 families and spreads over 400-800 dunams. The yishuv kehilati is a cooperative organization listed with the Israeli registrar of cooperatives. Its organizational structure is based on regulations binding on all members of the association. These regulations are usually identical for all such settlements, with the exception of small changes in accordance with the settlers' wishes.

The guiding principles are:
1. an elected management committee.
2. an elected supervisory committee.
3. a members' assembly as the top decision-making authority.
4. mutual economic guarantees.

The settlement is not based on agriculture. It is a closed system which accepts members according to defined acceptance procedures. The settler's candidacy lasts a year, after which a decision is made on whether to accept him.

The members' assembly is the decision-making body in all matters. Employment is by and large outside the settlement, in accordance with the wishes of each resident. Houses and land are purchased on private initiative.

The yishuv kehilati, adopted by Gush Emunim (see AMANA) and the Likud government as the preferred form of settlement on the West Bank, constitutes a historic turning point in the settlement of Eretz Israel. Kibbutzim and moshavim, pioneering, agricultural settlements with a socialist ethos, working the land and constituting their own labor force, are to give way to quasi-urban settlements based on a minimum amount of cooperation and on commuting. The yishuv kehilati is intended for the middle-class, white-collar worker. Many of them will eventually become suburban settlements and bedroom communities.

A list of community settlements, updated to September 1985:

Settlement	Regional Council	Number of People	Settlement Movement
Neve Tzuf	Benyamin	450	Amana
New Givon	Benyamin	241	Amana
Yitshar	Samaria	46	Amana
Ma'aleh Levona	Samaria	48	Amana
Neve Daniel	Etzion Bloc	110	Amana
Ofra	Benyamin	563	Amana
Michmash	Benyamin	163	Amana
Beit Horon	Benyamin	223	Amana
Ateret	Benyamin	92	Herut-Betar

28

Settlement	Regional Council	Number of People	Settlement Movement
Beit-Abba	Samaria	224	Herut-Betar
Beit-Arieh	Benyamin	61	Amana
Beit-El	Benyamin	586	Amana
Ma'aleh Amos	Etzion Bloc	116	Herut-Betar
Ganim	Samaria	100	Ha'Oved HaLeumi
Elon Moreh	Samaria	466	Amana and Housing Min.

COMMUNITY VILLAGE (Kfar Kehilati – Settlement Type)

A small-scale settlement intended for 150 families and founded upon the initiative of its members. The settlement is registered as a cooperative. An admissions committee chooses new candidates for the settlement.

The establishment of such a village is funded by the World Zionist Organization. According to the division of labor between the settlement division and the Ministry of Housing, the latter is responsible for construction and the World Zionist Organization for infrastructure and provision of employment. This type of settlement is a creation of Gush Emunim (See AMANA) and mainly serves the purpose of settling non-agricultural areas. A village can be set up quickly and with relatively small outlay, and it suits the needs of a population commuting to the central urban employment areas.

In principle, the community village emphasizes local sources of employment – industry, tourism, education, and services; in practice most residents hold on to their city jobs (See COMMUNITY SETTLEMENT). In 1985, 79 percent of the members commuted to the region and to the big cities.

The following is a list of community villages, updated to September 1985:

Community Village	Regional Council	Number of People
Hermesh	Samaria	60
Yakhin	Hebron	85
Yakir	Samaria	228
Kochav Ha'Shahar	Benyamin	190
Kfar Adumim	Benyamin	313
Yatir	Hebron	100

Community Village	Regional Council	Number of People
Mevo Dotan	Samaria	127
Mitzpeh Yericho	Benyamin	200
Nili	Benyamin	161
Susia	Hebron	86
Almon	Benyamin	91
Einav	Samaria	155
Ateret	Benyamin	92
Shavei Shomron	Samaria	320
Shiloh	Benyamin	389
Tekoa	Etzion bloc	234
Dolev	Benyamin	66
Otniel	Hebron	63
Homesh	Samaria	113

Settlement movement: Amana (with the exception of Homesh).

CONSTRUCTION (ARAB)

1. Private Construction

The lion's share of capital investment in the West Bank (some 55 percent) goes into the construction of private homes. Total building completions in 1983 (in the Arab sector) reached 672,000 square meters, with building starts at 600,000 square meters. The surge in construction in the territories began in 1974. It peaked in 1981 at about 800,000 square meters, 14 times as great as in 1968. Since 1982-1983 there has been some decline, and in 1984 total residential building completions came to 617,000 square meters. Private building starts may be divided by use: 80 percent for new apartments, 5 percent for additions to existing residences, and 15 percent for non-residential buildings. Some 58 percent are in cities and 42 percent in villages. Private residential construction in rural areas has grown faster in recent years than in urban areas. As a result of this building activity, residential density declined from 3.0 persons per room in 1972 to 2.6 per room in 1983. There has also been a noticeable improvement in the level of facilities in the home. In 1972, only 16 percent of residences contained bathrooms; by 1982 this had risen to 58 percent. The major consequence of this building activity on the West Bank is, however, the dramatic growth in built-up areas, both in towns and villages. In 1982 the built-up area of the West Bank stood at 260,000 dunams out of 5.5 million (See LAND USE). The building was not congested, but followed a pattern of ribbon development, with long, narrow, built-up areas along roads and access routes, and scattered building in cultivated areas. However, it also includes the filling in of vacant lots between existing buildings. Aerial photographs reveal the tremendous growth of construction in municipal areas. In 1967, the built-up area of Hebron was 7,000 dunams, out of a planning area of 73,000 dunams (9.6 percent); in 1982, the built-up area of Hebron covered more than 20,000 dunams (27 percent of the planning area). Growth in the built-up area of Beit Jala between 1968-1979 was 55 percent; in al-Bira, 67 percent; in Salfit, 162 percent; in Hebron, 185 percent; in Beit Sahur, 267 percent; in Bethlehem (outside the city center), 125 percent; and in south Ramallah, 76 percent.

The extensive development in private construction was funded, for the most part, from the savings of West Bankers employed in Israel, and from cash transfers from relatives working in Arab countries. Aside from the purpose of expanding the housing supply, the Palestinians see construction as a political strategy. Their experience is that the Israelis refrain from expropriating built-up, populated land. The PLO and Jordan take a similar view of the matter. For this reason, the Jordanian government and banks make loans available on easy terms through the JOINT COMMITTEE to every West Bank resident wishing to build a home and possessing a building permit (See SUMUD). In West Bank towns, construction cooperatives have been organized, also with Jordanian funding.

2. **Public Construction**

The rate of public construction is inversely proportional to the surge in private construction. In 1983–1984 there were no building starts at all in the public sector (for education, health, etc.). The total building starts in the public sector were 11,200 square meters in 1968, 5,000 square meters in 1978, and 1,500 square meters in 1981. This highlights the extremely low level of public investment in the West Bank, and the lack of initiative on the part of the military government regarding community development. The disparity between private and public construction is one example of the contrast between individual prosperity and communal stagnation typical of the West Bank (See ECONOMIC POLICY). See also PUBLIC CONSUMPTION AND INVESTMENT.

CONSULATES

The formal adherence of most countries to the United Nations 1947 resolution on the internationalization of Jerusalem has resulted in most embassies accredited to Israel being located in Tel Aviv rather than the capital. The few embassies and legations that were located in Jerusalem left after the Knesset passed the "Jerusalem Law" in 1980.

A few countries have consular offices in Jerusalem, among them the United States, Britain, France, Sweden, Belgium, and Spain. All functioned in the city during the Mandatory period and continued to do so after 1948. Since they recognized neither the partition of Jerusalem nor Israeli or Jordanian sovereignty over its two halves, but only *de facto* control, their area of jurisdiction was city-wide. They did not request, nor did they receive, diplomatic recognition of their status, with the exception of "courtesy calls" on the district commissioner.

The annexation of East Jerusalem in 1967 was not, of course, recognized by the foreign consuls. However, they did extend their activity to include the West Bank. A division of labor was devised between the consulates and the embassies in Tel Aviv, with the latter refraining from dealing with matters over the green line.

Since the consulates' jurisdiction involved the Palestinians, tensions naturally arose between the Jerusalem consulates and the Tel Aviv embassies, which saw their main task as fostering relations with Israel.

The Palestinian population saw the consulates as a means of making their views known to the outside world. On the other hand, the consulates' involvement in West Bank affairs has caused vexation among the Israeli public and resulted in tension between the consulates and the Israeli establishment. The Jerusalem consulates oversee the activities of a number of voluntary groups (See FOREIGN AID) and quasi-governmental foreign organizations working in the West Bank. They maintain a considerable range of social activities and ensure that foreign visitors meet representatives of the Palestinian population. It is worth pointing out that the consuls keep their social connections with Israelis and Palestinians separate. As a rule, members of the two groups are not invited to the same events.

COOPERATIVE SETTLEMENTS

The traditional forms of agricultural settlement, such as the kibbutz, the moshav, and the moshav shitufi. All are based on agriculture and industry, on their own labor and joint ownership on various levels, in accordance with the type of settlement. They generally consist of 3,000-5,000 dunams and 80-160 families (350-650 people).

Several settlement movements have founded agricultural settlements in the West Bank: HA'IHUD HA'HAKLAI, RELIGIOUS KIBBUTZ MOVEMENT, Takam (See UNITED KIBBUTZ MOVEMENT), The MOSHAVIM MOVEMENT, HA'OVED HA'LEUMI, POALEI AGUDAT ISRAEL and the Moshav Association of HAPOEL HAMIZRAHI.

These settlements are established and maintained by the WORLD ZIONIST ORGANIZATION.

COOPERATIVES FOR AGRICULTURAL MARKETING (Jam'iyat al-Taswik al-Zira'i)

Mainly founded in the northern West Bank, these cooperatives belong to the Jordanian Cooperative Organization whose headquarters is in Amman. That organization lends them money and also provides grants. Its declared intention is to help Arab farmers develop advanced agricultural methods, using modern equipment and improved varieties of crops. Many observers view these cooperatives as a political element designed to express support for the Jordanian administration when necessary.

The cooperatives receive American economic assistance through Anera (See FOREIGN AID). The largest are found in Nablus, Tulkarm and Kalkilya. The Israeli military government hinders the work of these cooperatives, in particular limiting the transfer of funds from Amman and refusing to authorize joint aid plans with Anera.

1. **The Cooperative for Agricultural Marketing in Nablus**
Founded in 1980, today it has 700 members in and around Nablus. Its purpose is to prepare land for agriculture, to pave agricultural service roads to transport produce from fields and to provide credit to farmers for the purchase of modern equipment.

2. **The Sikka Cooperative for Agricultural Marketing in the Hebron Region**
Established in 1978, in 1984 it purchased two tractors, a combine and a tank truck for weedkillers. It also built an office building and a garage for its equipment.

3. **The Cooperative for Agricultural Marketing and Irrigation in Kalkilya**
Although established in 1963, its activities were suspended after 1967 and only renewed in 1974. It now has 325 members and supplies farms with fertilizer, seedlings, agricultural equipment and weedkiller. It helps farmers obtain modern equipment for plowing, weedkilling, etc. and also issues permits allowing farmers to ship their produce to Amman.

4. **The Cooperative for Agricultural Marketing of Tulkarm**
Founded in 1982, in 1984 it had 482 members. The organization gave loans to its members totaling 250,000 dinars ($675,000) and is in contact with the Jordanian authorities to regulate the marketing of produce on the East Bank.

5. **The Azun Cooperative for Agricultural Marketing**
Founded in 1981 in the Azun area of Tulkarm, it has 131 members from 20

local villages. Its goals are similar to those of the other regional cooperatives for agricultural marketing.

COURTS (ISRAELI)

Empowered by emergency regulations enacted by the Knesset, to judge offenses committed in the occupied territories. According to the regulations, Israeli courts may try Israelis in the territories and foreign tourists visiting there, but not local Arab residents (See CREEPING ANNEXATION).

Courts for Local Affairs operate in the West Bank, in cases dealing with the authorities of the ISRAELI LOCAL AND REGIONAL COUNCILS. In 1985 two such courts were active, one in Kiryat Arba (with authority over the southern West Bank) and one in Ariel (responsible for the northern West Bank).

COURTS (LOCAL)

According to the proclamation issued by the Israeli military commander immediately after the occupation in June 1967, "the law, as it existed on June 7, 1967, will continue to apply on condition that it does not contradict this proclamation or any other directive or order that may be issued by the military government, or changes emanating from the establishment of IDF rule in the region."

Local law in the West Bank is composed of Ottoman legislation, Mandatory legislation and original Jordanian legislation. The Jordanians revised many of the Mandatory laws. In the Gaza Strip, local law is based mostly on Mandatory law, subject to changes by the Egyptian military governor (prohibiting, for instance, suits for damages against the army for physical injury).

INTERNATIONAL LAW forbids the military administration in an occupied territory to change existing law, which it must honor, "unless absolutely prevented." During the entire period of the protracted occupation of the West Bank and Gaza Strip, however, fundamental changes have been made in local law, not only with regard to security, but also in economic and civil law. The High Court of Justice has validated these changes, viewing them as essential for the preservation of "normal life" (See CREEPING ANNEXATION, SECURITY ENACTMENTS).

1. Court System

The Court of Appeal – sits in Ramallah and hears all appeals on judgements made in district courts and magistrates' courts. It has also been granted the powers of a high court of justice, once held by the courts in Amman. Its judgements are final.

The District Courts – may hear all civil and criminal cases not under the jurisdiction of the magistrates' courts. Appeals of judgements of the magistrates' courts are also submitted to the district courts, in two cases:
1. If the value of the suit is not more than 10 dinars.
2. In criminal cases, if the punishment meted out by the magistrates' court is not more than five dinars or 10 days' imprisonment.

All other appeals are submitted to the court of appeal in Ramallah. There are three district courts in the region, in Nablus, Hebron, and Ramallah.

The Magistrates' Courts – may hear civil suits in which the damages claimed are no higher than 250 dinars and, criminal cases in which the maximum penalty is no more than three years' imprisonment. There are nine magistrates' courts in the region: in Hebron, Bethlehem, Jericho, Ramallah, Nablus, Salfit, Jenin, Tulkarm, and Kalkilya.

2. The State Prosecutor

The "Naib 'Aam" is the equivalent of the state prosecutor. His responsibility is to appear before the court of appeal and supervise the work of the district prosecutors. The district prosecutors are responsible for criminal investigations and for representing the prosecution in matters under the jurisdiction of the district court. All other investigative files are submitted directly to the magistrates' courts and the prosecutors are exempt from appearing before them. In locations where there is no public prosecutor – such as Kalkilya, Salfit, Tulkarm, Jenin, and Jericho – the authority of the prosecutor is vested in the local judge himself.

3. Court Activity

Some 2,053 cases came before the court of appeal in 1984 and proceedings were completed in 2,063 cases. In the rest of the courts, the offices for executing court decisions and the office of the prosecutor, proceedings were initiated in 97,145 cases in 1984 and 91,589 reached completion.

There are 27 judges and prosecutors, including four court of appeal justices, nine district court justices, nine magistrates, one public prosecutor and four district prosecutors.

The local Arab courts on the West Bank have no authority to review decisions of the regional commander on the need for new legislation or changes in existing legislation. The regional commander has issued a special order stating that IDF authorities may not be sued before local courts, since they are not within the jurisdiction of these courts. This grants immunity to all IDF authorities before the Arab courts, and eliminates any possibility of the Arab courts judging the military government or its activities. In addition, the legal STAFF OFFICER is authorized to close any file and to halt any judicial procedure on cases already begun by transferring them to a military court, or by ruling that the investigation is not in the public interest. Various orders have removed powers from the local courts, particularly in cases involving land and land disputes. In addition, Israeli citizens may not be brought to trial or sued before a local court. As a result, Israeli residents are immune from any suit for damages or offense according to local law, or in matters involving a local resident or authority. The local courts are almost completely lacking in means of executing court decisions and, in many cases judgements are not carried out.

Palestinian lawyers have spoken out frequently on the poor state of the local judicial system and on the absence of centralized supervision of its activities. At the beginning of 1985, a number of appeals and district court judges were arrested on charges of bribery and perversion of justice. There is no doubt that the Israeli military government gives very low priority to the local judicial system.

COURTS (MILITARY)

Established by an order of the military government (Order 378, SECURITY ENACTMENTS), they are empowered to try residents of the territories for criminal offenses according to local law, and on security offenses as defined in the military government's legislation.

Hearings usually take place before a military court, comprised of three judges, one of whom must be a trained lawyer. They are also empowered to judge and penalize offenses committed outside the region, if their object was to harm the security of the region.

These courts are not restricted by the rules of evidence required in Israeli courts. When the accused is 18 or older, the military court may give the death penalty, on condition that the sentence be unanimous, and that two of the judges be trained lawyers.

Military court judgements cannot be appealed, although convictions and sentences require the approval of the regional commander. The commander may cancel the verdict, declare the accused innocent, reduce his punishment, or pardon him altogether. The commander may also, on the recommendation of the chief military prosecutor, order a retrial.

The military court occasionally comprises a single judge, in which case his powers are limited to sentences of up to five years in prison. The judge must have legal training. In these cases, the verdict does not require approval, but the accused may request a pardon or a reduced sentence from the regional commander.

COURTS (MUSLIM RELIGIOUS – SHAR'I)

Eight first instance Shar'i courts operate on the West Bank under the authority of the Shar'i Appeals Court, which operates in East Jerusalem. Israeli attempts to sever Jerusalem from the West Bank system have been unsuccessful.

The Shar'i system is completely independent of the Israeli authorities, subordinate rather to the Ministry for Waqf affairs in Amman (through the SUPREME MUSLIM COUNCIL and also directly). The salaries of the Shar'i qadis (religious judges) employed by the courts are paid directly by the Jordanian government. The Muslim judicial system's independence means that the Israeli administration does not enforce its rulings. It seems, however, that parties to disputes in most cases are willing to obey them voluntarily and sanctions are imposed, when necessary, by the Jordanian authorities.

CREEPING ANNEXATION

A term meant to describe the process by which Israeli administration, jurisdiction and law have gradually and incrementally been imposed on the West Bank in ever-expanding areas, without a comprehensive act of annexation. That process, which can also be termed *de facto* annexation, changes the status of the West Bank from an area under military occupation to one which is in fact subject to the Israeli system. Creeping annexation is generally seen in its demographic and physical aspect (See DEMOGRAPHY (ISRAELI)) but in that the term "annexation" is legal and constitutional, it should be described in that context.

The basic law on the West Bank is Jordanian. On the basis of the powers assumed by the MILITARY GOVERNMENT, more than 1,100 orders and many hundreds secondary regulations have been promulgated (See SECURITY ENACTMENTS). The law on the West Bank is therefore two-tiered. The Israeli administration on the West Bank also wears two hats: it acts on the basis of Jordanian law, whose authority it assumed upon the ousting of the Hashemite sovereign, and also on the basis of Israeli law, to which it is subject since it is one of its arms (See STAFF OFFICERS). The Israeli legal and administrative system was transferred to the West Bank in other ways too, chiefly in that Israeli settlers, although ostensibly subject to the territorial law in force in the West Bank (i.e., Jordanian law and the security enactments), actually have the rights and duties of residents of Israel. Those rights were conferred upon them by special Israeli legislation (See PERSONAL STATUS OF ISRAELIS). This is also the case regarding the Israeli administrative system applied in the Jewish settlements (See ISRAELI

REGIONAL COUNCILS). The dual situation is evident in that the Israeli Supreme Court considers itself competent to pass judgement on the actions of the administration in the territories although its judicial authority is limited territorially (See HIGH COURT OF JUSTICE) to the State of Israel. Below we present several examples of the application of Israeli law in the territories, either directly (through legislation by the Knesset) or indirectly (by promulgation of orders of the military government, which are merely copies of Israeli laws), or else, by the transfer of executive powers according to local law to Israeli statutory bodies and the usurpation of powers held by local (Jordanian) bodies.

Anyone physically present in the West Bank is subject to local law and the local judicial system – civil and military. The emergency regulations which were legislated by the Knesset granted parallel judicial authority (regarding Israeli citizens) to Israeli courts as well, subject to Israeli law. All Israeli citizens are tried only by Israeli courts. Moreover, according to the instructions of the legal STAFF OFFICER no local policeman may charge any Israeli citizen with any crime, including traffic violations. The Israeli election laws enfranchise citizens of Israel residing in the country. Israeli residents of the West Bank were thus not entitled to vote, for their permanent place of residence was not in Israel. Consequently the election law was amended so that any Israeli citizen listed in the registry of residents and living in an area occupied by the IDF would be included on the voting list.

For a long time the Israeli status of citizens of Israel living in the territories was not formally settled, though in fact they enjoyed all the rights of citizenship through extra-legal arrangements. In January 1984, that ambiguity was resolved through legislation in the Knesset, stating that for the purpose of certain laws, Israelis or those entitled to Israeli citizenship through the Law of Return (i.e., Jews) living on the West Bank would be viewed as residents of Israel. The main law mentioned in these regulations is the law of Israeli residents' registry. Thus the status of Jewish residents of the West Bank was made equal to that of residents of Israel.

Israeli tax laws, such as income tax and the tax on land appreciation, were applied to business transacted by Israeli residents of the West Bank.

The above are all examples of the application of Israeli law by means of legislation in the Knesset. The second way in which Israeli law is applied is the issuance of military orders identical to Israeli law. Thus, Israeli regional councils were established according to orders which are word for word copies of Israeli municipal laws. Similarly, local courts were established in the Israeli settlements by means of military orders and function according to Israeli law. Jewish religious councils were also established by military order.

The military government, in accordance with international law, assumed the powers of the Jordanian administration. However, contradictory to international law, no absolute distinction was made between Israeli civilian government bodies and military bodies acting on the basis of military occupation. On the contrary, the distinction between the two became increasingly vague until it virtually disappeared. One example concerning the Israeli police on the West Bank, is highly significant because the police are responsible for enforcing the law. Order 52, promulgated in 1967, placed the men and officers of the Israeli police under the command of the military governor and gave them authority to police the West Bank. That authority derived both from Jordanian law and from the security enactments. An amendment (105) to that order stated that every policeman and police officer on the West Bank was considered to be under the control of the military commander. That amendment meant that the entire chain of command of the Israeli police (which derives its authority from the Israeli police ordinance) was in force on the West Bank (See KARP REPORT, POLICE). Another example of the transfer of authority on the West Bank to Israeli statutory bodies is the power given to the Parks and Nature Reserves Authorities to supervise certain areas of the West Bank. However, the main instance of the blurring of the distinction between the military authority on the West Bank and the Israeli civilian administration is the institution of STAFF OFFICERS.

In addition to imposing the Israeli system by copying laws and granting authority, Israeli norms were also imposed through orders altering Jordanian law. Those changes were profuse, especially in the area of finance and taxation, but also in other areas (including insurance, motor vehicles, infrastructure and planning). Jordanian law, and the administrative structure which derived authority from it, were vitiated by usurping statutory powers from Jordanian bodies (the king, the council of ministers, statutory commissions, courts, authorities) and transferring them to the officers and employees of the Israeli military government.

Creeping annexation appears to be in violation of the HAGUE REGULATIONS (Section 43), but the HIGH COURT OF JUSTICE (HCJ) has chosen to interpret those regulations broadly and rejected the claim of the illegality of amending the Jordanian law. In the opinion of the HCJ, the regulations did not intend to freeze the law. The HCJ created a new test of the motives of the military legislator: if an amendment is made for the benefit of the local population, it is permissible. When the test relates to the substance of the amendment, the way is open for extensive change, whenever the HCJ is persuaded that the change is for the benefit of the population. How the local population is to be defined (Israeli settlers or Palestinians), whether the population is interested in the change, and whether the administration (and the HCJ) may determine what is in its interest is a different matter altogether.

The legality of legislation enacted by the Knesset has not been subjected to the test of the HCJ, for it has not been appealed.

After 19 years of Israeli rule, the administrative and judicial structure of the West Bank has been integrated into that of Israel so extensively that there is no practical need (judicial or administrative) for the formal step of applying the Israeli legal, judicial, or administrative system. On the contrary, such a step would be politically dangerous and create more complications than the continuation of the present, fluid situation. The major complications that would be entailed were the territories to be annexed would concern the personal and communal status of the Palestinian population.

DEFENSE STRATEGY

The security significance of the West Bank derives both from the topography of the area and from the vulnerability of the Israeli territory facing it.

The coastal plain of Israel, which is only a few meters above sea level, stretches out from the foothills of the mountainous area of the West Bank, and is only between 14 and 30 kilometers wide (as compared to the width of the West Bank, which is 55 kilometers as the crow flies, from Kalkilya to the Jordan). The area of the West Bank amounts to 28.4 percent of the area of the State of Israel within the green line, and to more than double the size of the "vital area" of Israel, i.e., the coastal plain between Hadera and Ashdod. In that area live two out of every three Israelis, and three out of every five factories in Israel are situated there.

The Israeli defense line along the Jordan River is much more convenient than along the green line, since there is no physical barrier between the West Bank and Israel similar to the river and valley that separate the West Bank from the kingdom of Jordan. The defense lines along the Jordan are 260 km. shorter than along the green line, and for that reason it also takes fewer forces to man it.

The Dead Sea, as an obstacle against Jordanian attack in Judea, diminishes the strategic importance of the southern Judean Hills. The area considered to be particularly vulnerable to attack and the transfer of forces hostile to Israel is northern Judea, including Jerusalem, and

Samaria. From all the western slopes of the mountains there are lookout points commanding a clear view of the coastal plain for the purposes of intelligence, air control, the direction of artillery fire, and battle movements.

From the Jordan Valley to the crest of the mountains (Jerusalem, Ramallah, and Nablus), there are five principal east-west arteries, including two first-class roads (from the Allenby Bridge to Jerusalem and from the Damia Bridge to Nablus). On each of those five roads it is possible to transport military units of division size or larger, when the dirt roads at the side of the main roads are also used. This means that there exists a possibility for simultaneous attack of five divisions. North-south axes allowing for the transfer of the thrust from one east-west road to another are fewer: the Jordan Valley Road, the Allon Highway, and the watershed road.

The most important battle in the first stage of such an attack would be to open up the roads. The presence of Israeli troops in the territories on the western slopes commanding the eastern slopes of Trans-Jordan could be decisive in a war and frustrate the entire attack.

In a monograph written by retired IDF Brigadier-General Arieh Shalev, six possible deployments of eastward-oriented defensive lines are analyzed, including one between the watershed and the green line and five to the east of the mountain plateau (close to the riverbed; on the eastern hills that overlook the entrances to the roads; along the Allon Highway; between the Allon Highway and the watershed and on the edge of the built-up areas on the mountain plateau overlooking the east). The easiest options from the military point of view are the first two to the east of the mountain summits; in the areas overlooking the entrances to the roads, making use of the hills in the Jordan Valley and the water line, which no attacker could circumvent. Shalev also points out the order-of-battle required for the deployments (See DEPLOYMENT).

This professional military analysis can be seen as representing a wide consensus, as apolitical as possible, among Israeli experts. Agreement is more limited when it comes to the analysis of possible solutions to the problem of formulating the security component in the political future of the West Bank. Israeli politicians who have a reputation for military planning and leadership disagree with regard to this matter, each according to his view of the Israeli-Arab conflict. It is therefore possible to speak only of an agreed-upon "security" approach to the basic facts of the topography and military capabilities, but not with respect to their significance and the degree of gravity with which Israel should relate to those facts.

The Maximalist Approach

Proponents of this approach wish to see the annexation of the West Bank to the State of Israel for ideological and national reasons. They use the security argument as proof of the necessity of annexation, since the non-security arguments have not succeeded in convincing sufficient of the international community or even of Israeli society that annexation is necessary.

Proponents of the maximalist approach occupy key posts in the areas of foreign policy and security in the LIKUD party. Yet despite the preponderance of the Herut faction within the Likud and in the Israeli government from 1977 to 1984, that party has not succeeded in attracting prominent military figures to its ranks. Two retired generals who served as minister of defense under the Likud government expressed, at different times, willingness to consider other solutions to the future of the West Bank.

There were five generals in the first Begin government, with Ezer Weizman and Ariel Sharon in office together with three former IDF colleagues – Yigal Yadin, Moshe Dayan, and Meir Amit. Although he was proud of having five generals in his government, Begin did not have a single advocate of the maximalist approach among them. The chief of staff who served during those five years, General Rafael Eitan, did actually support that approach in public, although in brief, and with emphasis on the ideological and nationalistic argument rather than the military ones.

Yuval Ne'eman, who served as the TEHIYA party representative in Begin's cabinet, is the most vocal exponent of the maximalist approach depending on the security argument. Ne'eman served in the IDF in planning and intelligence posts, reaching the rank of colonel, he held key posts in Israel's nuclear planning (he is a professor of physics), and he served as assistant to Shimon Peres when Peres was minister of defense (1974-75). Ne'eman claims that in 1953, when he served in the general staff as head of the planning department, he prepared an emergency plan in case of surprise attack from the east (over the 1949 borders). According to him, those plans were discussed by the general staff, with the participation of the minister of defense at the time, David Ben-Gurion, and "the conclusion was reached according to which within those borders we could not take the risk of being surprised in a war, and that in case of such a risk, Israel would have to launch a pre-emptive war." Ne'eman describes the wars of 1956 and 1967 as the application of that principle. He also claims "there were attacks which were not permitted to be made by the IDF, to our eternal regret."

The need for pre-emptive war in the borders that existed between 1949 and 1967 is explained, in Ne'eman's view, because the "Samaria arena is the vulnerable heart" of Israel. Ne'eman points out that the Jewish population of the State of Israel was, and still is, concentrated in the three big cities along the coast between Gadera and Hadera. "The dispersal of the population is of supreme importance for security reasons. The potential stored up in a few large centers offers strategic targets for bombing, for shelling, and even for conquest by land and winning the war. The overcrowding of the roads in the central areas necessarily impedes the capacity for maneuver and supply, especially during the stages of the mobilization of reserves and the deployment of the forces. Under those conditions artillery and aerial bombardment are of particular gravity, since they can prevent the mobilization of the IDF and the implementation of its entire military potential."

According to Ne'eman, Israeli defense "from the point of view of its potential for war is based on the mobilization of forces in the area and its transfer to the appropriate war zone. When the mobilization stage is over, that area (and especially the section between Gadera and Hadera) is the central logistical base for the campaigns, wherever they are waged. That is the heart of the state, both in the sense of its existence and in its ability to pump blood through the arteries."

Along with the physical imagery ("heart"), Ne'eman also describes the coastal plain as the "vital arc" whose center is Samaria. "For an Arab planner that arc represents a primary military goal… Whoever occupies Samaria threatens the inner lines of the whole center of the state. Clearly any force acting against us from Samaria would have to protect its flanks, but from the moment it launches an attack, it has the full possibility of retaining the initiative and even winning. Since the territory allows for the transfer of troops on internal lines from north to south and also from east to west, Israel must allocate considerable forces to the defense of the Sharon so it is not cut off, and to the area of Tel Aviv-Jaffa, so that it is not conquered, to Jerusalem and the corridor, and also to Haifa and the Jezreel Valley. Samaria is a classical strategic bridgehead, combining compactness and defensibility with direct access to the strategic objectives."

Ne'eman also makes use of the ancient history of Israel, of which one of the directions of conquest (in addition to the sea route from Egypt and from the north) has always been through Samaria: "The Book of Joshua offers a detailed scenario of the use of Samaria as a bridgehead and breaking out of it to all the vital areas of Canaan. However what took many years at the time of Joshua is liable to last only a few days with modern armored corps." Israeli deployment in the vital arc arouses for him "great similarity and worrisome associations" with the Crusader State "especially in its second phase."

While Israel is capable, according to Ne'eman, of repulsing local attacks at one point or another, or a military force which might attempt to penetrate it from Samaria, "from within the green line it is not possible to stop a massive enemy attack, when he has the initiative, in a sector where he can choose the principal thrust of his efforts," because to halt the advance of thousands of tanks a minimum depth of 10 to 20 kilometers is necessary.

Ne'eman claims that there is no substitute for high mountainous areas, not even in the age of electronic and airborne systems. He recalls the loss of the stronghold on Mt. Hermon complete with the electronic instruments for intercepting missiles. It had been under IDF control and was captured by Syrian commandos at the outset of the war in 1973, leading to the most serious losses sustained by the Israeli Air Force. The erection of electronic stations (as the Egyptians did in El Arish following their entry in 1980) in Samaria, would allow whoever controlled Samaria to inflict heavy damage on Israel's electronic communications and flight control systems. As evidence that even in the era of missiles strategic territories are still important, Ne'eman points out that the United States and the Soviet Union cling to every electronic base within their reach even though they both have intelligence satellites for flight control and reconnaissance. "The reason for this: only a small amount of apparatus can be placed in a satellite, a few dozen in a plane, but in a base on the ground, thousands and tens of thousands."

Ne'eman's principal conclusion is that Israel within the 1949-1967 borders cannot withstand a war in which the enemy could launch an attack from Samaria. The conditions for such an attack could come about, according to him, in two cases: firstly, strategic surprise, "like the Yom Kippur War, which could succeed not only if the enemy's armor were stationed in Samaria, but also if Samaria were not occupied by the IDF and the armor stationed in Jordanian bases on the east bank of the Jordan could reach the mountains in a few hours." Secondly, a local irregular force, or one that infiltrated into Samaria, could seize key positions in the first few minutes and provide assistance to the Jordanian armor on its way from the east. "Within four or six hours the enemy could be threatening Tel Aviv, Jerusalem, the Sharon, or Haifa, and from that time on it could prevent the mobilization of the IDF's potential by means of a direct attack."

Refraining from pre-emptive attack even when there is no surprise attack, because of "political circumstances, low morale or weak leadership," could bring about "results on the scale of a Holocaust," according to Ne'eman, if Israel should return to the green line. He claims that "there is no critical danger" in the present deployment of the IDF, in force since 1967. Ne'eman's approach denies any alternative to the annexation of the West Bank.

The Anti-Maximalist Approach

An approach that negates the security argument, upon which the maximalist approach is predicated. It is defined here as "anti-maximalist" in that the common denominator among its various proponents is the rejection of the maximalist argument rather than agreement on the extent of territory which should be left under Israeli control. Among the anti-maximalists, there are those who see the Jordan River as the eastern security border (but not necessarily a political border) of Israel, and there are others who would be satisfied with the deployment of a series of warning and control stations on the mountaintops of the West Bank and the demilitarization of Samaria by all Arab armies. The anti-maximalist approach is not identified with any particular political or military figures in Israel, although in private conversations certain senior military men, either in active service or in retirement, advocate it.

The anti-maximalist approach sees massive Jewish settlement on the West Bank as a security risk and not an advantage: "the bringing of a million Jews up from the coastal plain to the mountains (the West Bank)," as advocated by Yuval Ne'eman, would nullify the strategic depth which the West Bank was intended to offer Israel by keeping Arab armor at a distance from Jewish population centers. The anti-maximalists fear that the next step taken by the maximalists will be a plan to conquer the eastern side of the Jordan Valley and the mountains of Gilead, Ammon and Moab, with the argument that strategic distance from the Jewish settlements on the West Bank must be increased.

The anti-maximalists reject the dependence of the maximalists on historical examples. They claim that the military history of Palestine actually proves that the principle direction taken by conquerors has been from west to east, from the coast to the mountains. Control of "commanding areas" in the mountains has not helped against enemies from the plain below when their armies were more advanced technologically and possessed superior military doctrines. Allenby's campaigns of 1918 and the failure of the Arabs in the wars of 1948 and 1967 are used to refute the maximalist claim.

The lesson of the Israeli failures at the beginning of the Yom Kippur War also serves the anti-maximalists. The constant state of alert maintained by an enemy army on the other side of a line of contact (the Suez Canal in 1973, the Jordan River if the West Bank were annexed by Israel), and its preparedness as a result of its maneuvers in those positions, actually increase the chances that such an army – even if it did not achieve surprise – would act more effectively than if it had to set out from its distant, permanent bases and move along vulnerable roads. According to the anti-maximalist approach, there is an inverse relation between Israel's strategic depth and its political freedom of maneuver: as long as an Arab attack is not considered dangerous to the existence of the State of Israel, the Americans will be less willing to allow Israel to take pre-emptive action.

The security alternative to territories, according to that approach, is composed of political and security arrangements (demilitarization, buffer zones, guarantees, withdrawal of the Jordanian army 10 kilometers to the east of the river, prohibition on the entry of Iraqi or Syrian armies into Jordan) and an Israeli strategy based on rapid and decisive response to any infraction of those arrangements. The anti-maximalists, who are considered "doves" from the territorial point of view and because of their readiness to accept a compromise that would diminish the level of Arab hostility in the conflict with Israel, necessarily become "hawks" in the sense that they advocate a defense doctrine based on a strong and aggressive IDF. In the existing political circumstances, in which Israel does not enjoy freedom of maneuver between the great powers, that approach also entails the necessity of understanding the needs of the United States, Israel's major supplier of weapons and financial support.

The Nuclear Dimension

The fact that the Middle East is on the threshold of the nuclear age offers support for the assumptions of each of these opposing views. The maximalists claim that the dispersal of Israeli population to the West Bank from its present configuration would increase its ability to absorb a nuclear blow from the Arabs. But their basic claim is not meant to explain why the nuclear dimension makes Israeli control of the West Bank obligatory, but rather why it makes it possible: the mutual balance of terror will force the Arabs to accept Israeli annexation of the West Bank. The anti-maximalists advocate postponing the region's entry into the nuclear age, in which "the State of Israel would lose a great deal of its conventional military deterrent power since it would have to consider and reconsider a thousand and one times whether to undertake the risk of a significant attack," according to Meir Pail, retired colonel and former member of Knesset for the left-wing party, Sheli. "Nuclear arms will bring a renewed proliferation of terror and guerrilla warfare to our region and significantly limit Israel's military capacity to deter Arab states on the conventional level with armored attacking forces in coordination with the air force." The anti-maximalist conclusion is that it is preferable for Israel and the entire Middle East to enter the nuclear age as late as possible, and after peace has been reached in the region, peace for which, and in the framework of which, they advocate Israeli withdrawal from the territories on the West Bank.

The Territorial Compromise Approach

The Allon Plan is the best-known of the strategic plans which do not advocate total annexation of the West Bank, but at the same time rule out withdrawal to the old armistice line.

Israel's eastern border, according to the Allon Plan, would be the Jordan River and the line dividing the Dead Sea. Israeli sovereignty would apply to "a strip of 10-15 kilometers through the Jordan Valley to the Dead Sea," and also on the Hebron mountains, or at least to "all of the Judean Desert and the uninhabited portions of the Hebron mountains." The plan also proposed Israeli annexation of the Etzion bloc and adjustments of the border in the Latrun area. (For a description of the areas proposed by Allon to be annexed, see ALLON PLAN.)

From the security point of view, the Allon Plan allows for the erection of two forward defense lines or the combination of the two: on the foothills in the Jordan Valley, near the river, or in the areas commanding the entrances to the roads, in places where the routes first penetrate the eastern slopes of the hilly plateau.

The eastern security strip would prevent terrorist bands coming from Jordan from crossing the river by foot at night. They would have to pass through a system of military obstacles to the west and then reach hideouts beyond the strip. According to retired IDF Brigadier General Arieh Shalev, the strip proposed in the written plan is too narrow for that purpose, but the strip drawn on the map of the Allon Plan "alleviates that disadvantage." The map was published in 1972, more than four years after the formulation of the program.

In the case of war, the security strip is meant to allow for a defensive line along the Allon Highway. The principle battle in the Jordan Valley would be fought by armored forces from north to south. If the armored forces lost that battle, the advancing Arab armies would encounter Israeli infantry to the west, which would occupy the eastern slopes of the plateau.

Shalev points out that the Allon Plan does not consider the problem of intelligence warning stations, nor are solutions to the problem proposed, neither in the written plan nor on the map. The security strip, in both versions, does not include the highest places on the West Bank, which are necessary for the placement of electronic intelligence stations, radar installations for the air force, and batteries of ground-to-air missiles. According to Shalev, it is possible to place warning stations in lower areas which are within the Allon Plan. In his opinion the plan does not offer sufficient freedom of maneuver for the IDF along a number of routes, from the area of the Judean Desert in the security strip, in addition to the Jordan Valley (the central consideration for the widening of the strip in the south was to ensure Israeli sovereignty over Kiryat Arba, of which Yigal Allon was one of the political patrons).

The Sharon Plan

The Allon Plan was never adopted by Israeli governments under Labor, although the settlement policy of the Alignment embodied its principles. Moshe Dayan (defence minister 1967-1974 and foreign minister 1977-1980) did not accept its strategic concept. Dayan maintained that without a strong military presence on the watershed, the defensive line in the Jordan Valley is worthless. Ezer Weizman (defense minister 1977-1980) held the same views but supported a political compromise.

Ariel Sharon (defence minister 1981-1983) wished to annex larger portions of the West Bank, though not all of it. Official maps of the Sharon Plan (published in 1980) show that he defines "regions important for Israel's security" as encompassing three quarters of the West Bank.

Sharon's plan sees Jewish settlement in the mountain plateau as a principal requirement of Israeli security, in contrast to the emphasis placed in the Allon Plan on the role of settlement in the Jordan Valley in the framework of a security strip. It could be that the change in emphasis derives from the fact that by the time Sharon reached an influential position, Allon's conception of settlement in the Jordan Valley had already been put into effect. Sharon sought to hasten the settlement efforts on the mountain plateaus before the end of the autonomy negotiations. According to his plan, the security zones would only be durable if they were backed by Jewish settlements; almost all Jewish settlements in the West Bank are within the zones, for they include the Jordan Valley and the eastern slopes of the mountains, the western slopes of the plateau and Ramallah. The enclaves that would remain outside of Israeli control, according to the Sharon Plan, comprise a large portion of the Samaria plateau (including Nablus and Jenin), the area to the north of Ramallah and a strip of heavily populated land some five kilometers wide close to the green line (including Tulkarm and Kalkilya).

From the security point of view, the areas proposed by the Sharon Plan offer solutions to the military problems, countering possible threats from

Jordan. In fact, his program is close to the maximalist approach in that it leaves less than a quarter of the West Bank under Arab control. Although it does not call for the general annexation of the West Bank, it does represent a transition from the assumption behind the Allon Plan – that it would be possible to predicate an agreement on the West Bank upon territorial compromise – to the aim of unilateral reorganization on the part of Israel in some areas heavily populated by Arabs, although not in all of them.

DEMOGRAPHY (ISRAELI)

The number of Jewish settlers on the West Bank for the years 1972-85, is as follows:

1972 – 1,182	1976 – 3,176	1980 – 12,424	1984 – 42,600
1973 – 1,514	1977 – 5,023	1981 – 16,119	1985 – 52,000
1974 – 2,019	1978 – 7,361	1982 – 20,600	
1975 – 2,581	1979 – 10,001	1983 – 27,500	

Two major phases may be distinguished, the first from 1968-1977, concurrent with the Alignment government's term of office, the second from 1977-84, concurrent with the Likud administration. During the first period annual growth (1972-77) averaged 65 percent, and in the second period (1977-84) it almost doubled, averaging 121 percent. Since 1982, the rate of growth has considerably increased and the number of settlers has doubled within two years. The average absolute annual growth in the Alignment period was about 770 settlers and under the Likud about 5,400 settlers. In 1984, for the first time, the growth rate exceeded 10,000 settlers per year. These differing rates of growth highlight the differences in the extent to which public resources were distributed under the Alignment and Likud governments (See INVESTMENT IN SETTLEMENTS). They represent the differing approaches of the two political movements with regard to settling the West Bank. These divergent approaches are also clearly expressed in the location of the West Bank settlements. The growth rate of more than 50% between 1982–1983 and 1983–1984 slowed to 21.5% between 1984–1985. The absolute growth in 1985 was 9,165 compared with 15,000 in 1984.

With the fall of the last Alignment government in May, 1977, there were 34 settlement in the West Bank, 21 of them in the Jordan Valley and its western slopes, two in the Jerusalem area, six in the Etzion bloc, one in Kiryat Arba, two in the Latrun area, and two on the mountain ridge running in a southerly direction from Nablus to Hebron. In 1982, there were 71 West Bank settlements (including NAHAL outposts),16 of them in the Jerusalem area, 21 on the mountain ridge, 11 in Western Samaria (Tel Aviv area), 20 in the Jordan Valley, and three south of Mt. Hebron. In 1984 the number climbed to 114, distributed as follows: 24 in the

Jerusalem area, 26 on the mountain ridge, 20 in Western Samaria, 26 in the Jordan Valley, and 12 on Mt. Hebron (See ALLON PLAN, DROBLESS PLAN). The rest are nahal camps. Only one additional settlement had been added in 1985.

By 1984, 72.5 percent of the Israeli settlers were located in 15 large settlements (over 180 families per settlement), with 27.5 percent living in 99 small settlements. One quarter of all settlers were living within the municipal boundaries of Ma'aleh Adumim, an outlying suburb of Jerusalem. Distribution of the settlements by size reveals that 42.8 percent were populated by 20 or fewer families, 38.0 percent had between 20 and 50 families, 8 percent of the settlements had 50 to 100 families, 4.5 percent had 100-250 families, and 7.5 percent of the settlements had a population of more than 280 families. These data reveal the growth problems of the smaller settlements. By contrast, those planned as KIRIYOT or TOSHAVOT appear to have rapid growth potential. There has been no change in demographic distribution in this regard, since 1984.

In 1982, 57.0 percent of settlers were located in the metropolitan areas of Jerusalem and Tel Aviv. Forty percent were in the Jerusalem area (within a radius of 20 kilometers) and 17.5 percent were in the Tel Aviv area, within a commuting distance of 30-45 minutes. The rest were settled on the mountain ridge (29 percent) and in the Jordan Valley (13.5 percent). By 1985 there was a pronounced shift in the population center: 75.0 percent were living in the metropolitan areas, 17.5 percent on the mountain ridge and only 7.5 percent in the Jordan Valley. The growth in the metropolitan area of Tel Aviv was particularly rapid. There was almost no population increase in the Jordan Valley and, on the mountain ridge, settled mainly by members of Gush Emunim, growth was limited. In 1985 only 110 families joined COMMUNITY SETTLEMENTS. In July 1985 the World Zionist Organization published a demographic census of the community settlements in the West Bank. The socio-economic profile that emerges from this census is illuminating. Average family size in the settlements is 4.7 persons per family, average age 36; native-born Israelis – 63.1%; European or American-born – 22.4%, Asian or African-born – 13.8%.

If we include the origin of fathers of native-born Israelis, it emerges that about 29% are oriental and 61% are ashkenazim (the rest are third generation Israelis).

The inventory of houses and the projected rate of building starts permits the housing of 1,500 – 2,000 families per year. It is estimated that by the end of the 1980's, the number of Jewish settlers on the West Bank will reach 100,000. (See MINISTRY OF HOUSING).

DEMOGRAPHY (PALESTINIAN)

Data on the size of the population of the West Bank are based on estimates and statistical models and not on census. No census has been taken since 1967, even though during this period two full population censuses were conducted in Israel, in 1972 and 1983. Until 1972 three different figures had been published for the region's population. In 1980, the Central Bureau of Statistics published a population estimate of 704,000. The same year, the published Interior Ministry estimate was 871,000. The staff officer for statistics published his own figure – 750,000.

Publication of population data, other than by the Central Bureau of Statistics, was discontinued in 1982. According to the bureau's figures, the West Bank population at the end of 1984 was 787,000, not including Jewish settlers or the Arabs of East Jerusalem. This figure represents the population present at the end of the year and does not include 150,000 holders of West Bank identity cards residing abroad whose papers are deposited at the border stations. If these are included, the sum total of West Bank residents reaches over 900,000. At the end of 1967 there were 586,000 residents, in other words, there has been an increase of over 200,000 (present population), or 32 percent, in 18 years. Since the beginning of 1970, when war-related migration came to an end, the growth reached 34 percent. An examination of the annual growth rate reveals considerable changes from year to year. In the period 1969-1974, it stood at 2.4 percent, from 1975-79 at 1.5 percent, in 1980-81 at 0.8 percent and in 1982-83, at 2.4 percent. In 1984 the rate jumped to 2.7 percent – 3.1 percent natural increase and emigration of 0.4 percent. By comparison, between 1952 and 1967 under Jordanian rule, average annual growth rate was only 0.9 percent, half the rate under Israeli occupation.

The sources of population growth are fertility, live births minus deaths, and the migration balance. The fertility rate of the West Bank population has not changed over the last generation. The gross birth rate is 45 per 1,000 and total births are 30,000 each year (1974-1983). Under-registration of deaths, in particular of neonates and the elderly, makes estimates of natural increase and life expectancy controversial (See HEALTH). The Central Bureau of Statistics puts infant mortality at 60 – 70 per 1,000. Life expectancy is estimated at more than 60 for men and 64 for women. The annual rate of natural increase (live births minus deaths) averages 3 percent. The principal factor affecting population size and its growth rate is balance of migration.

During the Jordanian period, emigration from the West Bank was almost offset by natural increase. It is estimated that almost 400,000 persons left the West Bank between 1948 and 1966. Jordanian government economic policy, which accelerated East Bank development at the expense of the West Bank, created a strong incentive for emigration. This emigration was not uniform for all socio-economic groups. The number of Christians leaving was greater than that of Muslims and residents of refugee camps tended to emigrate less than permanent residents. Most emigrants during the Jordanian period were men under 40 years of age seeking a livelihood. During the 1960's women and children began to leave in order to reunite with their husbands. Between 1952 and 1961 the West Bank's population grew by only 63,000.

As a direct result of the 1967 war, 215,000 people left the West Bank – a fifth of its population. In the period after the war, emigration continued. With the exception of two years – 1969 and 1973 – there was a negative balance of migration each year. In total, 147,000 people emigrated between 1968 and 1983. Emigration was not uniform. In the period 1969-1974 it was of minor dimensions: 13,800 people, as against 69,100 in 1978-1979. During the years 1980-81 alone, 33,000 emigrated. In the years 1982-83 the level shrank considerably (10,600 people) and in 1984 the migration balance was 3,000. The emigration rate was especially high for men between the ages of 18 and 24, and those with secondary school and post-secondary education(See UNIVERSITY GRADUATES). Of West Bankers who were between the ages of 10 and 24 in 1961 (between 33 and 47 in 1983), only 27 percent of men and 40 percent of women have remained. Of the total initial cohort ages of 10 and 21 in 1967 (27–35 in 1983) only 30 percent of the men and 50 percent of the women continue to live in the West Bank. The causes of emigration are the classic socio-economic "push and pull" factors. It is commonplace to attribute emigration to the "repressive Israeli regime" but the reasons are more complex. The political pressures and the occupation do not directly affect emigration, but by means of economic policy and variables (See ECONOMIC POLICY, INDUSTRY, UNIVERSITY GRADUATES, AGRICULTURE).

The data on internal migration (from region to region) are scarce and unreliable. Even so, there are signs that there has been faster growth in the southern West Bank (Hebron and Bethlehem districts) than in the north (Nablus, Tulkarm and Jenin districts). The growth rate in the towns is greater than the average and there is no doubt that a rapid urbanization process is under way in the West Bank. This is particularly marked in the Jerusalem metropolitan area. In the city itself(SeeEAST JERUSALEM) there has been a constant annual growth of 3 percent.

Continued sustained fertility and decreasing mortality rates explain the very 'young' age structure of the territories' population: 46% of West Bankers and 48% of Gazans are children under the age of 14. Though the annual number of births has remained more or less constant in the last 10 years or so, the absolute size of the three younger 5-year age groups has still increased significantly: for instance, in 1977 the number of pre-school children (0-4 years) was 129,000 in the West Bank and close to 83,000 in the Gaza Strip; by 1984, the figures were 140,000 and 97,000, an increase of 9% and 17% respectively; the number of children aged 5 to 9 increased by 20-40% during the same period.

Following the decline in emigration, and the rise in survivorship, the number and proportion of people in their prime (20-34 years old) increased considerably in the last few years: since 1977 their number increased by almost 50% in the West Bank and by 35% in the Gaza Strip, and their proportion has increased from 20% or less, to 23%.

The immediate consequences of these trends were an expanded marriage market and an increased potential for natality; the availability of young men and women for wage labor also enlarged and dependency ratios steadily decreased (106-107 in 1977, around 100 in 1984).

An analysis of demographic trends reveals that the Palestinian population is almost totally dependent on outside forces, which determine its size and its age distribution by controlling factors affecting migration. Between 1948-1967 the Jordanians created and maintained incentives that led to continued emigration. After 1967, when Israel opened its economy to laborers from the territories, emigration came to a complete standstill. With the worsening economic situation in Israel (1974) and the outbreak of the Lebanese civil war, which had the effect of creating rapid growth in Jordan, there was a surge in emigration. Then, as the economic situation in the oil-producing countries began to get tighter, Jordan's own growth slowed, the entry of young people was restricted (1983), and emigration from the West Bank diminished considerably.

The demographic trends described above have brought about steady growth in the Arab population in former Mandatory Palestine. If population returns are accounted for (the return to Egypt of 37,000 Sinai residents), then Jewish majority status has been steadily eroded, from 65% in 1969 to 63% in 1984. In the younger age groups, up to age 15, which approximately forecast the overall situation a generation ahead, Jews now constitute 53% of the total population of this age living in the region as a whole, and Arabs constitute 47%, 31% of whom live in the occupied territories and the rest of whom are Israeli Arabs (including residents of East Jerusalem).

Distribution of children up to the age 15 by groups

	1982	1984	Difference % Absolute/Relative	
Total	100.0	100.0	–	–
Israel: Jews	53.7	52.9	–0.8	–1.4
Israel: Arabs and others	16.6	16.5	–0.1	–1.1
Occupied territories (Arabs)	29.7	30.6	+0.9	+3.2

As shown in the table, within two years the percentage of Arab children living in the West Bank and Gaza Strip was augmented by 3%, while the percentage of Jewish children declined by 1.4%. In fact, if a relatively moderate annual growth rate of 2.7 is assumed for the Arab populations in the forthcoming years (if fertility and mortality continue to decrease moderately and if net migrancy balance continues on the same level as in 1982-1984), then West Bankers could number over 900,000 persons by 1990 and Gazans, more than 600,000 (together more than 1.5 million). By the year 2000, assuming similar or even slightly lower growth, West Bankers and Gazans together would approach two million (1,986,000 according to assumed growth rates).

Based on these assumptions and realistic official population forecasts for the Jewish population, the share of the Jewish population in the area of Mandatory Palestine would decrease from 63% in 1984 to about 61% in 1990, 57-59% by 2000 and under 55% by 2005.

DEPLOYMENT OF THE IDF ON THE WEST BANK

Deployment is tailored to meet the threat of war on the Jordanian front, but also to meet the problems of day-to-day security and to exploit the possibilities for other military uses – such as training – of the land occupied by Israel.

54

The operational and intelligence data upon which the IDF bases its considerations are classified. However, a substitute for official data can be found in a monograph by a retired senior officer of the IDF (Brigadier General Arieh Shalev), who, during the decade following 1967, served consecutively as the officer responsible for intelligence evaluation in the IDF and as a regional commander on the West Bank. According to the monograph, the geographical and topographical given of the West Bank and the relations of power between the IDF and the Arab armies on the Jordanian front together comprise the potential geostrategic threat facing Israel on that front.

According to Shalev, "Against an enemy with offensive capabilities, Israel lacks sufficient strategic depth to defend the coastal plain, because Judea and Samaria are much higher and overlook it. The width of the State of Israel in those regions is between 14 and 20 kilometers. According to Soviet estimates, that is the depth of a defensive division, and according to the American estimate, of a brigade... Thus the defense of that area so vital to Israel from within the green line – strategic defense, taking everything into account – is possible merely on a tactical level because of the narrowness of the area. If the military threat against Israel persists, it is very doubtful whether it would be possible, over a long period of time, to succeed in the task of defending that vital area, where 67 percent of the inhabitants of Israel live, and to prevent a large number of casualties, unless the depth is increased and the potential threat is removed to the other side of the Jordan. Moreover, an enemy knowing that in a single tactical maneuver he might be able to achieve the strategic goal of dividing Israel in its vital territory and perhaps even occupying parts of it, would be strongly tempted to try. That knowledge alone would be enough to make the beginning of a war more likely."

In the balance of forces which, according to that estimate, pose a strategic danger to Israel, the IDF reckons four armies on the eastern front (Jordan, Syria, Iraq and Saudi Arabia, and, according to some scenarios, Iran as well). Despite the name "eastern front," it is, in fact, merely a geographical area with a significant potential for military alliances. Presently the aforementioned armies do not have a combined command, unified military doctrine, or significant experience in combined operations, but they do maintain connections (in recent years especially between Jordan and Iraq). If a political decision were made, the Jordanian government could offer the area from which to launch the war, and the main burden of the forces could be supplied by Iraq and Syria.

Shalev emphasizes that while in 1967 the Jordanian army had only a defensive capacity against Israel, today it has the ability to wage a fast and mobile war, with an advanced air force and anti-aircraft missiles. Its divisions are mechanized and armored, as opposed to infantry in the past, and they are mainly deployed in the triangle between the Sea of Galilee, the Dead Sea, and Zarqa/Mafraq, close to its emergency stations. The Jordanian deployment allows it to move westward and launch an attack without significant changes. The numerical relation between the standing armies, according to Shalev's monograph, gives clear superiority to the Arab land forces, until the full call-up of Israeli reserves: "In the event of a surprise attack by Jordan and Syria, and if, at the same time, an Iraqi expeditionary force began moving westward (without a clear picture of the behavior to be expected from Egypt), the IDF could place only two regular divisions as against four to five Jordanian divisions and seven to eight Syrian ones. Therefore Syria and Jordan would have a numerical advantage of some six to one for at least the first 48 hours of the war, with respect to regular land forces. That is a quantitative advantage which the Arabs could exploit, making gains on the ground."

The IDF Central Command is supposed to be prepared for limited Jordanian actions as well, the success of which would be measured in local gains, "actions such as seizing territory close to the cease-fire lines, which would hurt Israel and arouse international reverberations." According to that scenario, ever since Israel was deterred from accepting (in 1974) the American proposal of the "Jericho Plan" – which would have entailed voluntary withdrawal from an area in the Jordan Valley so that Jordan could point to some political success – the possibility has existed that Jordan might attempt to capture Jericho or a similar objective, where even a military defeat might provide a lever for setting a dormant political process back in motion.

The size of the regular forces which must be deployed by the IDF in the West Bank in order to delay an attack, according to this scenario – while mobilizing reserve forces and waging the war eastward of the green line (in addition to the observation stations manned by the intelligence corps, air radar stations, and anti-aircraft missile batteries) – is two armored or mechanized brigades, i.e., a force equal to a reduced division.

Immediately after the 1967 war, that number of brigades was in fact stationed on the West Bank, but the IDF did not need to use an entire division in that quiet sector secondary in comparison to the Golan Heights and especially Sinai and the Suez. Instead of a formation (brigade or division), training bases for infantry, NAHAL, combat engineers and basic training were transferred to the West Bank. It is customary to credit Ariel Sharon, who was then commander of the training division in the general staff, with the idea of transferring training bases to the West Bank as a stage in creation of political facts. However, according to Yitzhak Rabin, who was then chief of staff, it was actually Minister of Defense Moshe Dayan who initiated that action as early as June 1967, a few days after the war, in order to allow the demobilization of reserve forces and maintain day-to-day security in the West Bank by means of training bases (by nature part of the standing army). Evidence in support of that version can be found in the intention already expressed in 1966, or even before then, to remove training bases from densely-populated areas on the coastal plain. The officers' training school was actually transferred from Petah Tikva to the Negev. A "city of training bases" was supposed to be built around it. The economic recession of 1966-67 also affected the defense budget (the National Security Academy was closed because of a shortfall of about $300,000); and the plan for the city of training bases was deferred. The conquest of the West Bank brought new necessities and opportunities. Training bases were transferred to the West Bank and placed in abandoned Jordanian army camps – not in new facilities, the erection of which would have indicated different considerations with regard to deployment.

The most active war zone of the IDF in the West Bank, against PLO organizations between the summer of 1967 and the Black September of 1970, was the Jordan Valley. The sector was organized militarily as an infantry brigade command to which armored forces were attached, an arrangement maintained for more than a decade, during which most of the activity (after the defeat of the PLO in September 1970 and June 1971, and its expulsion from Jordan) was concentrated on preventing the infiltration of bands of terrorists trying to cross the Jordan and bring weapons into the West Bank or perpetrate acts of terror as part of the political bargaining. Those acts became less frequent after the 1968-69 period of hot pursuits.

The Israeli-Egyptian peace process brought about a change in the deployment of the IDF in the West Bank. The CAMP DAVID ACCORDS stipulated that after the establishment of autonomy in the West Bank, Israel could redeploy its forces in "defined security areas." The size of those areas and the forces stationed there was left to the autonomy negotiations. Some members of the IDF general staff feared that the bargaining would begin with the present state of IDF deployment and perhaps be determined by it. Chief of Staff at the time, Raphael Eitan, was opposed to any Israeli withdrawal from the West Bank. He thus ordered the immediate expansion of the areas designated for IDF training there. Minister of Defense at the time, Ezer Weizman, said that in

Major General Eitan's view, autonomy would consist of "one autonomous Arab riding on a donkey between fire zones."

Although the peace treaty between Israel and Egypt was not signed until March 1979, and the withdrawal from Sinai was carried out in two stages, being completed only in April 1982, the chief of central command at that time (afterwards chief of staff), Moshe Levy, realized that all IDF forces would be removed from Sinai, and that new locations had to be found. The construction of three new airbases in the Negev and the transfer of the main thrust of the military threat from the southwest to the northeast assisted Levy in convincing the chief of staff to transfer some of the regular army, previously based in Sinai, to the central command, i.e., the West Bank. The new deployment took the form of logistical infrastructure (camps, installations, emergency supply depots) and the more thorough use of training areas. The war in Lebanon halted the process, though it is likely that a portion of the troops withdrawn from Lebanon will be repositioned on the West Bank.

Incidentally, the shortage of training areas in Israel has been used as an additional reason for not withdrawing the IDF from the West Bank. It is claimed that since the strengthening of the IDF from 1967 on, the addition of thousands of tanks and other military equipment, and its enlargement by about 10 divisions, it is no longer possible to return to the narrow pre-June 1967 borders. However that contention is not accepted by all military experts. An alternative view is that more efficient use could be made of training facilities, bases could be better situated and the solution to political problems should not be made dependent on the apparent constraint of the IDF's need for training areas.

See also DEFENSE STRATEGY.

DETENTION AND INTERROGATION

Order 378 empowers any policeman or soldier to make an arrest without a warrant. A suspect may be detained for four days by any soldier or policeman. A police officer may extend the detention for another four days, and a senior officer may extend it for seven days. In all, a person may be detained for 18 days before being brought before a military judge. The court may extend detention for six months before trial. In Israel, in contrast, a suspect must be brought before a judge within 48 hours, and the judge may extend his detention by 15 days. After 30 days, the detention may only be extended by special request of the attorney general, and that for a period not exceeding 90 days.

Stages in Interrogation

Interrogation is generally carried out by members of the General Security

Services (Shin Bet). After a suspect admits his guilt, a policeman is brought in to record his confession. The General Security Service is required to keep an orderly record of the interrogation, but in more than a few cases no such record was kept, and there is no way of ascertaining what happened to the detainee from the day of his arrest. Consequently, a defendant is less able to deny the charges against him during his trial.

Treatment of the Detainee During Interrogation

Interrigation methods include: solitary confinement, transfer of the detainee from place to place in order to undermine his self-confidence, cold showers in the winter and at night, the arrest of relatives to put pressure on the suspect, threats, verbal abuse, and forcing the detainee to stand for long periods.

Few complaints have been lodged by detainees. The Red Cross estimates that about 6 percent of its visits to the detainees result in their lodging a complaint. Amnesty International reports improper treatment of detainees and an excessive extension of detention.

The Extraction of Confession

The confession and testimony of the accused are of critical importance in the trial. The confession is extracted during the interrogation by the detainee's interrogators and is generally central to the case made by the prosecution. It should be emphasized that the accused has no possibility of identifying his interrogators because they wear civilian clothes during the interrogation without any badge or identifying mark. Moreover, the confession is written in Hebrew, a language of which the accused is unlikely to have full command.

Condition of Detention

The central problem in the detention facilities is overcrowding. In the Gaza Strip there is accommodation for 58 detainees, whereas occupancy reached 123 in May 1984. At the same time, the West Bank facilities for 22 detainees were occupied by 68.

According to a 1977 agreement applicable on the West Bank and in East Jerusalem, the following guidelines were established for Red Cross intervention:

A. The Red Cross was to receive notification no more than 12 days after a person was detained.

B. The Red Cross would be allowed to visit the detainee within 14 days of his detention. The visit would take place without witnesses. A representative of the Red Cross would be permitted to ask only personal details about the detainee and his state of health. For his part, the detainee was permitted to lodge complaints. The representative was entitled to send a physician to the detainee.

C. The Red Cross was entitled to visit a detainee at 14-day intervals. Starting from the second visit the representative would ask any question about any subject whatsoever.

D. Israel undertook to investigate any complaint raised by the Red Cross about improper treatment. The complaint would be investigated by the attorney-general.

Israel does not honor all clauses of this agreement, particularly regarding reporting detention within 12 days. Requests made by the Red Cross to visit detainees within seven days of their arrest have been rejected. (See RED CROSS).

Legal Defense

In many cases, a detainee is not permitted to make contact with an attorney. Sometimes his first meeting with an attorney takes place after 18 days, when an extension of detention is requested. In such cases the attorney has no possibility of effectively representing the detainee.

There is no legal limit to the time it is permitted to prevent a detainee from meeting with his lawyer, although the detainee is entitled to legal defense at the time of the hearing for extending his detention. The warden of the prison may prevent a meeting between the detainee and his lawyer, "if it is justified by reasons of security."

The reports of Amnesty International indicate that in recent years there has been a two-month period between a person's arrest and his being permitted to consult freely with his attorney.

DEVELOPMENT CORPORATIONS (OF THE SETTLERS)

Established by Israeli local and regional councils on the West Bank, these companies are owned by the councils, by settlements incorporated within regional councils and by various public institutions within their own areas of jurisdiction. According to the articles of association of these companies (registered with the registrar of corporations in Jerusalem), their objectives are to develop agriculture and industry, initiate, deliver and maintain services, and initiate and carry out development plans and town planning schemes. An examination of the regulations of various development corporations reveals that council officials are identical with the companies' board of directors. For example, the regulations of the Kiryat Arba development corporation specify that, "In all cases, the chairman of the board of directors will be the person serving concurrently as chairman of the Kiryat Arba local council." The Mateh-Benyamin development corporation specifies that the owner of managing share B (the regional council) has the right to appoint a director who will serve as chairman of the board of directors.

The development corporations are entitled to submit bids for contracts (which they usually win), issued by the councils for supplying services (funded by government ministries), such as busing school children, garbage collection, and construction of public buildings. The capital investment needed for the purchase of equipment (buses, mechanical equipment) and working capital, are supplied by government and public authorities (including the Jewish Agency).

The supply of services to the regional councils brings the corporations profits enabling expansion into other areas. A fleet of buses (about 60) enables the councils to compete with private firms for transportation contracts (for workers and tourists). The mechanical equipment in the possession of the companies or rented by them and used for rural construction (funded by the Jewish National Fund), is also used for commercial infrastructure work.

A publication of the Central Company for the Development of Samaria, Inc., detailing its areas of activity and its objectives, reports that at the end of 1984 the company owned 22 buses, minibuses, small and large trucks and heavy equipment, being operated in the following divisions: transportation, development and earth-moving, trucking, gas stations and construction. The transportation division provided services to schools, various public institutions, workers, and subcontractors.

The development division paves roads and sidewalks, constructs roads for the Jewish National Fund and sports grounds for each settlement. The construction division builds public buildings and bomb shelters in the settlements. In partnership with a GENERAL FEDERATION OF LABOR corporation, Even Vasid, the company operates a concrete factory and deals in the marketing of fuel by-products to the Arab market.

After the regional development corporations established themselves, AMANA founded a parent company, SBA, run jointly with the Samaria, Mateh Benyamin, and Gush Etzion Regional Councils. This company initiated joint projects with large economic concerns, including the investment companies of Israeli banks. SBA established several subsidiary corporations: Or-SBA is a contractor, building industrial structures in the Barkan area, and constructing homes in the West Bank and Gaza Strip; SBA Investments has established a science park at Ariel; Tadir-SBA operates factories for ready-mixed concrete in Matityahu and Efrat.

According to statements made by directors of the development corporations, the economic activity aims at achieving operational independence for the settlers: It is important for us to build this kind of system, because if we do not do so, we shall be permanently dependent on the goodwill of the government. Today, we have the professional ability and expertise to establish settlements on our own.''

DEVELOPMENT PLAN, JUDEA-SAMARIA (1983-1986)

Prepared by the MINISTRY OF AGRICULTURE and the Settlement Department of the WORLD ZIONIST ORGANIZATION in April 1983.

The main points of the plan: the addition of 80,000 people or 5-6,000 housing units each year by 1986, paving roads at a rate of 100-150 kilometers annually, the addition of 23 settlements, 20 strongpoints and two TOSHAVOT, and developing 4-500 dunams of industrial zones annually. The planned investment is as follows:

Housing: $878 million
Industry: $457 million
Roads: $125 million
Infrastructure (electricity, water, communications): $104 million
Agriculture: $55 million
Community Services: $298 million
Physical infrastructure in the settlements: $48 million
Land Purchase: $30 million
Transportation, commerce and finance: $192 million
Unexpected and misc.: $428 million
    Total Expenditures: $2,615,000 ·

The bulk of the investment (82.5 percent) is planned for what is defined as the "high demand areas" surrounding Jerusalem and Tel Aviv. The plan seeks to exploit the "natural" tendency of city dwellers to settle in suburbs so as to improve their standard of housing and living. "Ideological" settlement, i.e., the mountain settlements of the AMANA movement, and those in the Jordan Valley (See ALLON PLAN) make up less than 20 percent of the planned population.

The impressive growth in the number of settlers between 1980-1985 (almost 40,000) should be evaluated with regards to the objectives set out in the plans of the Israeli authorities. Although one more year still remains for the final implementation of the "1983–1986 Plan", it is possible at this stage to evaluate its degree of success. A comparison of settler figures in 1985 with the plan's target (up till the end of 1986) shows that only 43% of the plan's objectives have been attained (11,400 families as opposed to the 26,300 originally envisaged).
See also DROBLESS PLAN.

DIRECTORS-GENERAL COMMITTEE

An inter-ministerial coordinating committee to deal with day-to-day management of economic relations and problems in the territories occupied by the IDF. It was established in June 1967 and is chaired by the director-general of the Ministry of Finance. Its members are the directors-general of certain ministries. The responsibility for setting its agenda lies with the coordinator of activities in the territories (the military government). In the first years of its existence it coordinated all civilian activity in the territories, activity which by its nature touched upon matters belonging to the areas under the jurisdiction of several of the ministries. Along with the task of coordination, it also served, under certain ministers, as a means of limiting the absolute rule of the Ministry of Defense in the territories, particularly the activities of Moshe Dayan as minister of defense.

With the establishment of the CIVILIAN ADMINISTRATION, particularly with the strengthening of the ties between the STAFF OFFICERS and their parent ministries in Israel, the importance of the committee declined. As the economic activities of Israelis increased in the territories, particularly in the settlements, the committee decided, with government approval, that "it does not deal with Israeli settlement in the territories, except for the granting of POLITICAL INSURANCE, authorizations for the establishment of enterprises (both Jewish and Arab), and the setting of license fees in the Arab sector."

In recent years the plenum of the committee has met very rarely, and all of its activities are carried out by sub-committees for insurance, enterprises, and licensing.

The actual responsibility for coordinating the activities of the government in the Arab sector on the West Bank lies in the hands of the coordinator of activities and the staff officers. The activity of the committee was not guided by a long-term master plan or even by clear policy guidelines. Its discussions dealt with matters of detail arising in various contexts, as well as with matters demanding inter-ministerial coordination.

DROBLESS PLAN

Drafted by the head of the settlement division of the WORLD ZIONIST ORGANIZATION (WZO), Matityahu Drobless, it first came out in 1978, and was updated in 1980 and 1981. It states: "There is to be not a shadow of doubt regarding our intention to remain in Judea and Samaria. A dense chain of settlements on the mountain ridge running southwards from Nablus to Hebron will serve as a reliable barrier on the eastern front (of Arab states). This buffer zone of settlements will also create security for settlers in the Jordan Valley. Both areas *between* concentrations of the minority population and the areas *around* them must be settled to minimize the danger of the rise of another Arab state in the region."

According to this plan, by 1985 there were to be some 80 rural and urban settlements housing some 120,000 Jews. By the beginning of 1985, more than 100 settlements had already been established in the West Bank (See DEMOGRAPHY), but the number of Jewish residents amounted to only 40 percent of the target. In 1983 a detailed plan was prepared, under the guidance of Drobless, consisting of a DEVELOPMENT PLAN and a "master plan for the year 2010." The essence of the Drobless Plan was a shift in emphasis in WZO investments, by increasing investment in the West Bank and giving development priority to the mountain ridge area rather than the Jordan Valley (in accordance with the Alignment plan). The change of direction is revealed in the following table of investments of the WZO (1974-1983 in the West Bank in millions of dollars):

Region	1974	1975	1976	1977	1978	1979	1980	1981	1982	1983
Jordan Valley	3.8	3.90	3.11	5.22	3.70	11.15	13.70	12.85	12.65	12.89
Mountain Ridge	1.22	1.20	0.72	5.06	10.14	18.59	23.40	28.20	22.14	21.24
Total	5.09	5.10	3.83	10.28	13.84	29.74	37.10	41.05	34.79	34.13
Mountain Ridge %	24	24	19	49	73	63	63	69	64	62

The emphasis on the development of West Bank settlements in general and settlements of the mountain ridge in particular, is clearly derived from the political philosophy of the Likud government (1977-1984). The investment rate follows both internal and external political developments. The massive investments on the mountain ridge at the end of 1977, in 1978, and 1979, were intended to establish settlement facts during the CAMP DAVID negotiations and the AUTONOMY talks. The record investments in 1981 are a result of the Likud's efforts to create facts before elections it feared it might lose.

The massive WZO settlement plan during the Likud years was based on the establishment of non-agricultural COMMUNITY SETTLE-MENTS and infrastructure, while at the same time creating a maximum spread of Jewish settlement points all over the West Bank. This constituted a fundamental departure from classic Zionist settlement philosophy which aimed at creating and developing settlements as self-sufficient social and economic units. For this reason the new settlement policy was subjected to trenchant criticism from loyalists of the classic approach, such as Ra'anan Weitz, who claimed that the community settlements were dummy towns without an economic base. The Drobless Plan and its successors, however, saw nothing wrong with the new settlements developing into suburbs, with their residents commuting to the major metropolitan areas. Hence minimal attention was given to creating self-sufficient settlements.

The rapid construction of small settlements did not attract a flow of settlers and their chances of attaining even half their population target by the end of the 1980s, seem slim. Nonetheless, the WZO, under the Likud's influence, continues to press for more settlements in the West Bank, though some of the existing ones still lack permanent housing (See WORLD ZIONIST ORGANIZATION, LIKUD, YESHA). The main thrust of settlement activity is focused in the towns, planned and financed by the MINISTRY OF HOUSING AND CONSTRUCTION.

With the establishment of the national unity government, there has been a noticeable change in the budgetary allocations to settlement areas. In 1984, 43 percent of the budget went to the Jordan Valley as opposed to 57 percent to the mountain ridge. In the 1985 budget, the first drafted by the unity government, precisely 50 percent is allocated to each area, apparently as a compromise between the supporters of the Drobless and Allon plans.

EAST JERUSALEM

On June 28, 1967, the Israeli government decreed, on the basis of a law passed the previous day by the Knesset, that Israeli law, jurisdiction, and administration applied to a 70 square kilometer area east of the 1948 armistice line. The area was put under the municipal jurisdiction of Israeli Jerusalem. In addition to the Old City and the municipal area of Jordanian Jerusalem, this area includes some villages that had previously enjoyed independent status. As far as internal Israeli law is concerned, East Jerusalem is part of the State of Israel. International law, however, does not recognize unilateral annexation and for this reason the rest of the world, including the United States, views Jerusalem as an area under occupation and part of the West Bank.

The Israelis, viewing East Jerusalem as part of Israel, combine demographic and other data on East Jerusalem with the general figures for Israel. Foreign sources, however, include them with West Bank data.

For example, foreign publications include Palestinian population figures for East Jerusalem in West Bank data and data on the Jewish population settled in the area over the armistice line in figures on the West Bank settlers.

In 1967, the number of non-Jewish residents of East Jerusalem was about 67,000, some 11.5 percent of West Bank residents. In 1983, their number reached 122,000, 16 percent of West Bank Arab residents. This statistic underlines the fact that Palestinian population growth rate in Jerusalem is greater than in the West Bank. The major reason for this is the low emigration rate, caused by favorable economic and employment opportunities.

Since 1967 there has been an increasing tendency to urbanization and tens of thousands of Palestinians have settled within the metropolitan area of the city, outside its municipal boundaries.

In this area (including West Jerusalem), the demographic ratio between Jews and Arabs is approaching equality, while in the city itself the Jewish majority has steadily decreased from about three quarters in 1967 to 71.5 percent in 1983.

About 80,000 Jews live in neighborhoods constructed after 1967 east of the armistice line (1985). Arab sources add this number to that of the settlers on the West Bank (See DEMOGRAPHY ((ISRAELI)).

East Jerusalem remains the largest and most important urban center in the West Bank, the focus of the economic, commercial, cultural, religious, social and political activity of the Palestinian community. Israeli efforts to detach East Jerusalem from the West Bank (in religious and political matters) have been unsuccessful. On the contrary, the fact that Israeli law applies to East Jerusalem has allowed the Palestinian press to operate with relative freedom (See PRESS (ARAB), CENSORSHIP). The personal legal status of East Jerusalem residents is equivalent to that of Israeli Arabs, with the exception of their citizenship, which remains Jordanian. They receive national insurance benefits and some are organized in the GENERAL FEDERATION OF LABOR. They are entitled to vote for and be elected to the Jerusalem municipal council, although only a minority (about 15 percent in 1983) have chosen to avail themselves of this right, and Arabs have never stood for election. In other matters (services, security, custody, land expropriation, personal religious status, etc.), East Jerusalem residents are no different from those on the West Bank. With the spread of Israeli settlement (and urban settlement in particular) in the metropolitan area, and the extension of Israeli norms to the Israeli settlers (See PERSONAL STATUS OF ISRAELIS), the difference between East

66

Jerusalem and the West Bank has been blurred even further. To all intents and purposes, the distinction insofar as it ever existed, has ceased being territorial and has become ethnic. Alienated islands of Arabs and Jews live side by side under a dual system, one for Jews and one for Arabs.

ECONOMIC POLICY

In the perspective of 18 years of occupation, Israel's economic policy appears on the surface to be clear, consistent, and deliberate. It can be summarized in a few sentences: freezing the economic development of the Palestinian sector along with encouragement of improvements in the standard of living, based on income from work in Israel; economic prosperity for individual residents alongside economic stagnation at the communal level; discouraging independent economic development that would enter into competition with the Israeli economy, and prevention of independent economic development that could enable Palestinian political forces to establish power bases, and eventually a Palestinian state. A relatively high standard of living, achieved by employment in Israel, is to create greater dependence on Israel and distract public opinion from politics; economic dependence is also to be achieved by the integration of infrastructure systems (roads, electricity, water); economic rewards and punishments form part of the political and security control system in the territories.

This policy appears to have been executed with great success, as is evident from an examination of the various economic sectors (See NATIONAL ACCOUNTS, FOREIGN TRADE, AGRICULTURE, INDUSTRY, EMPLOYMENT). Closer scrutiny of the economic decision-making process, however, shows that the "consistent" policy is merely a haphazard *post facto* consequence of decisions made without forethought, in response to pressures, or as compromises or concessions to Israeli pressure groups. This has been the pattern with decisions on the OPEN BRIDGES, EMPLOYMENT IN ISRAEL and BANKING. In actual fact, economic policy is inseparable from political and security policies, and derives from them.

Economic policy has conformed to political philosophy. In the years 1967-1973, Israeli rule in the territories was seen as temporary and the government therefore refrained from institutionalizing the economic relations between the territories and Israel. The belief that protracted Israeli government of the territories would create an insupportable economic burden upon Israel also contributed to this attitude.

As the years passed, it became apparent that the territories did not have to be an economic burden, but could provide obvious economic advantages as an outlet for Israeli goods and as a cheap labor market (See FOREIGN TRADE). They even proved not to be a FISCAL BURDEN. The political decision "not to decide," and to keep all options open for economic separation (the economic expression of the "territorial compromise" approach), eventually became a long-range policy to integrate the economies insofar as Israeli interests were concerned, but without granting a system of incentives and Israeli assistance to the local population and its productive sector.

This dual system characterizes economic activity in the West Bank.

EDUCATION (ARAB)

The Arab educational system operates according to the Jordanian system existing before the occupation. Three different systems function in the region: government, UNRWA, private.

Arab education comprises three levels:

I) elementary: compulsory, six years; II) prep school: compulsory, three years; III) high school: compulsory but not free, three years.

The number of students in the West Bank in 1984 reached 278,500 in 8,185 classes. The number of teaching jobs was 7,310, and the number of administrative and service workers 836. In vocational schools and teachers' colleges, the number of students grew from 3,163 in 1967/68 to 6,098 in 1982/83.

The highest educational authority in the West Bank is the Examination Committee in Nablus. This authority operates the matriculation system and the final examinations for teachers' colleges according to the Jordanian system. It is headed by a chairman to whom the matriculation examination directorate and college affairs directorate are responsible. Members of the committee include the directors of the bureaus of education in the six sub-districts, and of the three teachers' colleges. The committee sets examination papers and arranges examination halls, proctors and examiners. It coordinates the entire regional system, including East Jerusalem.

The UNRWA Educational System operates mainly in the refugee camps and is maintained by UNRWA (the United Nations Relief and Works Agency). The system is similar to the government one except that students go on to government high schools after completion of prep schools. The system includes a teachers' college in Ramallah and a vocational school in Kalandiya. There are 39,882 students in 97 schools, 1,178 teachers and 79 administrative workers.

Private Schools are mainly communal and Christian. They are located principally in the Bethlehem and Ramallah sub-districts. The Christian institutions are supported by world organizations and comprise all levels including high school. There are 269 kindergartens for 9,454 children, which operate in conjunction with the private schools. The total number of students is 23,526 in 822 classes. In spite of the Christian sponsorship, the vast majority of the students are Muslim – 15,872, as against 7,636 Christians. The teaching staff numbers 1,106, with 123 administrative workers.

Government Vocational Education – These schools are attended by 659 students in 20 classes. The majority are Muslims and 140 of them are from refugee camps.

The vocational school in Nablus was founded in 1960 and serves 290 students in 11 classes in the following subjects: electricity, auto mechanics, carpentry, plumbing, construction, metalwork, and draftsmanship. There are 23 teachers and 10 administrative workers. The school has 14 workshops.

The vocational school in Tulkarm was founded in 1975, with the aim of raising consciousness with regard to vocational education. There are 183 students in six classes, 13 teachers, and six administrative and service workers.

The vocational school in Deir-Dibwan was founded in 1976, with the same policy of expanding vocational education. There are 91 students studying in three classes. UNRWA operates a vocational school in Kalandiya, and in Hebron there is a private Polytechnic Institute, in addition to other private schools teaching technical subjects.

Government Teachers' Colleges operate with funding from the civilian administration, which includes upkeep of the dormitories attached to them. They serve 608 students, including 130 from the refugee camps. There are 31 classes and 53 teachers.

The following data reflect developments in Arab education in the West Bank: the number of those with no education fell from 47.5 percent in 1970 to 26.6 percent in 1983 and the illiteracy rate has fallen from 27.8 percent to 13.5 percent for men, and from 65.1 percent to 38.9 percent for women (1970-1983). In 1983 the number of men with post-secondary education was 12.4 percent, as against 1.4 percent in 1970, and for women 5.3 percent, as against 0.5 percent. In 1983 men between the ages of 18 and 24 were educated as follows: illiterate, 1 percent; elementary school, 17 percent; prep school, 16 percent; high school, 43 percent; post-secondary, 23 percent. Among women of the same ages, the breakdown was: illiterate, 7.5 percent; elementary school, 31 percent; prep school, 14 percent; high school, 34 percent; post-secondary, 13.5 percent. See also EMPLOYMENT, DEMOGRAPHY, UNIVERSITY GRADUATES.

EDUCATION (JEWISH)

The educational system of the Jewish settlers in the territories is organized along the same four divisions as in Israel proper:

1. Pre-school division – including day care centers and kindergartens, both preliminary and compulsory.
2. Elementary division – Grades 1 through 6.
3. Junior high division – Grades 7 through 9.
4. High school division – Grades 10 through 12.

All these include the various educational "streams" existing in Israel (i.e. state and state religious). In most of the settlements there is a local educational system, at least up to elementary school age. Where the settlement's population is small, students are bused to a nearby school. Because of the transportation problems, there is a trend to concentrate the junior high and high schools in regional schools or blocs, depending on distance between settlements, or educational stream (state, state-religious, independent ultra-Orthodox). Children through the second grade may not be bused further than 15 kilometers, and from third grade may not travel longer than half an hour. Dozens of vehicles (buses and taxis) are involved in transporting settlers' children within the region itself and from it to the cities (Jerusalem and Tel Aviv areas), and the cost to the taxpayer is estimated at millions of dollars each year. The settlers' educational system is managed by a special department in the Ministry of Education. From its inception, the department has seen that yeshivot and ulpanot (schools for religious studies for boys and girls, respectively) such as Shomron College in Ariel and Kedumim, and Orot College in Elkana, are built in almost every settlement requesting them. A separate teacher-training system was also set up for the West Bank and Gaza Strip, including continuing education for teachers, national service (alternative service for religious girls), branches of the Bnei Akiva religious youth movement, community centers and extensions, schools and institutes, libraries, and instructional centers, all financed by the government.

The number of employees in the West Bank educational system is based on the following criteria: in day-care centers, one staff member for every six children; in pre-school, two staff members for each class; in kindergarten, two staff members for each class; in elementary school, 1.5 for each class; in junior high, 2.5 for each class; in high school, 2.5 for each class. These ratios are on the same order as those within the green line. However, in Mateh Benyamin for instance, there are about 400 employed in education, or 10 percent of all employed persons (a staff student ratio of 1:4.6). The average number of students per class in Mateh Benyamin is as follows: day-care centers – 8.9 children; pre-school – 26.4 children;

kindergarten – 10.4 children; elementary school – 8.5; junior high – 4; high school – 1.7 (for the school year 1983-84). The Israeli standard is 30 children per class in kindergarten and 35-40 in elementary, junior high and high schools.

During the 1984-85 school year all Israeli schools in the West Bank were under-utilized. According to Ministry of Education reports, 16 students attended the Mt. Hebron School; there were 72 students in the six elementary grades in Ofra; 80 students in the junior high and high school in Kedumim, and 95 students in grades 7-10 in Kiryat Arba. High school students preferred to travel to schools within the green line rather than attending schools in the region.

ELECTIONS (ISRAELI)

According to Israeli law (See CREEPING ANNEXATION), Israeli residents of the West Bank have the right to participate in Knesset elections in their places of residence. In the 1984 elections, for the first time, it was possible to discern the voting patterns of both types of settlers: the ideological – in the outlaying settlements, and the suburban – in settlements close to metropolitan areas.

Altogether, about 10,000 Israelis voted in the territories. The breakdown was as follows: Likud – 33 percent; Tehiya – 20.6 percent; Morasha – 16.8 percent; Alignment – 6.5 percent; National Religious Party – 5.9 percent; Kach – 5.1 percent; Shas – 3 percent; others – 1-2 percent.

These results underline the success of the lists supporting settlement of Judea and Samaria, which received a much higher percentage of the vote than they did nationally. The bloc of parties to the right of the Alignment (Likud, Tehiya, Morasha, NRP, Shas, and Kach) won 86 percent – compared with the Alignment (7 percent) and the other center and left parties which altogether received 7 percent. Analysis of the election results by type of settlement reveals the following trend: in the urban settlements close to the metropolitan areas the Likud won a majority and the Alignment an insignificant minority. In Ma'aleh Adumim, 5 kilometers from Jerusalem, the Likud polled 1,239 votes and the Alignment 373. In Ariel, the Alignment polled 8 votes and the Likud 348. In the ideological settlements right-wing parties Morasha, Tehiya, and Kach were in the majority while the Likud polled a minority of votes. However, because of the decisive weight of the urban settlers among the total Israeli settlers in the West Bank, the Likud won the greatest number of votes in the West Bank.

The results of the Knesset elections of 1984 support the argument that a bloc of West Bank voters is being created who oppose territorial compromise. This bloc is divided between those whose vote is ideological and those whose vote is not ideological but based on a desire to secure their property and quality of life in the suburban settlements. If these trends continue, the settlers will become an important factor in preventing a political solution based on withdrawal from the territories.

ELECTIONS (PALESTINIAN)

According to Jordanian law three local bodies in the West Bank are elected: MUNICIPALITIES, VILLAGE COUNCILS, and CHAMBERS OF COMMERCE. Municipal and chamber of commerce elections are held every four years, and village council elections every three years. The last elections held before Israeli occupation were in 1963 for municipalities and in 1965 for chambers of commerce.

1. Municipal Elections

Before the legal end of the term of the municipal councils elected under Jordanian rule (1967), the military administration issued an order (80) stating that "all local bodies will continue to serve until a new order is issued." At the end of 1971, it was felt that the time was ripe for holding municipal elections, in light of the political calm in the territories and Jordan's acquiescence. Order 454 fixed a date for the conclusion of the municipal council's term and for the elections, which were held in Samaria and Jericho in March 1972, and in Judea in May 1972. No changes were made in Jordanian election laws. Some 21 cities held lively election campaigns and voter participation reached 80 percent. In Hebron and Salfit a single list was submitted; hence, according to Jordanian law, elections were unnecessary. For the most part, the incumbent councils and mayors were re-elected (See MUNICIPALITIES).

Despite the notable change in the political climate, the military government decided to hold elections in 1976, as scheduled, but this time with revisions in the Jordanian law: women were given the vote, and local tax payment – which qualifies a citizen to vote, under Jordanian law – was reduced. As a result of these changes, the number of eligible voters increased from about 31,000 to 88,300.

The election campaign aroused great interest, and focused on the struggle between the radical bloc and the traditional leadership, which in several localities did not, in the end, put up candidates. The turnout was 72 percent, and the radicals, supported and guided by the PLO, won a stunning victory. Even though the results did not please the Israeli authorities, they did not exercise their right to appoint mayors of their own choosing, or even alter the make-up of the municipal councils. The military government's attempt to reach a *modus operandi* with the radical mayors was not successful. The 1976 elections were the last held in the West Bank, and eventually, many officials then elected were dismissed or suspended from their posts. The High Court of Justice in 1984 rejected the petitions of residents of several towns to order the military government to hold elections.

2. Chamber of Commerce Elections

Last held in 1972-73. In light of the military government's experience in the municipal elections, it preferred to freeze the existing state of affairs (1977, Order 697) and extend the terms of the chambers of commerce. These included the prominent chambers in Bethlehem, Hebron, Ramallah, and Tulkarm, where elections were not held in 1973. Consequently, these chambers of commerce have served since 1965.

3. Village Council Elections

In October-November 1975, elections were held in 51 villages. In six others a single list was submitted. These councils have served ever since, as the military government has not called for new elections.

ELECTRIC CORPORATION (JERUSALEM)

A company that originated in a concession granted to a Greek merchant during the period of Ottoman rule, for the supply of electricity to Jerusalem and its surroundings. After World War I the concession was sold to a British company. Following the founding of the State of Israel, the Israeli Electric Corporation purchased the British company, but the Jordanian authorities did not recognize the deal insofar as it concerned East Jerusalem and the West Bank, where the Jerusalem company became publicly-owned and continued to operate. After the Six Day War the Israeli government decided to recognize the East Jerusalem Electric Company's concession in East Jerusalem and nearby West Bank communities. The government also registered the company with the Israeli registrar of corporations, and coopted two representatives of the Jerusalem municipality to its board of directors. Other members of the board are public figures and mayors from the West Bank, and its chairman since 1979 is Anwar Nuseibah, a former senior Jordanian minister.

In 1971, a legal dispute broke out over the supply of electricity to the Mt. Hebron area, including the towns of Hebron and Halhul. This area lies outside the original concession area of the company. While the Jordanian parliament authorized the Jordanian economic minister to extend the Jerusalem company's concession to this area before the Six Day War, the extension was not implemented and Mt. Hebron continued to receive its electricity from local generators. The Israeli military government decided to grant the concession in the area to the Israeli Electric Corporation. The East Jerusalem Electric Company appealed the decision, arguing that it contravened Jordanian legislation. They also argued that the military government's decision constituted a "permanent change" in the status of the occupied territories, forbidden by INTERNATIONAL LAW.

The High Court of Justice rejected the East Jerusalem Electric Company's petition in December 1972. The justices ruled that the Jordanian law of 1967 simply "empowered" the government to grant the company the concession in the Hebron area but did not "oblige" it to do so. The justices also accepted the military government's contention that it was "absolutely impossible" from an economic point of view to continue supplying electricity to the area from local generators. Since the end of the occupation was not in sight, the court ruled that there was no choice but to make the investment and restructure the electricity supply to the Mt. Hebron area.

In April 1979, the East Jerusalem Electric Company encountered a serious financial crisis, and the supply of electricity to new Jewish neighborhoods in East Jerusalem and the surrounding settlements was disrupted. The government offered to purchase the company's rights to supply electricity to the new Jewish areas. After long negotiations, the offer was turned down.

On December 30, 1979 the government notified the Jerusalem company that it would expropriate its concession for East Jerusalem as of January 1, 1981. Concurrently, the military commander served a similar notice, concerning the West Bank. The principal grounds for the action were ostensibly inefficiency and disruption in electricity supply.

In July 1980 – some six months before the expropriation was due to come into effect – the company petitioned the High Court. On December 30, 1980 the court ordered a postponement. In February 1981, the court ruled that the company's concession would not be revoked in the West Bank, and would be revoked in East Jerusalem only if doing so would not harm the company's operations in the West Bank. The court rejected the economic argument for the expropriation and ruled that the real motive was political, and therefore unacceptable according to international law: while the government may act on political considerations in East

Jerusalem, it may not do so in the occupied territories.

The court's decision prevented the takeover of the Jerusalem company, because it was manifestly impossible to expropriate its facilities in East Jerusalem without affecting its ability to operate in the West Bank (See ELECTRICITY).

By 1984, the company generated only 10% of its electricity supply, and purchased the rest from the Israeli Electric Corporation. Due to mismanagement and internal disputes it was unable to meet its financial obligations, and the debts to the Israeli company reached $11 million in 1986. Its concession is due to expire in 1987 and will, probably, not be renewed by Israel.

ELECTRICITY

The West Bank's electricity comes from three sources: the national Israeli grid (The Israeli Electric Corporation), Arab municipal and regional grids, and small diesel generators in Arab villages. At the beginning of 1983 power sources for the West Bank were as follows: a) power stations – Nablus and environs, 21 megawatts; Jerusalem and environs, 15 megawatts; Jenin, three megawatts; Jericho, three megawatts; 200 generators (about one quarter-megawatt each) in Arab villages; b) high tension lines (national grid): two high tension lines of 5.5 megawatt-amperes from Jerusalem to Hebron, three high tension trans-Samaria lines (7.5 megawatts-amperes) and a 3.3 kilovolt line from the Beit She'an station along the Jordan Valley. Under construction: lines from Jerusalem to the Jordan Valley, from Hebron to Yata, from Tapuah to Elon Moreh, and south and west Mt. Hebron. The towns of Kalkilya, Tulkarm, Halhul, Hebron, Jenin, and part of Nablus are connected to the Israeli national grid, as are 33 Arab villages (three in the Jenin sub-district, 10 in the Nablus sub-district, 16 in the Tulkarm sub-district, and four in the Hebron sub-district). A number of other Arab villages are also in the process of being connected. The Jewish settlements outside the concession area of the East Jerusalem Electric Company are connected to the national grid. All Gaza's electricity is supplied by the national grid.

In 1967, the power stations in the West Bank supplied 10.5 megawatts. Nablus and Jerusalem consumed 77 percent, Hebron 9 percent, and the rest of the West Bank, 14 percent. Beginning in the mid-1970s, the authorities began connecting up the West Bank to the national grid. The Palestinian local authorities launched a campaign against the incursion of the Israeli Electric Corporation, seeing linkage with the national grid as creating a permanent political fact. A petition submitted to the High Court of Justice by the East Jerusalem Electric Company against the connection of Hebron and environs to the Israeli grid was rejected; the efforts of Arab towns and the East Jerusalem company to open and expand power stations were confronted with obstacles and several requests for the import of new diesel generators were turned down. It may be assumed that with the expiration of the East Jerusalem Electric Company's concession and the development of infrastructure for the Jewish settlements, local production of electricity will gradually be eliminated.

There has been considerable growth in the consumption of electricity in the West Bank since 1967. In 1970 it was estimated at 37 million kilowatts hours, and in 1980 reached approximately 130 million kilowatts (without the Jewish settlements but including East Jerusalem). In Nablus, consumption rose from 10.5 million kilowatts in 1970 to 32.0 million kilowatts in 1980, and in Hebron from 1.5 million to 19.2 million kilowatts. The major change, however, came in the expansion of electric supply to outlying towns and villages, whose consumption rose from 0.7 million kilowatts in 1970 to 11.5 million kilowatts in 1980. A peak demand of 25 megawatts was estimated (1983) for the West Bank (not including East Jerusalem). The Israeli Electric Corporation reported a growth of 33.8 percent in West Bank consumption between 1983/4 and 1984/5, from 94.6 million kilowatts to 126.6 million kilowatts.

In 1981, 96 percent of city households had regular electric supply and 72 percent of village households were supplied electricity for at least a few hours a day. The percentage of houses supplied with electricity (for at least a few hours per day) was 23.1 in 1967 and 48.0 in 1975. The percentage owning electric refrigerators rose from 14 percent in 1974 to 60 percent in 1983, and the percentage of television owners from 13 percent in 1974 to 75 percent in 1983. Industrial electrical consumption also grew rapidly. It should be noted that growth in electricity consumption was higher in towns connected to the Israeli grid (Hebron, Tulkarm) than in Nablus. This indicates that had more electricity been supplied to the other towns, their consumption would have been even higher. According to the development plan of the Israeli Electric Corporation, the Arab family's participation at peak demand will be 0.45 kilowatt (1986), 0.60 kilowatt (1990) and 1.00 kilowatt (2000). This is less than half the rate calculated for a Jewish family (in each target year) and lower still considering the size of an Arab family (on average 50 percent larger than a Jewish family). This planning indicates that the disparity between Jews and Arabs in standards of living and levels of electrical supply to industry will persist into the 21st century.

Israeli Electric Corporation projections call for a tripling of electrical supply to the West Bank by the end of the century (an average supply of 70 megawatt-amperes) to the Jewish and Arab population.

In addition to approximately 150 kilometers of high tension lines already constructed in the West Bank by the Israeli Electric Corporation, and lines scheduled for 1984-85 (see above), two sub-stations of 30 megawatts each are planned for the present decade in Tapuah – which is connected by high tension lines 40 km to Petah Tikva – and in Kiryat Arba (60 megawatts). Kiryat Arba is connected by high tension lines to the sub-station at Even Sapir, near Jerusalem. Two more sub-stations, at Kedumim and Givon, are planned for the next decade.

EMERGENCY REGULATIONS (1945)

Enacted by the British high commissioner to fight the Jewish underground movements. They give the administration the broadest authority to infringe upon basic rights of the population. The Knesset has defined them as "undemocratic," and in the decisions of the Israeli Supreme Court reservations have been expressed several times regarding their draconian character. In Israel a few of those regulations have been rescinded (those dealing with expulsion and administrative detention). According to the Israeli view, those regulations are in force throughout the area of Mandatory Palestine, and they were part of the existing law when the West Bank was occupied. In the opinion of Palestinian jurists and international organizations, however, the Jordanian constitution completely abolished the security regulations. In order to impose the Israeli interpretation, the military government issued an interpretative order according to which any law applying on the West Bank which has not been explicitly cancelled by another law, will be regarded as valid. To make doubly certain, the government promulgated the Order Concerning the Security Enactments (378) in which most of the 1945 regulations are included.

The regulations provide the legal basis for an extensive series of individual and collective punitive measures such as expulsion (par. 112), curfew (par. 124), demolition of houses (pars. 119, 120), house arrest (pars. 111-115), closing off areas, preventive and administrative detention (pars. 16, 72, 132), and censorship (pars. 87, 88) (See ENFORCEMENT AND PUNISHMENT). Characteristic of the security enactments is that people can be punished for holding opinions or refusing to inform on their friends rather than be convicted for acts which they themselves committed or are proven to have committed. The enactments also permit collective punishment and are subject to no judicial review except that of the HIGH COURT OF JUSTICE.

Moreover, that court tends to give the military governor considerable freedom of action in applying the regulations.

EMPLOYMENT IN ISRAEL (PALESTINIAN)

Employment in Israel, or, as the economists say, "the export of labor services," is a decisive factor in the economy of the West Bank, contributing 20 percent to the Gross National Product of the region, only slightly less than the contribution of the main economic branch, agriculture, 22 percent of GNP (See AGRICULTURE). Income from employment in Israel compensates for most of the negative balance of trade of the area ("excess imports"). That income has been a decisive factor in the constantly rising standard of living of the residents of the West Bank, and its growth is conspicuous in comparison to the stagnation in the productive sector and the West Bank's Gross Domestic Product.

In 1982, according to official statistics, 43,000 workers from the territories worked in Israel, 30 percent of the West Bank labor force. In 1984 the number came to about 50,000, 31.5 percent of the labor force that year. To that figure must be added approximately 20,000 illegal workers, i.e., those not employed through the official labor exchanges.

In 1972, 14,700 West Bank workers were employed in Israel (12.8 percent of the West Bank labor force); in 1975 there were 40,400 (30.5 percent of the labor force), a proportion remaining unchanged until 1984. In contrast to the relative stability in the number of workers from the West Bank during the past decade, there has been a constant rise in the number of workers from the Gaza Strip employed in Israel (17,500 in 1972, 22,700 in 1973, 35,900 in 1981, 40,000 in 1983). Consequently, the proportion of workers from the West Bank among total workers from the territories in Israel fell from two-thirds in the mid-1970's to one-half in the mid-1980's. That is because, in contrast to the Gaza Strip, employment in Israel is not the only source of employment for residents of the West Bank. They can maneuver among four options, depending on economic and political circumstances: employment in Israel, in the West Bank, in agriculture in the West Bank villages, or work in Arab countries abroad. The decrease in employment in the Arab oil-producing states, for example, brought significant growth in employment in Israel in 1983-84. Every job-seeker on the West Bank found work in Israel. According to administration reports, in 1983-84 the demand for workers from Israel exceeded the number of job-seekers applying to the labor exchanges, despite the increase in unemployment in Israel. That is because the employment of West Bank Arabs in certain branches of the Israeli economy has become institutionalized, and Jewish workers are not generally willing to accept those jobs.

When Israel emerged from the recession of 1966, workers from the territories took the place of Jewish workers in construction and services who had lost their jobs because of the recession and did not return because of the low pay and low status. Workers from the territories comprise no more than 5-6 percent of the Israeli labor force (8 percent of workers in production), but they are concentrated in certain branches: half of the workers from the territories are employed in construction, 18 percent of all workers in that sector in Israel. West Bank workers are even more preponderant on the building site itself. In municipal sanitation services, in the hotel industry and in other services, their proportion is also very high. By far the majority (79 percent) are employed in the Jerusalem and Tel Aviv metropolitan areas. Only about 18 percent are employed in industry, and there too workers from the territories are concentrated in unskilled jobs.

The structure of the job market limits competition between West Bank workers and Israeli labor. Israelis would rather receive unemployment compensation than perform the low-status, manual jobs in which the Arab workers are employed. In fact, reports of the Israeli labor offices show that thousands of jobless Jews choose to forfeit the right to unemployment compensation by refusing to take what they regard as "Arab work."

The employment of workers from the territories in Israel has thus had a structural, sociological impact rather than a purely economic effect. Their contribution to the Israeli labor force is marginal, but they alone are willing to perform certain vital jobs in sectors perceived by Israelis as beneath their dignity or too low paying. For that reason workers from the West Bank employed in Israel are resistant to growing unemployment. Moreover, they have other employment options, as noted above.

Most of the West Bank workers employed in Israel are male (97 percent), aged 14-34, and married. Half are the sole wage earners in their households.

About a third of the workers from the territories have been employed in Israel more than 10 years, and a fifth have worked for the same employer for more than four years. This demographic stability shows that employment of workers from the territories has become a way of life, facilitated as travel time for most of the workers does not exceed an hour and about 80 percent return home every evening.

The increase in the pace of construction of Israeli settlements on the West Bank and the establishment of industry there has increased the number of workers from the West Bank who do not need to travel to

Jewish centers across the green line. These workers are included among those employed in Israel, as the statistics are ethnic, rather than geographical (See NATIONAL ACCOUNTS).

EMPLOYMENT IN ISRAEL – WAGES

Wages and Salary

There are no exact statistics, but the declared policy of the employment service is equal pay for equal work without distinction of citizenship (See GENERAL FEDERATION OF LABOR (HISTADRUT)). Most of the residents of the territories are hired on a daily basis in all branches, except for agriculture, where it is obligatory to go over from a daily to a monthly basis after five years. In most of the other branches the transition from a daily to a monthly basis depends on the employer, and in general employers prefer the daily basis, where the pay is lower and does not include social benefits. A significant number of the workers receive the minimum wage or less. On the first of the month the worker receives an advance equal to a third or a half of his monthly wage, and in the middle of the month he receives the rest from the employment service. The Arab worker receives premiums equal to only 30 percent of his daily wage, whereas the Israeli worker's premiums are about 50 percent of his daily wage.

Tenure

The maximum permitted daily employment period in Israel is five years. However, a worker who is not a permanent resident of the State of Israel is not entitled to tenure at work. Consequently a resident of the territories is not entitled to sick leave or paid vacations from his employer. His wages are lower; he is entitled to severance pay equal to 12 days' wages for every year he has worked, whereas a worker employed on a monthly basis is entitled to a month's severance pay for every year of employment. The day laborer is in greater danger of being fired than the monthly worker, and when a worker from the territories is fired after less than six months any severance pay is dependent on the good will of his employer.

Seniority

Workers from the territories rarely receive pay increases for seniority except in the construction industry, where the worker must prove his seniority by means of work examinations. Unless the union is influential or the employer has some specific interest, a worker from the territories receives less for seniority than one from Israel. As of the twelfth year of employment, a West Bank worker is entitled to no increase in seniority pay, even if he works for a longer period.

Sick Leave

A worker from the occupied territories is entitled to receive his salary from the labor exchange during the period he is sick. His rights are identical to those of any day worker, including Israelis.

Mourning Periods and Festivals

Payment for the mourning period of a worker from the territories is not obligatory and depends on the employer's good will. Unlike an Israeli, a worker from the territories is not entitled to three days of paid vacation. As for festivals, only in the construction industry and agriculture do the same conditions apply to Israelis and workers from the territories. In other sectors, the decision depends on the employer's good will.

Pension

A pension is paid to a worker from the territories only if he has worked for at least 10 years in Israel. The worker may receive a monthly pension six months after the day of his retirement. Alternatively his heirs may receive the entire sum in one payment from the day of his death. It is not clear whether his wife is entitled to a pension, or, if his wife dies, whether his children are entitled to receive it, as is the case in Israel. A resident of the territories is not entitled to a pension if his health forces him to retire before retirement age (65), even though part of his salary may have been set aside for that purpose.

Recuperation Allowance

Unlike Israeli workers, who receive a fixed and standard sum annually, a resident of the territories receives a recuperation payment, which is a function of the size of his salary over the past year. Moreover, because of inflation, the value of that payment is eroded, which is not the case with an Israeli worker.

Clothing Allowance and Vacation

Only in agriculture is the worker entitled to a clothing allowance (2 percent of his annual salary). In other sectors it depends on the employer's good will. Since workers from the territories are paid on a daily basis, they are entitled to up to 14 days of annual vacation, less than received by an Israeli worker.

National Insurance

There are no clear statistics about national insurance arrangements regarding the 50,000 legal workers from the territories. A sum equal to 20 percent of the worker's net pay is transferred to the employment service, the same sum as is transferred by Israeli employers and workers. However, whereas for the Israeli worker the payments are transferred to the National Insurance Institute, those made in the name of the worker from the territories are transferred directly to the Treasury. That money, the "withholding fund," covers part of the budget of the occupied territories (See FISCAL BURDEN). A resident of the territories is entitled to accident insurance and insurance against the employer's bankruptcy to the same extent as an Israeli worker. Residents of the territories also receive childbirth benefits and 12 weeks' paid maternity leave, but this applies only to women giving birth within the State of Israel, not in the territories. A resident of the territories is not entitled to payments for old age, widowhood, dependent children, survivors, general disability, unemployment, or social benefits. That money, set aside from the worker's salary, is kept, according to Ministry of Labor policy, for the time when "the future of the territories is decided and talks are held in the framework of peace negotiations."

EMPLOYMENT ON THE WEST BANK

1. Israelis

The first settlements established in the West Bank according to the Allon Plan were based on the traditional settlement model of the Labor movement. That movement seeks to establish communities with an agrarian way of life (including agriculture and industry), supporting themselves socially and economically and providing employment within the settlement itself or in regions composed of cooperative settlements of all kinds, i.e., kibbutzim, collective moshavim, and cooperative moshavim.

Settlement based on this model requires large allocations of agricultural land and supply of water and the establishment of industrial enterprises as well as housing and public institutions. Since the settlement area chosen for ideological and security reasons (See ALLON PLAN) was the relatively inaccessible Jordan Valley, it demanded considerable capital. That settlement model, predicated upon settlers with strong ideological motivation, did not attract large numbers, and its growth potential was low. Because of the crisis in Israeli agriculture, the shortage of public investment funds, and the harsh topography and climate, there was a large turnover among the settlers, who ran into economic difficulties. The number of settlers in the Jordan Valley has never exceeded a few thousand.

The proponents of "settlement in all parts of the Land of Israel," Gush Emunim and the first Likud government, were not constrained by Alignment settlement policy. Their goal was to populate the West Bank with Jewish settlers en masse, quickly, extensively, and in any way possible. The members of Gush Emunim were older than the products of the Labor youth movements, they were urban, white-collar workers not attracted by agrarian life. What did attract them was the idea of being within commuting distance of their jobs in the metropolitan areas. They developed a new type of "pioneering settlement," the COMMUNITY SETTLEMENT. Settlements of this type established between 1977 and 1984 were open, semi-urban bedroom communities within 30-45 minutes of the urban centers on the other side of the green line. Because of the shortage of land and water few of those settlements were based on agriculture.

Liberal allocations of public funds made it possible for many of the Gush Emunim settlers to earn a living in the public sector in their settlements and region. According to the WZO (1985) census most of the families (over two thirds) have two breadwinners (husband and wife); 74% are employed in the public sector, 13.2% in industry and 1.5% in agriculture.

Twenty-nine percent of family heads define their occupations as "managers", 23.3% white-collar, businessmen and service workers; 15.5% are professionals, 9% are academics and 16.6% are in industry and agriculture (professional employees).

About 79% travel to work each morning outside their own settlements; about 62% commute to the nearest big city and 17% travel to another West Bank settlement. About three quarters are salaried employees and approximately 12.5% are self-employed. Fifty-three percent have postsecondary education.

By comparison, in Jerusalem, which is known as a "white-collar city", 43.7% of employees were in public and community services in 1984. The percentage in the veteran urban Jewish settlements within the Green Line is 29%. The percentage of "managers" in the total Jewish population nationally (native-born Israeli) is 5.4%; the percentage of white-collar workers and businessmen is 27.7% and the percentage of academics is 8.6%.

The percentage defining themselves as housewives in the settlements is surprisingly low, given that the majority have at least three children. Out of the entire female population in the yishuvim kehilatiyim, 65% were salaried employees (as compared to 47% of Jewish women with three children, nationally) and in this group 93% worked in the public sector in the settlement itself or in the immediate vicinity.

Settler spokesman claim that this profile represents the "initial settlement phase," while the economic and occupational base are still undeveloped. However, an earlier census conducted in 1982 and reported by us in a previous publication, shows that the three intervening years of massive investment have produced no substantial change in the picture. In 1982, 47.8% of Mateh Benyamin settlers commuted to Jerusalem and Tel-Aviv and 5.4% to other settlements in the region; 60.6% of salaried employees in the settlements were in the public sector. In Gush Etzion (1982) 41% commuted to work, and 36% of workers in the settlements were employed in the public sector (21% of the total labor force). Comparison of the 1982 and 1985 censuses indicates that the economic viability of the settlements (excluding the large urban centers,) as reflected by the percentage of commuters, has even declined somewhat.

The government wished to employ at least part of the settlers in industry. In the relatively old settlements (Mishor Adumim, Kiryat Arba, Ma'aleh Ephraim), industrial facilities were built, but the plants there were labor intensive and most of the employees are Arabs from the surrounding area. The development plan for industry in the West Bank is based on high-technology industry and the transfer of industry from the metropolitan areas to the new industrial zones in the West Bank. In 1984 industrial parks in the territories covered 1,500 dunams and employed 2,500 workers, 70 percent of whom were Jews. According to the plans, thousands of Jewish workers are supposed to be employed by industry in the West Bank. However they will not necessarily be residents of the West Bank. Since the conception is metropolitan in nature, the planners expected that there would be daily commuting in both directions between the settlements in the West Bank and the big cities. Some of the settlers will continue to work in the cities, and some of the residents of the cities will commute to industry concentrated within relatively close range.

See also INCENTIVES FOR SETTLEMENT.

2. Palestinians

The total population of working age (14 and up) in the West Bank reached 436,000 in 1984, and the labor force was 154,000. Thus the level of participation in the labor force was 36.7 percent. Participation of women was lower (12.5 percent) than that of men (66.5 percent). About a third of this working population is employed in Israel and two-thirds in the West Bank or abroad. The unemployment rate, which fluctuated between 1 and 2 percent from 1972 to 1983, rose to 3.6 percent in 1984 according to official figures. Though, in general, it may be said that full employment has been maintained on the West Bank, Palestinian sources claim that the unemployment rate is 10 percent.

The division of labor among various branches shows continuing decline in the number employed in agriculture on the West Bank, from about 42 percent in 1970 to about 30 percent in 1981, and 28.5 percent in 1984. The percentage employed in industry has remained relatively constant at 15 percent, and there has been growth in employment in construction and in sectors such as personal services. The division can be explained by the changes which took place in the economic activities in the productive branches of the Paletinian sector (See AGRICULTURE, INDUSTRY, CONSTRUCTION).

An examination of the wage structure of Arabs employed in the West Bank compared to wages in Israel proper shows a rapid narrowing of the gap during 1970-77 and a widening in 1977-1982. In agriculture and construction, the wages of those employed in Israel in 1970 was double that of those employed on the West Bank. That gap disappeared in 1977 but in 1982 wages in Israel were 10-15 percent higher than in the West Bank.

The number of West Bank residents employed in Arab countries was high in the mid-1970s (See DEMOGRAPHY) but declined in 1983-84 with the deterioration in economic conditions in the oil-producing countries. The rise in numbers employed in Israel at that time (See EMPLOYMENT IN ISRAEL (PALESTINIAN)) indicates that most of the workers returning from abroad were absorbed into the Israeli economy and did not find employment in the West Bank itself.

ENFORCEMENT AND PUNISHMENT

Curfew:

Intended to facilitate the activities of the military government during arrests or searches for suspects these may be authorized by the general commanding the region. Starting in the mid-1970s, the curfew was widely used as a means of collective punishment in response to disturbances of the peace and demonstrations. Areas which have experienced lengthy periods under curfew are the Dehaishe refugee camp, Hebron, and Dhahariya. The curfews there lasted several weeks and applied only to local residents, while Jewish settlers were allowed freedom of movement. Imposition of a curfew often causes disruption in food supply and medical services. Children and teenagers cannot attend school and wage-earners cannot get to work.

Demolition of Houses:

According to the EMERGENCY REGULATIONS (1945), the military commander is empowered to order the confiscation and demolition of buildings, if there is reason to believe that shots were fired or bombs thrown from them. In addition, he may order demolition if a building lies on a road or in an area in which inhabitants have committed security offenses. The language of the regulations allows, in effect, for the demolition of any building in an area in which an inhabitant has committed a security offense. The commander may issue an order to blow up, confiscate, or seal a house without having to make a report, and without charging the owner of the house with any offense.

The use of demolition or sealing of houses has lessened since the 1970s. Between 1967-1978, 1,224 houses were demolished or sealed, but from 1979 to 1983, the number was considerably less:

1979: 9 houses destroyed and 9 sealed
1980: 19 houses destroyed and 11 sealed
1981: 17 houses destroyed and 17 sealed
1982: 32 houses destroyed or sealed

In late 1984 and especially in 1985, the authorities again made wide use of this punitive measure.

Demolition or sealing of the houses generally precedes legal proceedings against a suspect. It is carried out shortly after the residents of the house receive notification. There is not sufficient time to clear the house of possessions, and the resident is not entitled to any compensation. In a small number of cases the military government has permitted reconstruction of a demolished house.

Opening and Closing of Stores:

The opening and closing of stores or businesses sometimes functions as a means of punishment or reward, as in the following cases:

1. Where stores or businesses are located in areas where stone-throwing or other disturbances either have occurred or are likely to occur.
2. Where material prohibited by the censor is sold on the premises.
3. As a means of collective punishment for politically-motivated business strikes. The army may also force shopkeepers to open for business against their will.

Deportation:

Under the emergency regulations (1945) and security enactments (378), the military government is authorized to issue a deportation order "whenever necessary or desirable to preserve public security, defend the area, secure public order, or to put down sedition, revolt, or riots." A resident against whom an expulsion order has been issued may appeal to an advisory committee, which will look into the matter. The committee has, however, only advisory powers, and the authority in the area is not bound to adopt its recommendations. The resident may also apply to the High Court of Justice.

In two appeals to the High Court of Justice residents of the territories argued that authority to deport was repealed in Jordan even before the Six Day War. The argument was based on a Jordanian legislative order from 1953 which forbade the deportation of a Jordanian citizen from the kingdom. However, in 1980 the High Court rejected the argument.

Since 1967, nearly 2,000 people have been deported from the area under the regulation. After a long period (1980-85), during which no deportations were carried out, the military government re-instituted the measure in August 1985. By February 1986, 35 persons had been deported to Jordan.

Restrictions on Movement and Closed Areas

The military commander is authorized to declare any area or region in the occupied territories a "closed area." According to the SECURITY ENACTMENTS, paragraph 90, entrance to a declared "closed area" is forbidden without explicit written permission. From the time an area is declared closed, only permanent residents of the location are allowed to remain there. Anyone there on a temporary basis must leave at once. In general, the order has been used to isolate a population from the outside world, in particular from the media. It has also occasionally been used in the early stages of establishing a settlement (See INTERFERENCE WITH PRIVATE LAND OWNERSHIP).

Restrictive Orders

The military commander is authorized to issue a restrictive order against a resident of the occupied territories "if necessary for security purposes." The order may forbid the resident to associate with a certain person or to disseminate news or ideas. The order may also require the resident to report on his movements. Preventing movement from the territories to Jordan also constitutes a means of punishment (See OPEN BRIDGES).

Those affected by a restrictive order may appeal to an appeals committee.

The military authority may order the detention of a resident of the occupied territories without trial "if necessary for security purposes." An administrative detention order must be reported within 96 hours to the regional commander's counsel. The detainee may appeal the order to an appeals committee, headed by an attorney qualified to sit as a judge on a court of appeal. The committee reviews each detainee's case every six months, even in the absence of an appeal. It should be noted that in Israel itself, administrative detention must be approved by a district judge within 48 hours of the arrest. There is no such constraint in the occupied territories. In 1978 there were 30 such detainees; in 1979, 25; in August 1980 the number went down to 1; in 1984 there were no administrative detainees. In July-August 1985, more than 60 persons were placed in administrative detention, and by the end of the year their number rose to over 100.

House Arrests

A means of confining an inhabitant to his place of residence, it forbids him to leave his house at night and requires him to report to the police station at regular intervals such as twice a day. House arrest is within the jurisdiction of the regional military commander, according to paragraph 86 of military order 378. It is issued for a six-month period and is intended as a deterrent, but there is reason to believe that it is used as a penalty. The individual concerned is not brought to trial and does not know the charge against him. There is no obligation to specify the grounds for the order. Likewise, the individual does not have recourse to appeal the penalty. Between 1979 and 1983, 105 people were put under house arrest – 91 men and 14 women. Among them there were five newspaper editors. On an average, there were 66 people under house arrest in the years between 1980 and 1984 inclusive. In summer 1985 there were 70.

The grounds for house arrest are open criticism of Israeli policy and support of the PLO.

Exile

The military commander has the authority to remove a person from his permanent place of residence and confine him to a location decided upon by the commander. This penalty is seldom imposed.

FAHD PLAN

Proposed by Crown Prince Fahd (afterwards king) of Saudi Arabia, in August 1981. It was taken from previous resolutions, including General Assembly Resolution 3226. Its main points are as follows:

1. Israeli evacuation of all Arab territories seized during the 1967 Six Day War, including the Arab sector of Jerusalem.

2. Dismantling the settlements set up by Israel on the occupied lands after the 1967 war.

3. Guaranteeing freedom of religious practice for all religions in the Jerusalem holy shrines.

4. Asserting the rights of the Palestinian people and compensating those Palestinians who do not wish to return to their homeland.

5. Commencing a transitional period on the West Bank of Jordan and in the Gaza Strip under United Nations supervision for a duration not exceeding a few months.

6. Setting up a Palestinian state with East Jerusalem as its capital.

7. Affirming the right of all countries of the region to live in peace.

8. Guaranteeing the implementation of these principles by the United Nations or some of its member states.

FAMILY REUNIFICATION

Between June and September 1967 some 200,000 people left the West Bank. This is in addition to those West Bank residents who were, at the time of the 1967 war, out of the country. Approximately 140,000 of them have since submitted applications to reunite with their families living permanently in the area. During the first years (1967-1972) after the war, some 45,000 were allowed to return. By 1979, however, the number of unprocessed applications remained at 150,000. The military government declared the following petitions acceptable: application for the return of a spouse; of an unmarried child aged 16 or younger; of orphan grandchildren aged 16 or under; of an unmarried sister; and of parents over the age of 60. Under no circumstances is the return of a male between the ages of 16 and 60 permitted. At the beginning of the 1980s between 900 and 1,200 applications were approved per year. In 1985 the authorities drastically curtailed approval of family reunification permits, and only a few dozen persons were admitted.

Family reunification permits serve as rewards for cooperation with the military government. The administration granted the "right of recommendation" for family reunification to the VILLAGE LEAGUES, thus allowing them to wield considerable power, this being one of the most sensitive issues on the West Bank. The Palestinian population sees family reunification, according to more liberal criteria – for all who desire it – and the return of entire families, as a natural right.

At the time of the CAMP DAVID negotiations, the right of the "1967 refugees" to return to the West Bank was recognized in principle. A joint Israeli-Egyptian-Jordanian committee (with the participation of Self Governing Authority representatives), was supposed to deal with their return, its decisions being arrived at by mutual agreement.

FATAH (ACTIVITIES IN THE TERRITORIES)

In addition to military and terrorist actions, Fatah also carries out a series of activities in the West Bank and Gaza Strip of a varied, open, and public character.

Propaganda and mobilization of public opinion: the daily newspapers **al-Fajr,** and **a-Sha'ab**, published in East Jerusalem, are thought to be Fatah organs. In addition there are a number of other organs: **al-Fajr** in English (a weekly), **al-Fajr al-Adabi** (a literary magazine), and for about a year (in 1983), **al-Fajr** published a weekly Hebrew magazine. **Al-Awdah** is published by the Palestinian Press Service, the information and press service run by Raymonda Tawil, as well as **al-Bayader** and **al-Bayader a-Siyassi** (See PRESS (ARAB)).

The Center for Palestinian Research, run by Faisal al-Husseini, deals mainly with the listing and documenting of press clippings and providing services for academic research.

There is also Fatah influence in the Union of Journalists (which split in 1984 with the departure of rejectionist opponents of the seventeenth congress in Amman), the Writers' Union (which underwent a similar split), and the new Union of Painters and Sculptors.

Fatah has strong student organizations in all of the colleges and also "voluntary committees" active in urban neighborhoods, villages, and refugee camps. Their main activity is the organization of strikes, demonstrations, ceremonies, volunteer action to pave roads, cleaning, and mutual assistance.

Fatah also has a PALESTINIAN TRADE UNION headed by Shehadeh Minawi of Nablus, which competes with the Communist and REJECTION FRONT trade unions.

FEZ SUMMIT RESOLUTIONS

The Arab summit meeting in Fez, Morocco, adopted an eight-point peace plan. Below are the plan's points according to the conference's official English version, as published in **The Jerusalem Post** of September 12, 1982.

1. The withdrawal of Israel from all Arab territories occupied in 1967 including Arab al-Kuds (Jerusalem).

2. The dismantling of settlements established by Israel on the Arab territories after 1967.

3. The guarantee of freedom of worship and practice of religious rites for all religions in the holy shrines.

4. The re-affirmation of the Palestinian people's right to self-determination and the exercise of its imprescriptible and inalienable national rights under the leadership of the Palestine Liberation Organization, its sole and legitimate representative, and the indemnification of all those who do not desire to return.

5. Placing the West Bank and Gaza Strip under the control of the UN for a transitory period not exceeding a few months.

6. The establishment of an independent Palestinian state with al-Kuds as its capital.

7. The Security Council guarantees peace among all states of the region including the independent Palestinian state.

8. The Security Council guarantees the respect of these principles.

This plan was also accepted by the PLO, which views it as a "minimum condition for political action of the Arab states, which must be accompanied by military action, with everything that implies... These decisions at Fez do not contradict support for the political plan of the Palestinian National Congress," i.e., the Algiers decisions (See PLO POLITICAL PLANS). Paragraph 7, mentioning guarantees for all states in the region, has been construed as indirect recognition of Israel, but it mentions, of course, only "Security Council guarantees."

FISCAL BURDEN

Defined here as the net transfers of the Israeli government to the West Bank, this is an item in the "balance of payments" of the West Bank (See NATIONAL ACCOUNTS). In that balance the net direct transfers of the Israeli government are listed. These transfers show the deficit of the civilian budget of the military government (both regular and development) spent in the Palestinian sector (See MILITARY GOVERNMENT BUDGET), less income tax and national insurance payments collected from workers from the territories employed in Israel. It should be recalled that the budget of the military government is a "closed system," in that all income from taxes and imposts collected in the region is used for its activities (See TAXATION), the deficit alone being made up from the budget of the Israeli Ministry of Defense.

The extent of net government transfers (i.e., the fiscal burden placed on the Israeli taxpayer as a result of the activities of the military government) has not been uniform during the years of the occupation. In general it can be said that the burden is inversely proportional to the increase in the number of workers from the territories in Israel and their income, and the decrease of the budgets of the military government. In the mid-1970s the burden was negative, i.e., the residents of the territories contributed to Israeli public expenditure. In the late 1970s the burden came to $10-15 million per annum. In the early 1980s the burden decreased and was generally negative. It can be estimated that over the years the military government of the West Bank has cost the Israeli taxpayer about $180-200, or no more than $10 million annually.

In this context it must be pointed out that current public expenditure and government investment in the Israeli sector (settlements, infrastructure) are not included in the fiscal burden. While it can be said that some of that expenditure benefited the Palestinian sector, the official accounts (See NATIONAL ACCOUNTS) attribute them to the Israeli sector alone since they are intended to develop that sector.

Net direct transfers of the Israeli government do not fully describe the burden involved in retaining the territories. To arrive at the total financial burden one must calculate the indirect Israeli taxation levied on goods produced in Israel and marketed in the West Bank as well as the duties imposed on imports to the West Bank through Israeli ports and the Jordan River bridges. From those sums must be deducted the subsidies given to food and agricultural produce. In 1983 alone manufactured products valued at $400 million were sold in the West Bank. The value added tax on those goods came to about $50 million. In that year the value of manufactured products imported through Israeli ports and the Jordan River bridges was some $40 million, upon which duties of 50 percent were charged, or $20 million. Imports of agricultural produce from Israel to the West Bank came to about $50 million that year. If one assumes a subsidy of 50 percent, about $25 million must be deducted from the indirect taxes paid to Israel, and the surplus credited to the West Bank comes to $45 – $50 million. If one deducts the burden of direct transfers, one finds that the residents of the West Bank contributed a total of about $600 –- $700 million to Israeli public consumption over 19 years of occupation. This means that occupying the territories is not a burden on the Israeli taxpayer, rather the contrary: the residents of the territories pay an "occupation tax" to the occupying authorities. This fact refutes the Israeli claim that the low level of PUBLIC CONSUMPTION AND INVESTMENT derives from budgetary limitations. If the net fiscal transfers from the West Bank were invested in services and physical development, it would be possible to improve the civilian administration significantly, particularly in promoting the development of the economic infrastructure of the West Bank. The fiscal profit derived from retaining the territories is, of course, part of the economic profit gained by Israel from the prolonged occupation (See ECONOMIC POLICY).

FOREIGN AID

A large number of foreign relief organizations are active in the West Bank and Gaza Strip. They may be divided according to whether they belong to foreign governmental, public, private, religious or secular organizations and institutions, and also as to the area of their activities: development, education, relief or health. Some of them have worked in this area for decades, some began after 1967. Some have offices locally, others operate from abroad. Below is a partial list of the organizations, their major area of activities, and the countries which fund them:

AMIDEAST: higher education, training of students abroad; U.S.

ANERA: development of economic infrastructure, agriculture,

industry, water works (see below); U.S.

CDF: development of local infrastructure, water, electricity, agriculture, education, health (see below); U.S.

CRS: welfare, food distribution, clinics, charitable associations (see below); U.S.

Mennonites: agriculture, drip irrigation, water reservoirs, education, community work, access roads; Canada, U.S.

Friends (Quakers): legal aid, kindergartens; U.S.

NECC (Near Eastern Council of Churches): schools, clinics, mother-and-child care; U.S.

CARITAS: schools; Switzerland

EFTA: school for the deaf and dumb; Italy

UNDP: UN development plans, health, welfare, education, equipment, professional training; UN

UNICEF: mother-and-child care, kindergartens, training centers; UN

SOIR (welfare organization): aid to retarded children, welfare; Sweden

OXFAM: relief, education; Britain

Talitha Kumi: school; Germany

Holyland Christian Mission: hospital; U.S.

French Hospital; France

Christopher Blind Mission: education for the blind; Germany

Silesiana: vocational school; Franciscans

Shiloah: school for the blind; Germany

The Evangelical Church (Anglican): school, hospital; Anglican Church

Dom Bosco: school; Italy

LWF: the Augusta Victoria Hospital, clinics, professional training; Germany

Various church groups are active in the field as part of their religious communal services. These organizations are called Private Voluntary Organizations (PVO). The aid funds are contributed by private and public bodies. The larger sums are contributed by the United States government through its foreign aid programs, (AID – the State Department foreign aid program) but also by the governments of Canada and Germany.

Voluntary organizations with local offices must receive authorization from the military government for all activities they initiate. Without that approval they are not permitted to make contact with local bodies. A number of European and other organizations circumvent that supervision by transferring funds directly from their centers abroad. Since the PVOs provide assistance and relief to the Palestinian population, and their teams are composed of activists with ideological motivation, it is not surprising that they identify with the Palestinians emotionally and sometimes also politically. On the other hand, the Israeli authorities are suspicious of the activities of the relief organizations and keep very careful track of what they do. In 1983 a special unit was established in the military government to supervise the work of the international relief organizations.

The problematic nature of foreign assistance on the West Bank and in the Gaza Strip emerges clearly from a survey of the 1984 activities of the three largest American organizations – CRS, CDF, and ANERA. An investigation of 358 projects planned by those organizations between 1979 and 1983 produced these findings:

A. The basic condition for the approval of projects by the AID agency is the availability of matching funds, ostensibly provided by the population, though in fact they come from the JOINT COMMITTEE (PLO-JORDAN).

B. The overall budget approved by the United States government in 1983 was $6.5 million, and in 1984, $8.4 million, but in fact less than half of that sum was actually spent.

C. The budgeted plan was not carried out because of selective approval by the Israeli government. Analysis of the approved projects reveals the approach of the military government and its priorities.

D. About half the projects were originally designed to develop economic infrastructure, about a quarter were devoted to social goals, education, and relief, and about a fourth to the improvement of services (running water, electricity). As a result of the government's selective policy in approving projects, the proportion of those aimed at improving services rose from a quarter to a half, and that of projects in the area of economic infrastructure fell from half to less than a third.

E. These findings show clearly that the Israeli authorities attempt to block projects for the development of economic infrastructure, preferring those which improve services. That policy supports the political line taken by Israel, permitting individual prosperity but stifling community development (See ECONOMIC POLICY). In addition, that policy decreases the budgetary burden upon the administration, for otherwise it would have to provide funding for access roads and water mains for domestic consumption. In fact the reports of the military government list projects subsidized by the voluntary agencies and the joint PLO-Jordanian committee as projects financed by the administration itself.

These conclusions have direct effects on the policies for IMPROVEMENT OF THE QUALITY OF LIFE in the territories. In 1985 a certain easing was reported in the approval of projects which had been ignored for a long time. According to a report of the military government, 85 projects were being carried out in 1984: 17 involving water; three, electricity; 21, agriculture; 11, education; seven, health; and 14, grants. The total investment was $8 million, 51 percent from foreign aid funds and 49 percent self-financed (including funds from the Jordanian-PLO fund (See SUMUD). The proportion of projects for improving services remained very high relative to those for development.

FOREIGN TRADE

This involves the sale of goods and services of the Palestinian population to foreign markets. The trade, despite the label given to it, has no territorial significance, for Israeli activity in the West Bank is not considered part of the area's trade. Trade between (Palestinian) Hebron and (Israeli) Kiryat Arba, for example, appears in the official statistics as foreign trade between the Israeli economy and that of the West Bank. Moreover, all statistics on trade between Israel and the West Bank are approximate and unreliable, for there is no supervision of commercial movement, except for the transfer of certain agricultural produce.

The patterns of foreign trade of the West Bank have not changed significantly since 1967 in either the sources or composition of its commodities. That is because the economic, administrative, and political patterns instituted in the early 1970s remain in force (See ECONOMIC POLICY). Most imports come from Israel (90 percent in 1984), 8 percent come from abroad through Israel, and 2 percent come from Jordan. In contrast, 55 percent of the exports go to Israel, and about 45 percent to Jordan. About 84 percent of total imports and 75 percent of total exports are manufactured goods, and the rest is agricultural produce. In trade with Israel, 16 percent of total imports are agricultural products, as are 28 percent of exports to Israel; in trade with Jordan 36 percent of exports are agricultural, and 64 percent are manufactured goods.

Israel "exported" goods valued at $363 million to the West Bank in 1984, compared with $400 million in 1983 and $380 million in 1982. In 1984 commerce with the West Bank and the Gaza Strip totaled 10.6 percent of Israel's total exports. The West Bank alone purchased goods in Israel equal in value to those purchased by Britain, Israel's second largest foreign customer. That fact points to the importance of the West Bank market for Israeli industry. Israeli "export" is possible because the economic integration of the two economies ensures massive protection for Israeli industry. According to research carried out in 1977, that protection (imposts and various taxes on competitive imports) reached 60 percent of the value of the products on the international market.

95

In contrast, "exports" from the West Bank receive no protection. Industrial manufacturers from the West Bank have little or no chance of competing with Israeli industry. Agricultural exports are subject to strict administrative limitations, in addition to the almost total absence of incentives, subsidies and minimum prices characterizing Israeli products (See AGRICULTURE, INDUSTRY). Exports to Jordan also encounter many obstacles. Under the pretense of observing the Arab boycott, the Jordanians have not permitted export from the West Bank except from factories established before 1967, and it also made all import from the West Bank conditional upon the purchase of raw materials and machinery in or through Jordan. For their part, the Israelis impose customs duties on commodities imported through Jordan and brought across the bridges (upon which Jordanian customs have already been paid). Agricultural export from the West Bank is also limited by quotas, to avoid competition with Jordanian agriculture. Imports from the East Bank are extremely limited, mainly due to security limitations. Manufactured commodities exported to Jordan are mainly olive oil, samna (liquid margarine), dairy products, soap, and cut building stones. Industrial exports to Israel consist largely of goods produced by sub-contractors for Israeli producers, mainly textiles, leather, and shoes.

The foreign trade of the West Bank and its difficulties demonstrate the absolute dependence of the Arab economic sector on both Israel and Jordan. Its chances, and the growth potential of the entire Palestinian economy, depend on political and economic decisions made by the two adjacent sovereign states. Under the conditions of the 1980s, foreign trade of the West Bank is squeezed between the Israeli hammer and the Jordanian anvil. The terms of trade which they dictate not only fail to encourage the growth and consolidation of an independent Palestinian economic sector, they also perpetuate its dependence and backwardness.

FUNDAMENTALIST MUSLIM GROUPS

The Muslim Brothers

A generic term for groups of an Islamic-religious nature, operating on the West Bank and in Gaza. These groups gained in momentum and strength at the end of the 1970s as a consequence of the Iranian revolution. A great deal of Muslim activity is concentrated in the Gaza Strip and centers on a group called "The Islamic Congress," which brings together a range of preachers and mosques. Muslim religious activities are vigorously pursued at Gaza University (formerly called the al-Azhar Institute), which maintains connections with al-Azhar University in Cairo. The activity in Gaza is essentially similar to extremist Muslim activity in Egypt and has links with it. It also affects the West Bank; the active "Muslim Bloc" at Bir-Zeit University, for instance, is centered on students from Gaza.

In contrast with the centralized, organized activities in the Gaza Strip, Islamic fundamentalist activity in the West Bank lacks a general organizing body. It takes place around the two Islamic colleges, in Hebron and Beit Hanina (East Jerusalem) and through various preachers and Muslim groups concentrated around the mosques on Mt. Hebron and in Hebron itself.

The fundamentalist Islamic groups in the West Bank can be divided into those with views similar to the Muslim Brothers – advocating the establishment of a state based on Islamic law and therefore regarded as anti-nationalist (those in Gaza are mainly of this type) – or those which are the heirs of the Liberation Party – such as The Eternal Torch – which are religious-nationalist and support current national frameworks, including Palestinian nationalism.

Most Islamic activity centers on the individual personalities of preachers with followings in the mosques, with no organizational links.

The Eternal Torch Association

The only significant remnant of the Islamic Liberation Party which operated in the West Bank during the Jordanian period. It is active in Hebron and has weak and unofficial links with people with a similar religious outlook in traditional areas – Kalkilya, Tulkarm, Jenin, and Nablus sub-districts (mostly in the villages).

Sufis

This concerns the activities of a mystical nature of several preachers and of dervishes, mostly in the villages around Hebron and Northern Samaria. The Tariqs (Sufi groups) particularly active in the West Bank are "Rafa'iya" and "Shazaliya." They are also active in villages in the Israeli Triangle, especially Umm al-Fahm. They are very much under the influence of Egyptian Sufis. They have no particular political leanings and concentrate on mystical-religious activity.

GENERAL FEDERATION OF LABOR (HISTADRUT)

This trade union federation does not function on the West Bank. After the occupation, its leaders contributed to setting the policies regarding the employment and wages of workers from the territories. Those policies are meant to ensure that the expense to the employer of hiring workers from the territories will not be less than that of hiring organized Israeli labor, hence a distinction must be made between the expense to the employer and the wages received by the worker. That distinction is blurred in many people's eyes and viewed as "the equalization of wage conditions" of workers from the West Bank and Israeli workers. In fact the wages paid to workers from the West Bank are not equal (See EMPLOYMENT IN ISRAEL (PALESTINIAN)) and the interest shown in retaining the practices which have evolved is intended only to prevent West Bank workers undercutting Israeli workers and competing with them. The Israeli labor unions do not represent West Bank workers in relations with their Israeli employers. This is carried out by the government labor exchange officials, who are inexperienced in such matters. In any case they show little interest in the conditions of employment of Arab workers. It should be pointed out that the Histadrut receives "organization fees" from the Employment service, deducted from West Bank employees "to look after their professional interests".

The Histadrut does not accept workers from the West Bank as members of its trade unions, and therefore the workers do not belong to the Histadrut pension funds. The pension and retirement funds accrued in the name of the Arab workers are administered by officials of the Ministry of Labor and Social Affairs, but in fact they are transferred to the Israeli Treasury. The following data are indicative of the processing of social security claims of workers from the West Bank, working in Israel, by Israeli officials: in 1982-83, 2,000 claims for severance pay were treated, 2,866 claims for sick pay, and six suits in the labor court. In that year about 43,000 workers from the West Bank were employed in Israel (See EMPLOYMENT IN ISRAEL). Although a third of the workers (about 15,000) have been employed for more than 10 years (the minimum period for eligibility for old age pensions), only 122 currently receive old-age pensions for work in Israel. Since residents of the territories may not become members of the General Federation of Labor, neither can they be members of the General Sick Fund. In place of this health insurance there is a program administered by the staff officer for the Ministry of Health in the CIVILIAN ADMINISTRATION. About 40 percent of the population (80,000 households) were ensured through that program in 1983.

In the early 1980s, when Histadrut pension funds ran into financial difficulties, Histadrut leaders began demanding that pension funds of the West Bank workers be transferred to them. However, the LIKUD government rejected their demand, as those funds were being used by the Israeli Treasury. For national insurance payments to West Bank workers, see EMPLOYMENT.

The General Federation of Labor does function in EAST

98

JERUSALEM. See also PALESTINIAN TRADE UNIONS.

GENEVA CONVENTION (FOURTH)

International treaty (signed August 12, 1949) regarding protection of civilians in wartime. The following is a brief summary of some of the articles of the Convention:

Article 49:

Individual or mass forcible transfers, as well as deportations of protected persons from occupied territory to the territory of the Occupying Power or to that of any other country occupied or not, are prohibited, regardless of their motive.

    Nevertheless, the Occupying Power may undertake total or partial evacuation of a given area if the security of the population or imperative military reasons so demand… Persons thus evacuated shall be transferred back to their homes as soon as hostilities in the area in question have ceased… The Occupying Power shall not deport or transfer parts of its own civilian population into the territory it occupies.

Article 147:

Grave breaches… shall be those involving the following, vif committed against persons or property protected by the present convention: willful killing, torture or inhuman trxatment, including biological experiments, willfully causing great suffering or serious injury to body or health, unlawful deportation or transfer… compelling a protected person to serve in the forces of a hostile Power, or willfully depriving a protected person ofnthe rights of fair and regular trial prescribed in th present Convention, taking of hostages and extensive destruction and appropriation of property, not justified by military necessity and carried out unlawfully and wantonly.

Article 85: (From Section II of Appendix III Protocol Additional to the Geneva Convention of 12 August 1949, and relating to the Protection of Victims of International Armed Conflicts [Protocol I] of 8 June 1977).

4. In addition to the grave breaches defined in the preceding paragraphs and in the Convention, the following shall be regarded as grave breaches of this Protocol, when committed willfully and in violation of the Conventions or the Protocol:

a. The transfer by the Occupying Power of parts of its own civilian population into the territory it occupies, or the deportation or transfer of all or parts of the population of the occupied territory within or outside this territory, in violation of Article 49 of the Fourth Convention.

HAGUE REGULATIONS

An international convention signed in 1907. An annex, "Regulations Respecting the Laws and Customs of War on Land" – and especially Section III (Articles 42-56) – has been accepted as universal principles for the conduct of an occupying power. According to a decision of the High Court of Justice, Israel is required to observe the Hague Regulations (unlike the GENEVA CONVENTION).

Here is an abbreviated list of the relevant articles, quoted from the official English text (which is not identical in all its details to the French text):

Article 43. The authority of the legitimate power... having in fact passed into the hands of the occupant, the latter shall take all the measures in his power to restore, and ensure, as far as possible, public order and safety, while respecting, unless absolutely prevented, the laws in force in the country.

Article 46. ... Private property cannot be confiscated.

Article 50. No general penalty, pecuniary or otherwise, shall be inflicted upon the population on account of the acts of individuals for which they cannot be regarded as jointly and severally responsible.

Article 52. Requisitions in kind and services shall not be demanded from municipalities or inhabitants except for the needs of the army of occupation. They shall be in proportion to the resources of the country and of such a nature as not to involve the inhabitants in the obligation of taking part in military operations against their own country.

Article 55. The occupying state shall be regarded only as administrator and usufructuary of public buildings, real estate, forests, and agricultural estates belonging to the hostile state, and situated in the occupied country. It must safeguard the capital of these properties and administer them in accordance with the rules of usufruct.

HA'IHUD HA'HAKLAI (Agricultural Union – Settlement Movement)

A national organization of private agricultural settlements, founded in the 1940s. The Agricultural Union's thinking on West Bank settlements conforms to the principles laid down in the ALLON PLAN.

Settlements of Ha'Ihud Ha'Haklai on the West Bank, as of September 1985, are:

Settlement	Region	Number of People
Ro'i	Jordan Valley	114
Rimonim	Allon Road	140
Mekhora	Jordan Valley	146
Khamra	Jordan Valley	168
Bekaot	Jordan Valley	170
Vered Yericho	Jericho Road	126

HA'OVED HA'LEUMI (SETTLEMENTS)

A settlement organization belonging to the Nationalist Workers' Organization (LIKUD), established in the 1940s. In accordance with Likud views, it establishes settlements on the West Bank. The settlements of Ha'Oved Ha'Leumi, as of September 1985, were as follows:

Homesh, Shomron: 120 people
Ganim, Shomron: 100 people

HAPOEL HAMIZRACHI, MOSHAVIM AND RELIGIOUS KIBBUTZIM

The settlement movement of Hapoel Hamizrachi was founded in the 1920s. The movement is an integral part of Hapoel Hamizrachi and its members are associated with the National Religious Party (NRP). The movement establishes moshavim (communal settlements) and deals with all aspects of life in them: religion, social matters, maintenance, financing, etc.

The moshavim of Hapoel Hamizrachi, like the kibbutzim of the Religious Kibbutz Movement, are particularly attentive to the religious problems involved in working the land and seek solutions within the framework of Jewish religious law. The movement is connected with the Bnei Akiva youth movement.

The movement seeks to form blocks of religious communal settlements which in turn permit the establishment of comprehensive religious and educational frameworks.

The Religious Kibbutz Movement

The national organization of the religious kibbutzim founded by Hapoel Hamizrachi in 1938, with the goal of establishing settlements with a Zionist, religious and communal character. The members of the Religious Kibbutz Movement have also formed a political faction within the NRP. Both the moshavim and the Religious Kibbutz Movement have established settlements on the West Bank and in the Gaza Strip:

Settlement	Established	Region	People	Type
Kfar Etzion	1967	Mt. Hebron	400	kibbutz
Kfar Mekhola	1968	Jordan Valley	156	moshav
Shadmot Mekhola	1978	Jordan Valley	161	m. shitufi
Rosh Tsurim	1969	Mt. Hebron	240	kibbutz
Katif	1978	Gaza Strip	32	m. shitufi
Elazar	1975	Mt. Hebron	170	moshav
Netser Hazani	1976	Gaza Strip	241	moshav
Migdal Oz	1977	Mt. Hebron	130	kibbutz

Settlement	Established	Region	People	Type
Ganei Tal	1977	Gaza Strip	238	moshav
Gadid	1983	Gaza Strip	122	moshav
Gan Or	1983	Gaza Strip	77	moshav
Netzarim	1980	Gaza Strip	31	kibbutz
Morag	1984	Gaza Strip	94	moshav
Karmei Tsur	1984	Samaria	60	moshav
Kfar Tapuah	1978	Samaria	130	kehilati
Peduel	1984	West Samaria	50	moshav
Neveh Daniel	1982	Judea	110	kehilati
Psagot	1981	M. Benyamin	210	kehilati

HEALTH

Both the quality and the problems of the health system on the West Bank and in the Gaza Strip are determined by the socio-economic infrastructure of the community, physical infrastructure, water supply, waste collection, sewage and sanitation, level of employment, standard of living and, wages (See DEMOGRAPHY, EDUCATION, STANDARD OF LIVING, EMPLOYMENT). It is also, of course, dependent on the operation of the health system itself – hospitalization, mother-and-child care, hygiene, and sanitation supervision. All these systems affect life expectancy, level of illness, infant mortality rate, chronic diseases, and so on. The functions and achievements of the health system are, for this reason, a subject of controversy between the Israeli administration and Palestinian researchers. In addition to the political aspects of the controversy – in which Israel's goal is to highlight the improvements made under its rule, and the Palestinians' goal is to emphasize the occupying power's neglect – the dispute arises from the different criteria applied by the two parties. The Israelis compare the situation in the territories with the period before the occupation. The Palestinians, on the other hand, evaluate the system relative to international standards, and relative to the standards prevalent in Israel itself. There is no doubt, according to Israeli methodology, that there has been a significant improvement in the level of public health on the West Bank and in the Gaza Strip, but according to the methodology applied by the Palestinians this improvement is illusory.

The problem is that the data themselves are open to dispute. Some essential statistics, such as those on infant mortality and morbidity, are incomplete. This is because less than half of West Bank births take place in hospitals, and the infant mortality rate outside the hospitals is very high. The lack of proper recording of non-hospital births and the failure to enforce the law against burial without a death certificate mean that birth and death rates, which form the basis for demographic calculations, are inaccurate, and the Central Bureau of Statistics (CBS) must use theoretical statistical models instead. Such models are far from reliable (See DEMOGRAPHY). As a result, the published data are suspect and give rise to the claim that misleading data are being cited for political purposes.

The following data are taken exclusively from official publications.

The health system in the West Bank is based on seven hospitalization areas, not including large hospitals in East Jerusalem. Clearly, this organizational framework reflects the Israeli political concept of East Jerusalem as part of Israel and separate from the West Bank. The actual state of affairs is, of course, completely different. Hospitalization, preventive medicine, and Arab clinics in East Jerusalem as well as the foreign voluntary system, are an integral part of the West Bank system. This arbitrary division is reflected in the administration's statistics, not always in its favor. According to official figures, 17 hospitals were operating in the West Bank in 1984, including eight general government hospitals (654 beds), one hospital for the mentally ill (320 beds) and, eight private hospitals (391 beds), a total of 1,365 beds. The number of beds per 1,000 residents in 1983 was 1.8, as against 2.15 in 1970 and 2.01 in 1975. The decline reflects the freeze in new beds, (an actual drop of 30 beds between 1974 and 1983) as against a growth of 100,000 in the population.

The number of beds per 1,000 residents in Israel was 6.4 in 1983. In the general hospitals the proportion was 2.8 in Israel as compared to 1.3 in the West Bank (1983); for hospitals for the mentally ill, 2.0 in Israel as against 0.4 on the West Bank. The number of person-days of hospitalization per 1,000 West Bank residents remained stable (542 in 1970, 593 in 1975, 544 in 1981), as against 1,913 in Israel (1983). The surgery rate per 1,000 West Bank residents rose from 15.7 (1972) to about 20 in 1977 and has remained at that rate ever since. The occupancy rate rose from 69.2 percent in 1970 to about 80 percent in 1982. There was a rise in the hospitalization rate per 1,000 residents, from 65.8 in 1970 to 81.2 in 1983, and average length of stay declined.

Medical staff per West Bank bed rose from 0.36 (1968) to 0.78 (1982) and the rate of hospital births rose from 20.7 percent in 1970 to 45.7 percent in 1982, as against almost 100 percent in Israel (Jews and Arabs). There was a growth of 40 percent in the rate of hospital admittance per 1,000 population and, a rise of 100 percent in visits to clinics. There were 140 general clinics on the West Bank as of 1983, 95 mother-and-child care clinics and three tuberculosis prevention clinics. In addition, there were

90 non-governmental clinics in the region. Infant vaccination reached 90 percent in 1983.

The infant mortality rate, estimated at 15 percent in 1967, was estimated by the CBS to have dropped to 7 percent in 1983. The mortality rate per 1,000 live births was estimated by the Ministry of Health to be 25.6 (1982). This figure is not accepted by the CBS. In Israel, the rate in 1983 was 13.9 per 1,000. Palestinian sources give higher infant mortality figures. The reason for the difference is the persistent incomplete recording of deaths in the region. The infant mortality rate has turned into a contentious political issue, owing to its emotional overtones. According to CBS models, life expectancy on the West Bank and in the Gaza Strip at the beginning of the 1980's was 60–65 years for men, as against 72.8 for Jewish men, 76.2 for Jewish women, and 70.8 and 73.3 for male and female non-Jews respectively, in Israel. Data on infectious diseases indicate a decline in almost all types of illness, but the level per 1,000 for tetanus, diphtheria, measles, and polio remains significantly higher than in Israel (according to 1982 figures). Intestinal diseases, especially in small children, remain problematic.

The number of beds per 1,000 residents in the Gaza Strip was 2.4 in 1974 and dropped to 1.8 in 1983. This is a result of a decline in the number of beds in the same period, from 1,004 to 899, while the population increased by 80,000. The number of person-days of hospitalization per 1,000 residents in 1983 was 425, as against 607 in 1974. By contrast, hospitalization per 1,000 rose from 84.2 in 1974 to 108.8 in 1983, indicating greater access to medical centers. The incidence of surgery in 1983 was 34.4 per 1,000 residents as against 31.4 in 1974. The rate of hospital births also grew, from 46 percent to 70 percent (1982). There are 35 clinics in the Gaza Strip, indicating better access to health care than on the West Bank.

The number of professional medical workers in the Gaza Strip per 1,000 residents is also higher than on the West Bank. The reasons are, apparently, the density of the population, reducing the distance to hospitals and clinics and UNRWA's well-established work in the refugee camps. However, the data show that infant mortality in the Gaza Strip is higher, perhaps even double that of the West Bank, contrary to the CBS estimate that they are equal. On the other hand, the incidence of severe illness caused by improper sanitation (viral hepatitis, polio, tetanus, typhus, etc.) is no greater than on the West Bank, despite the poor sanitary conditions in the refugee camps.

In 1981-82 total expenditure for health per capita on the West Bank, (regular and development budgets, by government and non-profit organizations) was estimated at 23 percent of Israeli public health expenditure per capita.

HERUT BETAR (SETTLEMENTS)

The settlement movement of the Herut Party. Its settlements are deployed according to its ideology, which holds that Israeli sovereignty must be established in the whole of Eretz Israel, and its entire area must be settled.

Its West Bank settlements are as follows (as of October 1985):

Settlement	Region	Number of People
Salit	Benyamin	230
Shaked	Samaria	150
Ma'aleh Shomron	Samaria	200
Ma'aleh Amos	Gush Etzion	150
Betar	Gush Etzion	15
Beit Abba	Samaria	280
Beit Arieh	Samaria	400
Argaman	Jordan Valley	100

HIGH COURT OF JUSTICE

Israel's Supreme Court, sitting as the High Court of Justice (HCJ) has ruled, since 1968, on petitions from West Bank and Gaza Strip residents, against activities and orders of the Israeli military administration.

The authority of the HCJ to rule on these petitions remains in doubt and is a subject of controversy; this is because its jurisdiction is restricted, generally, to the territory of the state. Indeed, there exists no precedent anywhere in the world for an occupying power's supreme court to hear pleas from the residents of an occupied area. It is also accepted that the HCJ cannot review or invalidate primary legislation, and military orders have the status of primary legislation. In spite of all these reservations and doubts, the HCJ ruled that it is competent to review military government actions on the grounds that the latter had never argued that the HCJ lacks jurisdiction – in effect accepting its competence. The decision to accept the authority of the HCJ was mainly that of Meir Shamgar, who was chief military counsel at the time of the occupation and later became attorney-general (today he is president of the Supreme Court). The legal basis for HCJ authority is paragraph 2 of the Court's Law, 1957.

The impact of the HCJ on the legal status of residents of the territories has been marginal. Since military government orders and international law both give wide powers to the military administration, the HCJ has had to reject the overwhelming majority of petitions. In some cases, however, its involvement brought about the repeal of illegal decisions of the administration, most notably the decision to confiscate the West Bank installations of the East Jerusalem Electric Company and transfer them to the Israeli Electric Corporation, and the establishment of the Jewish settlement of Elon Moreh on private land requisitioned from the village of Rujeib near Nablus. In other instances, the mere appeal to the court by residents brought about a change in the position of the military government (as with the cancellation of the decision to expel Nablus Mayor Basam Shak'a). Indeed, the possibility of HCJ interference has forced the military administration to coordinate its activities in the territories with the government prosecutor and attorney-general in advance.

Jewish Settlements Cases in HCJ

The legal battle over the right of Jews to settle in the occupied territories began in 1969, when Arab residents of the Rafah salient submitted a plea to the HCJ against land confiscations for the purpose of establishing Jewish settlements in the region. In that instance the HCJ decided that according to INTERNATIONAL LAW the right of settlement on private land is conditional upon the existence of a definite **"military and security need."**

In 1978, during the hearings concerning a petition against the establishment of Beit-El (see below), the HCJ added a further condition to the legality of settlement – that it be of a **temporary** nature.

In 1979, for the first time, the HCJ annulled land confiscation for the purpose of settlement and ordered the dismantling of Elon Moreh (see below), established on land confiscated from the residents of the village of Rujeib near Nablus. The confiscation was ruled invalid both because the motive for establishing the settlement was not military but political and because the settlement was intended to be permanent.

Following this incident, the Israeli government has abstained from confiscating private land for settlements, and has focused its settlement activities on lands declared "state land" (See INTERFERENCE WITH PRIVATE LAND OWNERSHIP), and land purchased from local residents. Since then, residents claiming ownership of "state lands" have been obliged to refer their claims to REVIEW BOARDS and their channel to the HCJ has been blocked.

In this way, the HCJ has been prevented – almost completely – from intervening in settlement activity in the territories.

1. Elon Moreh Case

The first attempts to establish Elon Moreh were made in the mid-1970s in the area of Sebastiya, near Nablus. The settlers squatted several times in the area without government permission and in violation of military orders which forbade Israelis to remain on the West Bank for more than 48 hours without a special permit. In 1974 the then attorney-general, Meir Shamgar, decided that there was no public interest in prosecuting Israelis for violating the order regarding stay without permit. In November 1975, a petition to the HCJ presented by a plaintiff, an Israeli citizen, to order the military authorities to remove the settlers, was rejected, on grounds of "no standing." Finally, the settlers were evacuated, with their consent, to the military camp at Kaddum.

In January 1979, after repeated demonstrations by the settlers, the government decided in principle to establish Elon Moreh and to confiscate private land for that purpose. On May 30, 1979, the final decision was approved by the ministerial committee on settlement, fixing the location of the settlement on the lands of the village of Rujeib, five kilometers southeast of Nablus. Deputy Prime Minister Yigal Yadin appealed the decision to the cabinet, but his appeal was rejected on June 3, 1979.

On June 7, 1979, the lands were confiscated and settlers took possession of the area. Within a week a petition was submitted to the HCJ against the confiscation. The plea was supported by a statement of former chief of staff Haim Bar-Lev, who declared that "Elon Moreh, to the best of my professional knowledge, does not contribute to Israel's security." The settlers themselves joined the hearing on the plea, at their request, and submitted a statement declaring that their primary motive for establishing the settlement was not security but ideology, and that they had been given assurance that the settlement would be permanent.

The HCJ heard the plea in a special session of five judges, headed by President of the Supreme Court Moshe Landau. During the hearing, in an unusual move, the judges instructed Chief of Staff Rafael Eitan, to answer in writing questions submitted by the plaintiffs. From his answers, it became clear that the settlement was decided upon initially under pressure from Gush Emunim. Only later was a military justification found.

In October 1979, the HCJ unanimously ordered the cancellation of the land confiscation and the dismantling of the settlement within 30 days. This was for two main reasons: lack of a security justification for the confiscation, and the fact that the settlement was meant to be permanent. On December 5, 1979, the government and the settlers agreed upon the transfer of the settlement to state land nearby (Jabal Kabir).

2. **Beit-El Case:**

In 1970 the military government seized 2,400 dunams from the residents of al-Bira, near Ramallah, and in 1972 began to build a Jewish settlement on this land. After construction got under way, a petition was made to the HCJ against the confiscation.

Government attorneys submitted a signed statement from the coordinator of activities in the territories, General Avraham Orly, to the HCJ. Orly confirmed that the settlement was located "on a site of great security importance."

The hearing on the plea took place before five justices, who reached a unanimous decision to reject the plea and approve the confiscation. They based their decision on General Orly's statement testifying to the "security necessity" of the confiscation, and upon the declaration of the Government Prosecutor Gavriel Bach that it was to be a "temporary" settlement for the duration of the military occupation only.

3. **Matityahu Case:**

In the case of the Matityahu settlement, a senior Israeli army reserve officer came to the aid of West Bank residents for the first time in their legal battle against Jewish settlements.

In September 1977, some 500 dunams of land belonging to the residents of Kfar Na'alin, in the Ramallah sub-district, were confiscated. In March 1979, the land was leased for the establishment of the Jewish settlement Matityahu, and the owners submitted a petition to the HCJ against the confiscation. They included with their plea a statement by General (Res.) Matityahu Peled denying the security importance of the projected settlement.

Opposing this statement, the government counsel submitted a statement by the coordinator of activities in the territories, General Dani Matt, pointing out Matityahu's strategically commanding position near Ben-Gurion International Airport, hence the security requirement for establishing it.

In July 1979 the plea was rejected; the justices of the HCJ preferred Matt's opinion on the grounds that the court must prefer "the spokesman for those actively engaged in the preservation of security in the administered territories and within the green line."

HOLY PLACES

The West Bank contains more than 550 Christian sites, including 75 churches (31 in the Bethlehem area), 77 monastaries (39 in the Bethlehem area, 16 in the Jordan area). There are more than 500 mosques, at least one in every village and town on the West Bank. There are 15 Jewish holy places, and in every Israeli settlement, at least one synagogue has been built. In Nablus (and on Mount Grizim) are Samaritan synagogues. There is no sectarian friction involving the holy places except for the Cave of the Machpela in Hebron, which is sacred to both Jews and Muslims. There, over the years of the occupation, Jews have steadily asserted control over the chambers of the "Haram Ibrahimi" and the atmosphere has been tense, with occasional incidents.

HUSSEIN-ARAFAT AGREEMENT

An agreement reached between Jordan and the PLO in February 1985, intended to encourage the United States to renew its efforts for a solution to the West Bank and Gaza Strip problem. It reads as follows:

Proceeding from the spirit of the Fez summit resolutions approved by the Arabs and from UN resolutions on the Palestinian question, in accordance with international legitimacy, and proceeding from a joint understanding toward building a distinguished relationship between the Jordanian and Palestinian peoples, the government of the Hashemite Kingdom of Jordan and the PLO have agreed to march together toward a just, peaceful settlement of the Middle East issue and toward the termination of the Israeli occupation of the Arab territories, including Jerusalem, in accordance with the following bases and principles:

1. Land in exchange for peace as cited in the UN resolutions, including the Security Council resolutions.
2. The Palestinian people's right to self-determination. The Palestinians should exercise their inalienable right to self-determination when the Jordanians and Palestinians manage to achieve this within the framework of an Arab confederation that is intended to be established between the two states of Jordan and Palestine.
3. Solving the Palestinian refugees problem in accordance with UN resolutions.
4. Solving all aspects of the Palestinian question.
5. Based on this, peace negotiations should be held within the framework of an international conference to be attended by the five UN Security Council permanent member-states and all parties to the conflict, including the PLO, which is the Palestinian people's sole legitimate representative, within a joint Jordanian-Palestinian delegation.

HUSSEIN'S FEDERATION PLAN

Basic principles of a plan to establish a United Arab Kingdom of Palestine and Jordan, announced by King Hussein, March 15, 1972. Excerpts:

The Hashemite Kingdom of Jordan shall become a United Arab Kingdom. Amman shall be the central capital and Jerusalem shall become the capital of the Region of Palestine. The king shall be head of state. The central legislative authority shall be vested in the king and in the National Assembly, composed of an equal number of members from each of the two regions. The kingdom shall have a single armed forces and its supreme commander shall be the king. The responsibility of the central executive power (the king and Central Council of Ministers) shall be confined to matters relating to the kingdom as a sovereign international entity. The executive power in each region shall be responsible for all its matters with the exception of such matters as the constitution requires to be the responsibility of the central executive power.

The Federation Plan was rejected by the PLO. The Jordanians view it as a basis for future Jordanian-Palestinian relations, after Israeli withdrawal. The plan is not acceptable to the PLO. Palestine National Council Algiers resolutions speak about "confederation." The HUSSEIN-ARAFAT AGREEMENT uses the term "Arab confederation", which, according to Palestinian sources, mean the creation of two independent and equal regions loosely united.

IMPROVEMENT OF THE QUALITY OF LIFE

A policy launched by American Secretary of State George Shultz in 1982. Its official wording:"[The Palestinians] must be given a stake in their future by greater opportunities for economic development, fairer administrative practices and greater concern for the quality of their life." This policy is closely linked to the Egyptian demand that Israel take "confidence-building measures," with regard to the Palestinian population, as a condition for improving relations between the two countries, and the implementation of AUTONOMY (See CAMP DAVID).

This initiative was interpreted in conflicting ways. One interpretation (voiced by some State Department officials and by the American Consulate in Jerusalem) sees it as an attempt to create an independent Palestinian economic infrastructure which will not be completely dependent on the Israeli economic system, and to widen the resource base of the Palestinian population on the West Bank and in the Gaza Strip. The second, (voiced by the Israeli government and the American Embassy in Tel Aviv) defines "quality of life" as the improvement of individual welfare and hence, complementary to the ECONOMIC POLICY Israel has been pursuing in the territories. The political leadership on the West Bank and in the Gaza Strip has regarded the

American initiative with suspicion. It is seen as acquiescence in the status quo and the end of American attempts to seek a comprehensive political solution for the territories. Others see it as disguised American support for the "pacification" of the local population through economic benefits to collaborators. At the same time, local entrepreneurs endeavor to reap advantages both from the aid monies and from American interest in the improvement in the quality of life, in order to advance their own commercial interests (See FOREIGN AID).

INCENTIVES FOR SETTLEMENT

The West Bank is regarded by the government as an A+ or A development region for investment in industrial enterprises and facilities for tourism. Therefore enterprises established across the green line receive a grant of 30 percent and loans at a real interest rate of 0.5 percent, or if dollar linked, at 6 percent. These enterprises are also entitled to a grant for land development, structures, and equipment, and a 5 percent rebate on financial charges.

The A+ development areas within the green line are: Eilat, Beit She'an, Hatzor, Metulla, Ma'alot, Mitspe Ramon, and Shlomi, all of which are in remote, poorly developed regions. In contrast, on the West Bank, the A+ development areas include settlements such as Yakir, Elkana, Kedumim, Karnei Shomron, and Neve Tsuf, all of which are in the Tel Aviv metropolitan area (35-40 minutes away). The other settlements in Samaria are A development areas. In comparison, places such as Acre, Kiryat Gat, and Beit Shemesh are B development areas, whereas Kfar Sava, which is only 15 minutes away from Yakir, is not entitled to any government aid at all.

A similar situation is found regarding housing. In areas of "high demand," within the metropolitan areas of Jerusalem and Tel Aviv, government assistance reaches an average of about 75 percent of the value of the apartment, whereas in more distant areas the assistance in its various forms covers the entire cost of the apartment and its development. The aid consists of a mortgage (11.5 percent) unlinked to the cost of living index, a linked but interest free loan (65.5 percent), and a linked loan bearing 6 percent interest (11.5 percent). Moreover, the price of the apartment is also subsidized in that the cost of the land is only 5 percent of its actual value, and the infrastructure is provided to the settlement free of charge. Thus one can purchase an apartment only 30-45 minutes from Jerusalem for a cash payment of $2,500.

INDEPENDENT LIBERAL LABOR MOVEMENT (SETTLEMENTS)

The settlements of this movement are of two types, the kibbutzim of the Zionist Youth and the Moshav Organization of the Zionist Worker.

The Kibbutzim of the Zionist Youth:

First established in the 1930's, tower and stockade settlements were built. In 1954 a cooperation agreement was signed between its kibbutzim and those of the Labor Party covering all areas of kibbutz life except the youth movement.

The Moshav Organization of the Zionist Workers:

Also founded in the 1930's, this organization has placed two moshavim on the West Bank: Reihan, in the Samarian hills, with 50 people, and Massuah, in the Jordan Valley, with 174 people (September 1985). Its political views are identical with those of the Labor Party; thus it opposes settlement in areas with dense Arab populations. The organization has two central financial institutions: Mifal Ha'Oved Ha'Tsioni, the movement's settlement fund, and Mishkei Ha'Oved Ha'Tsioni, a company concerned with the organization's citrus and orchard plantations.

INDUSTRY

In the economy of the West Bank industry does not play a major role. Despite rapid growth in Gross National Product (GNP) (See NATIONAL ACCOUNTS), industry has not grown. On the contrary, its proportion of GNP fell from 9 percent in 1968 to 6.7 percent in 1984. Productivity calculated by added value, is less than half of the added value in agriculture. The number of workers employed in industry has remained constant at 15,000 since 1970. In 1984 only 9,550 (9% of the total employed in the West Bank) were employed in industrial plants. The rest worked in quarries and olive presses: 22 percent are employed in processing olive oil, 25 percent in textiles, 18 percent in quarrying, 10 percent in food manufacture, 4-5 percent in matallurgy, and the rest in carpentry, tailoring, etc. Of 2,000 enterprises, only five employ more than 100 workers. Of the industrial labor force, 23 percent lives in Nablus, 20 percent in Hebron, 18 percent in Ramallah and al-Bira, 16 percent in Bethlehem and Jericho, and 10 percent in Jenin. In absolute terms there has been some growth in industry since 1967, but that growth must be divided into three periods: relatively rapid growth till the mid-1970s, a sharp decrease in the mid-1970s, a slight improvement at the end of the decade, and an additional decline in the first half of the 1980s. This business cycle closely follows the fluctuations of the Israeli economy, pointing to the absolute dependence of West Bank industry upon Israel.

The local market on the West Bank and in the Gaza Strip is the major outlet for goods produced by Palestinian industry. The factories of the West Bank sell more than twice as much on the local market than in Israel (excluding East Jerusalem). Goods sold in Israel are mainly sub-contracted for Israeli factories, particularly textiles and shoes (12 percent of the income from the industry of the West Bank in the 1970s).

The Jordanian market does not import manufactured goods from the West Bank on a large scale. Total exports to Jordan are no greater than in 1967 (See FOREIGN TRADE). Of 201 West Bank companies surveyed, only 12 exported to Jordan.

Some factories selling locally have managed to develop markets despite intense competition from Israeli goods. However, in general, the industry of the West Bank is unable to withstand Israeli competition, which enjoys massive protection as well as government subsidies and credit. In 1984 Israel sold manufactured goods worth $363 million on the West Bank (See FOREIGN TRADE). Moreover, lately the industry of the West Bank has had to compete with Israeli enterprises located in the territories and enjoying far-reaching benefits (See INCENTIVES FOR SETTLEMENT).

INTERFERENCE WITH PRIVATE LAND OWNERSHIP

This can be subsumed under the following categories:
  I. Expropriation of Ownership
  II. Seizure of Possession
  III. Restriction on Use

I. Expropriation

A. Absentee Owned Lands

In accordance with the 1967 Order Concerning Abandoned Property (58), property, the legal owner or tenant of which left the region, is transferred to the Custodian of Abandoned Property. "Property" includes land, movable property and other economic interests. Ignorance of the identity of the owner or tenant of the property does not prevent it from being considered abandoned property. The Order Concerning Abandoned Private Property (150) adds directives, stating, among other things, that property belonging to a corporation controlled by people active in an enemy country may be taken by the custodian as though it were abandoned. Property belonging to a resident of an enemy country who is not in the region is also considered abandoned. The burden of proof of ownership or tenancy of the property lies upon the person claiming rights.

In the area of the West Bank about 430,000 dunams of land were identified after the Six Day War as abandoned property, including 350,000 dunams of stony, inarable land (some of which was later declared state land, (see below). About 70,000 dunams are arable (some were leased to the families of the absentee owners and some were leased to Jewish settlers), and another 12,000 dunams were transferred to the possession of relatives of the absentees. In addition, there were about 11,000 houses, stores and storehouses, most of which were transferred to relatives of the absentees. The Custodian of Abandoned Property also administers property which had been held by the Jordanian Custodian of Enemy Property (mostly Jewish lands purchased before 1948). The Jewish lands came to about 33,000 dunams, with 88 structures.

B. Government Lands

In the Jordanian land registry, 527,000 dunams were registered in the name of the Jordanian government. Over the years about 160,000 dunams of land were added to these, land which could be viewed as state land according to old archives. By 1973 official Israeli publications indicated that the area of state lands was about 700,000 dunams, of which more than 600,000 dunams were stony, 55,000 dunams arable and 33,000 roads, forests and ravines. Three hundred thousand dunams of state lands are in the Jordan Valley and the eastern slopes of the mountains of Judea and Samaria (the districts of Jericho, Ramallah, Nablus, and Jenin), as well as the stony hills in Western Judea and Samaria.

C. The Declaration of State Lands

In 1980 the Israeli government adopted a new legal approach to state lands (as opposed to registered government lands). The custodian began (on the authority vested in him by Order 59, 1967) to declare uncultivated, unregistered land as state lands. That was on the basis of the Israeli interpretation of the Ottoman Land Law of 1855. According to that law (par. 103), "Vacant land which is not in possession of anyone by title deed or assigned *ab antiquo* to the use of inhabitants of a town or village and lies at such a distance from towns and villages from which a human voice cannot be heard at the nearest inhabited place, such as rocky mountains, wild fields, and bushland is called *mawat* (dead). Anyone who is in need may cultivate it as sown land gratuitously, with the leave of the official. On the condition that the ultimate ownership *(raqabah)* shall belong to the sultan and that all the laws concerning cultivated lands shall apply to this land."

Paragraph 103 of the Ottoman Land Law speaks of *mawat* lands. However, *miri* class lands (to which the abstract right of ownership is

114

reserved to the sultan) are also liable to be declared state lands according to the Israeli interpretation of the law. In that case, though, the test is whether they were cultivated during the past 10 years. Thus, according to that test, any unregistered and uncultivated land on the West Bank may become state land, unless someone can prove ownership in a matter satisfactory to the special adviser to the Ministry of Justice and the REVIEW BOARD composed of administration officials. It must be pointed out that the Israeli definition of state lands was not used by the Jordanian government in whose name, ostensibly, the land was seized. Moreover, the declarations are not made in an orderly, judicial process of land registration, but they preempt it. They could not have been carried out if Israel had continued the process of land registration which had been interrupted in 1968 (Order 291).

According to the double test of registration and cultivation, 2,150,000 dunams of land on the West Bank (some 40 percent of the total area) were located and mapped. That area also includes government lands (See above), which means that the new legal approach located an additional million-and-a-half dunams of land which can be declared state land. Of this, by mid-1984, some 800,000 dunams had been declared, bringing the total lands declared and seized to 1,800,000 dunams. Tens of thousands of dunams are in the process of being so declared. Once sufficient land for unlimited Jewish settlement was assured, the pace of declaration slowed, nonetheless it continues unabated. As noted, until 1980 the government did not view uncultivated lands of the *mawat* and *miri* categories as government lands, since it continued Jordanian practice. With the proliferation of declarations, a judicial problem arose, as the custodian had been appointed to administer only "government property," as understood in June 1967, and not "state property," as subsequently declared. To remove that difficulty Order 1091 was published. That order changed the wording and declared that not only land which was registered in the name of the enemy state on the determining day (June 7, 1967) but also that which was registered **after that day**, would be administered by the custodian.

D. Land Expropriation for Public Use

Land expropriation (or, in legal language, "purchase") is carried out according to Jordanian law (Land Law – Purchase for Public Use, No. 2, 1953) as amended by Military Orders 321 and 949. Jordanian law created and supervised multi-staged processes for expropriation for public use. Israeli military orders transferred the authorities of the Jordanian council of ministers and the king to an authorized body (the assistant head of the CIVILIAN ADMINISTRATION) and, above it, as the "authorizing body," the regional commander (later the head of the civilian administration). Thus the structure of checks and balances existing in Jordanian law (pars. 5, 6, 8, and 9) was removed. Moreover, the administration makes constant use of par. 12, according to which the council of ministers (namely the assistant head of the civilian administration) is entitled to decide upon "immediate purchase and possession" without being limited by the processes of negotiation, judicial process, or appeal, if it is "convinced that there are reasons obligating immediate possession of the lands."

The orders of the administration did away with the need to publish the proposed seizure in the official gazette and to notify the owners of the property through the registry clerk. It was not until 1981, when the Arab residents of the West Bank appealed to the HIGH COURT OF JUSTICE, arguing, among other things, that they were not notified of the condemnation, that the administration published Order 949, determining that notification of land condemnation would be published in the "collected proclamations" of the administration and given to the owners through the registry clerk and the MUKHTARS. Jordanian law states explicitly that expropriation must be for the public benefit, for example for roads. Thus the administration may not use it as a method for the establishment of Israeli settlements. However, it is able to make extensive use of it for expropriating lands for access roads, public institutions and particularly for a network of arterial highways planned and paved for the expansion and proliferation of Jewish settlements. Arab settlements were purposely bypassed (See ROADS). The use of land expropriation is closely connected to the structure of physical planning and zoning (see below). Any land which, in the statutory zoning plan, is destined for public use, can be expropriated according to law.

The lands expropriated and those of which immediate possession has been taken, amount to approximately 50,000 dunams; in addition, about 100,000 dunams are designated for expropriation.

II Seizure of possession
A. Closed Areas

By virtue of Article 90 of Order Concerning Security Regulations (378, 1970, previously Article 70, 1967), a "military commander" (not necessarily the regional commander but any officer) is empowered to proclaim an area or place a closed area for the purposes of the above order. Any person entering or leaving a closed area or place without written permission of the military commander is committing a crime. The declaration is made by written order with an attached map of the area, however it can also be so declared by an oral order. In early 1985, 23 closure orders were in effect, encompassing about one million dunams. Most of the closed areas are also state lands and are used as military training areas, but about 80,000 dunams were closed within populated areas as a first step towards their seizure (see below) and the establishment of Jewish settlements, for example, the Latrun zone and Ma'aleh Adumim. Most of the closed areas were also declared "combat zones" (see below). Ownership of closed areas remains in the hands of the residents, but they are deprived of use of the land without any compensation or payment, excepting the option of applying to the REVIEW BOARDS.

B. Requisition for Military Purposes

The regional commander, "on the basis of his authority, and in that he is convinced that it is necessary for military purposes," promulgated several dozen orders for the requisition of property from 1968 until 1979, encompassing about 50,000 dunams. The authority of the regional commander is based on HAGUE REGULATIONS No. 52 (1907). Requisition orders, unlike closed areas, stipulate that the owners or tenants of the land are entitled to demand payment for use and compensation for any real damage caused by the requisition. Requisition does not cancel rights of ownership, only the rights of possession and use.

The requisition of property for immediate military purposes was the principal method by which private property was seized between 1968 and 1979 for the purpose of establishing Israeli settlements. In that the seizures were anchored in the Hague Regulations, which state that they are permissible only for military purposes, it was claimed that the establishment of Israeli civilian settlements was inconsistent with the regulations.

The HIGH COURT OF JUSTICE accepted the position of the military government and ruled that "Israeli settlements in the territories occupied by the IDF are part of the territorial defense system, and therefore Jewish settlement serves a defense need *par excellence*." It was also argued that the establishment of permanent settlements violates the rule that requisition must be temporary, until the end of the state of war. Here too the High Court accepted the military government position that, although a civilian settlement may remain in place only so long as the IDF holds it by virtue of the requisition order, the fate of the settlement will be determined in international negotiations leading to a new arrangement. The use of requisition orders to establish Israeli settlements suited the political conception of the ALIGNMENT (1968-1977), but not that of the LIKUD (1977-1984). The latter could not use the requisition method since it implied the temporary nature of Israeli presence. Therefore, when the area of ELON MOREH was seized, the representatives of the military administration did not conceal their main intention, which was to establish a permanent settlement there. For that reason alone, the seizure was revoked by the High Court. At the same time the use of requisition orders to seize property ceased and was replaced by the method of declarations of state lands (see above).

It should be pointed out that according to the 1982 Order Concerning Work on Requisitioned Areas (977), all excavation, construction or use is forbidden without a permit. That order does not apply to an agency of the IDF or one acting under the orders of IDF forces. The Israeli settlements on the requisitioned lands were erected on the basis of that order.

III. Restriction of Use

A. Prohibition of Building and Construction

By virtue of Order 393, 1970, on the supervision of building in Judea and Samaria, any military commander (not necessarily the area commander) may prohibit construction or order a halt in construction or impose conditions on construction if he believes it necessary for the security of the Israeli army in the area or to ensure public order. Orders prohibiting building were issued regarding areas around IDF camps and installations, around Israeli settlements and around whole settlement areas (Gush Etzion, Givat Ze'ev), similarly in a 200-meter strip along both sides of main roads. Orders were also imposed on built-up areas of Arab municipalities when the authorities wished to curb building expansion. Prohibition of building can also be effected by designating margins of 100-150 meters on either side of a planned road in the statutory plan. In the outline scheme for the Jerusalem metropolitan area (see below), margins of that sort were actually stipulated, limiting the use of tens of thousands of dunams of land. The total area around Israeli sites affected by prohibition orders amounts to 293,500 dunams. With "road margin" regulations, the total area affected is 580,000 dunams.

B. Restrictions Based on the Statutory Zoning Plan (See PHYSICAL PLANNING)

Changes made by the military administration in the zoning ordinances applying to the territories (Mandatory plans in the open areas and Jordanian plans in the cities) set severe limits on the use of land.

Although no statutory plan prepared by the administration has received legal force, the administration planners act as though their plans have been approved. In that context it should be noted that in 1985 the physical planning unit (serving the "supreme planning council") which

118

had been subordinate to the STAFF OFFICER for interior affairs in the civilian administration, was transferred to the responsibility of the infrastructure branch, responsible, among other things, for the seizure and expropriation of property. That administrative change makes the goals of the administration's physical planning quite manifest.

It should be pointed out that the supreme planning council has the authority to decide which lands are destined for expropriation and to request their purchase according to par. 56 of the Jordanian Land Law (See above). Whereas the supreme planning council is an institution whose members belong to the administration, the expropriation is initiated, deliberated upon, and approved by the same body. The district commander does not view himself as limited by statutory plans. He issues building regulations which purport to be based on the Jordanian Planning Law (for example, Order 912, as well as the regulations on building height in Ramallah).

C. **The Prohibition on Rebuilding Demolished Houses**

According to the 1972 order prohibiting building (456), no building or part of a building may be built on land on which there had been a building which had been confiscated and razed according to an order issued by the military commander on his authority according to regulation 119 of the EMERGENCY REGULATIONS (1945), except with the authorization of the district commander. That order has retroactive application and it is meant to ensure that buildings demolished as punishment will not be rebuilt.

D. **Combat Zones**

Combat zones or fire zones are areas regarding which the administration is not responsible for damage incurred by military action. An order regarding liability (271, 1968) states that a resident who claims to have suffered damage as a result of the actions of IDF soldiers, of a force acting in coordination with the IDF, or a citizen working for the IDF, and who is entitled to compensation for that damage, may demand compensation from the staff officer in charge of claims. However, section 2c of that order states: "No claim may be made, and none will be considered, and no compensation will be paid for damage incurred in an area declared by the district commander as a combat zone." The combat zone was declared in Order 270/1 and an attached map. The area defined as a combat zone extends over about a million dunams in the eastern part of the West Bank (the Jordan Valley and the western slopes), as well as other areas. The combat zones are largely co-extensive with the closed areas. It should be pointed out that the specific combat zones have lost all significance in terms of claims for damages. In the order regarding claims (Amendment 4, 1984), the reservation disclaiming liability for damage caused in an area declared as a combat zone was rescinded. According to that amendment, no compensation at all will be paid, throughout the West Bank, if the commander of the IDF forces in the area declares that the damage resulted from military activity. Thus, for the purposes of claiming compensation for damage, the entire West Bank has become a combat zone.

While no change has been made in private property rights in the combat zones, clearly no one would consider remaining in a fire zone, and consequently no use can be made of the land.

E. Nature Reserves

The Order Concerning the Protection of Nature (363, 1969) imposes severe restrictions on construction and land use in areas declared as nature reserves. The registrar of lands attaches a "warning notice" to the lands in the registry, thus diminishing the value of the land. No compensation for damages is specified. Although declaration of a nature reserve is aimed at protecting the environment, it is considered by the authorities as an integral part of the land seizure program. As of mid–1985 the authorities have declared 250,000 dunams nature reserves. An additional 90,000 have yet to be declared. (See PARKS AND NATURE RESERVES).

F. Restrictions on Cultivation

According to the Order Concerning Supervision of Fruit Trees and Vegetables (1015, 1982), no fruit tree may be planted in an orchard without written permission issued by the authorities. The authorities are empowered to impose conditions for issuing permits. The prohibition applies to the planting of vegetables in the Jordan Valley (eggplants and tomatoes) and to plum trees and grapevines throughout the West Bank. Order 818 (1980) states that the officer responsible shall set quotas for the planting of ornamental shrubs. These orders were issued in order to plan agricultural production, but the officer responsible uses them for other purposes as well. One of the conditions for receiving permission to plant is producing documentary proof of ownership of the land to be cultivated. That measure is intended to prevent the cultivation of lands which the government claims for itself as unregistered, uncultivated land.

Summary

The judicial and administrative structure described above assured Israeli control over 52 percent of the area of the West Bank. Some 2,268,500

120

dunams, or 41 percent of the area, is under direct Israeli possession. 570,000 dunams, or 11 percent of the area is placed under severe restrictions. It also assured a virtually unlimited reserve of land for Israeli settlement. Moreover, severe limitations were imposed on the use and development of the lands remaining in the hands of the Palestinian population. Although the system for controlling the land is made up of a great number of juridical components, it is viewed by the military government, by the settlers, and by the Palestinians as a single system, and the use of various judicial means merely suits the convenience of the administration, and the needs of the settlers. Land seized by order for military purposes is converted into state land by another order. "Closed" areas are turned into "requisitioned" land by another order. The Israeli settlements are made up of lands which were requisitioned, expropriated, closed, and upon which constrution is forbidden. For example: the area of the Shiloh settlement is composed of 740 dunams "requisitioned" for military purposes, 850 dunams declared state lands and 41 dunams expropriated for public purposes. Ofra, another settlement, contains 350 dunams requisitioned by a Jordanian order (as a military camp), 20 dunams of expropriated land, and 140 dunams declared state lands. The built-up area of Ofra is surrounded by an area of about 1,000 dunams in which building is forbidden.

The Gush Etzion area is composed of "Jewish-owned lands," "expropriated lands," "closed areas," "requisitioned lands," and "state lands." The entire bloc is surrounded by an "order forbidding construction."

INTERMINISTERIAL COORDINATION

West Bank settlement involves the parallel activity of the MINISTRY OF HOUSING AND CONSTRUCTION and three separate branches within it; the settlement division of the WORLD ZIONIST ORGANIZATION; the MINISTRY OF AGRICULTURE (directly, and through the Israel Lands Authority and the Mekorot water company); the Ministry of Defense and the CIVILIAN ADMINISTRATION; the Ministry of Industry and Trade; the Ministry of the Interior and the regional councils; the Ministry of Justice (in land matters); the Ministry of Energy (through the Electric Corporation) and also the Ministries of Health, Communications and Education and Culture.

The MINISTERIAL COMMITTEE FOR SETTLEMENTS, theoretically responsible for settlement and construction on the West Bank, has laid down general rules, but has refrained from dealing with fiscal matters or interministerial coordination. Likud government policy, aimed at bringing about total integration of bureaucratic management of the West Bank with the Israeli system (See MINISTERIAL RESPONSIBILITY), created a situation in which each ministry acts within its own jurisdiction with virtually no interministerial coordination. The formation of the national unity government contributed ideological differences to the personal and institutional rivalry and conflicting interests that existed during the Likud's term of office.

According to the state comptroller report of 1984, despite the multiplicity of authorities involved in settlement activity, no coordinating committee or office has been established to monitor the way decisions are carried into effect or to coordinate the functions and budgets of the different authorities. The lack of interministerial coordination enables the various settler institutions (See ISRAELI REGIONAL COUNCILS, YESHA) to play one body off against another and reap the benefits of duplication and wastefulness.

INTERNATIONAL LAW

The two main documents determining the principles of international law applying to occupied territories are the HAGUE REGULATIONS of 1907 and the GENEVA CONVENTION (FOURTH) of 1949. An Israeli general staff order of 1954 stipulates that IDF soldiers must obey the strictures of those conventions in any area occupied by IDF soldiers.

The conventions require the occupying power to maintain public order and security as far as possible, respecting the law in force in the area. It must respect those laws unless absolutely unable to do so. The occupying power may not force the residents of the occupied territory to swear allegiance to the occupying power, nor may it seize private property except for military purposes.

Israel holds that from a juridical point of view the West Bank and the Gaza Strip are not subject to international law applying to "occupied territories" since they do not belong to that category. Israel claims that there was never Jordanian sovereignty on the West Bank, because Jordanian annexation was recognized by only two states. The Gaza Strip was never annexed by Egypt, and therefore it was never under Egyptian sovereignty.

It should be pointed out that the attitude towards the Fourth Geneva Convention of 1949 was not unequivocal during the early years of the military government. Only in Order 144 did the military government cancel the supremacy of the convention over the orders of the military commander of the West Bank. International organizations, including the RED CROSS, which supervises the implementation of the convention, do not accept Israel's arguments, responding that the convention sets norms for behavior applying to all occupied territories, regardless of the issue of sovereignty. Similar international organizations, both legal and political, judge the actions of Israel in the territories according to the criteria of the two aforementioned conventions.

In 1971, Attorney-General Meir Shamgar stated that Israel took it upon itself to observe the humanitarian directives of international law regarding occupied territories. In the course of time that position has been eroded, and cases have been heard before the HIGH COURT OF JUSTICE in which the government has opposed the attempt to subject its actions to the directives of the Geneva Convention on the West Bank. It has argued that the convention is binding only between governments, and therefore individual residents of the territories cannot bring legal action for its application. The HIGH COURT OF JUSTICE has accepted this argument, and some actions in the territories do contradict those conventions.

INVESTMENT IN SETTLEMENTS

It is difficult to specify exact figures for Israeli investment in settlements, since the official sources do not itemize their development budgets by region (except the Ministry of Agriculture). Even so, it is possible to estimate the size of the various types of investment, by multiplying the published figures on the scope of physical construction by the price per unit, according to official publications.

It is estimated that $2,000 million has been invested in the territories between 1968-1985, not including defense investment. Of this, $750 million was invested by the Alignment governments (1968-1977), about $1 billion by the Likud government (1977-1984), and about $250 million by the National Unity government (1984-1985).

These sums do not include the huge investments of the Ministry of Defense, part of which serve civilian needs. The extent of these investments is, of course, classified information.

Since 1979 the level of annual capital investment has been $200-$250 million a year.

According to figures of the state comptroller's office, a total of $220 million was invested on the West Bank in 1983 in the following manner:

Direct construction activity of the Ministry of Housing and Construction	$40.0 million
Intermediate financing to contractors	$18.5 million
Assistance to settlers	$33.5 million
Road development	$45.5 million
Water development	$5.5 million
Land purchase	$1.5 million
Settlement division (community settlements and villages)	$40.5 million
Ministry of Industry and Trade	$26.0 million
Communications	$10.5 million

Analysis of the 1985 budgets of the government ministries (a year of severe cutbacks in public spending) shows that the extent of gross annual investment decreased to approximately $150 million, two thirds for new projects and the rest for funding projects initiated in previous years. In some sectors, i.e. the WORLD ZIONIST ORGANIZATION and industry there is an increase over the 1984 budget. Investment in West Bank settlements represented, under the national unity government almost one third of total public investment in infrastructure for the whole country.

ISRAELI EXTRA-PARLIAMENTARY BODIES

Ha'Derech Le'Shalom (The Way to Peace)
A small Israeli political action group founded in 1983 in the aftermath of the refusal of the CIVILIAN ADMINISTRATION on the West Bank, headed by Brigadier General Shlomo Ilia, to permit groups of Palestinian notables connected with the VILLAGE LEAGUES from establishing a Palestinian political party advocating peace (The Palestinian Democratic Movement for Peace). The Derech Le'Shalom movement regarded that step as an expression of misconceived Israeli policy regarding Palestinians seeking peace with Israel and rejecting terror. The movement's goal was to encourage moderate elements in the territories and to speak with any people or groups supporting them. The movement views dialogue as a first step towards peace and arranges joint meetings with moderates in the territories. It was founded by kibbutz members, with active members from development towns, kibbutzim, and cities, as well as the Israeli Arab population.

Ha'Mizrach Le'Shalom (The East for Peace)
A non-parliamentary movement, founded May 29, 1983 by a group of Israeli Jewish intellectuals, educators, and community activists of oriental

and North-African origin. It is essentially an ideological forum seeking to change the negative image of oriental Jews regarding peace and to air ideas about the integration of Israel within the Middle East. The movement's goal is to encourage the peace process in the region. It perceives settlements across the green line as a danger to that process and opposes all activities harmful to the chances for peace and any act of terror and extremism committed by either side. It supports dialogue between Jews and Arabs to find a solution to the Palestinian problem.

Most of its activities are in the area of information (meetings in homes, on campuses, etc.) articles and research. The movement has published a book in Hebrew called **The Mediterranean Sea.**

Netivot Shalom (Paths of Peace) – **Oz Ve'Shalom** (Strength and Peace)
Oz Ve'Shalom is a religious, ideological forum founded in 1975 in opposition to nationalist religious movements and Gush Emunim. Through articles and public meetings the movement seeks to spread its own religious and national view regarding Zionism and the Jewish-Arab confrontation. According to its view, peace must be achieved through agreement between neighboring states, based on territorial compromise, to prevent Israeli rule over an Arab population, rule which would ultimately entail a moral decline in Israeli society. Its members are mainly religious academics.

In 1984 it joined forces with Netivot Shalom, a more broadly-based movement which emerged in the course of the Lebanon War. Its founders included students at the Hesder yeshivot (which combine religious studies with military service) as well as prominent rabbinical figures.

Its assertion of the primacy of peace and its critique of the messianic determinism of Gush Emunim and the political chauvinism of Meir Kahane and the far right, derive from a religious rather than pragmatic perspective. Its most widely-publicized activities were to press for a commission of inquiry following the Sabra and Shatilla massacres and to denounce the emergence of the JEWISH UNDERGROUND.

Zionut Aheret (Alternative Zionism)
A group based in Jerusalem which began operation in 1977, one of the founding elements of Peace Now. It arose in protest against the settlements and the growing power of the extreme right. The movement reacted to events in the territories and fostered Jewish-Arab relations, working through home meetings, activities among youth, and contacts with the Oz Ve'Shalom movement and circles within the Labor Movement and Ha'Kibbutz Ha'Artsi; however it received little public support.

Gush Emunim (The Bloc of the Faithful)

A political and settlement movement with a strong religious underpinning. It views the establishment of Jewish settlements on the West Bank and in the Gaza Strip as a political and social means of preventing Israeli withdrawal from those areas and also as a means of reforming the image and character of Israeli society.

Gush Emunim was first established within the NATIONAL RELIGIOUS PARTY in early 1974 in reaction to the political crisis and protest movements which emerged in the aftermath of the Yom Kippur War. The founders of Gush Emunim were religious youth associated with the NRP (former members of the Bnei Akiva religious youth movement, students at the yeshiva high schools and the Hesder yeshivot), often called the "generation of the knitted **kipot** (skullcaps)", as opposed to the black-hatted students at the ultra-Orthodox, non-Zionist yeshivot. Gush Emunim adopted a political and religious doctrine forbidding withdrawal from any part of the Land of Israel on the basis of national-religious commandments. They founded settlements as political demonstrations, adopting the method first used by Rabbi Moshe Levinger in Hebron (Kiryat Arba) in the spring of 1968, before the establishment of Gush Emunim.

Most of the members of Gush Emunim and its central activists studied at the Merkaz HaRav Yeshiva in Jerusalem. Their spiritual mentor was the yeshiva head, the late Rabbi Tsvi Yehuda Kook who guided them according to his interpretation of the doctrines of his father, Rabbi Avraham Hacohen Kook (the first Ashkenazi chief rabbi of Palestine). These rabbis regarded Zionism and the settlement of the Land of Israel as the beginning of redemption and a sign of the imminent arrival of the Messiah. The members of Gush Emunim display elements of a fanatic, messianic faith, which impelled them to violent action in demonstrating against the policies of Yitzhak Rabin's government in 1974-75. The climax of those actions took the form of demonstrative settlement attempts in areas where the government had forbidden Israeli settlements (mainly in central Samaria) focused around the village of Sebastiya near Nablus.

The religious activists of Gush Emunim, including many young rabbis, were conspicuous in their willingness to cooperate (exceptional for religious leaders in Israeli politics) with non-religious political movements who advocated a "Greater Israel." This joint effort forced the ALIGNMENT government, headed by Rabin, to make concessions and help them establish settlements on the West Bank.

The struggle between Gush Emunim and the government continued under the first LIKUD government headed by Menachem Begin, ending with the collapse of the coalition (the crises with the Democratic Movement for Change and the resignations of Moshe Dayan and Ezer Weizman) leading to the 1981 elections. In the winter of 1980-81 the Begin government started implementing the Gush Emunim settlement plan, giving its activists considerable material aid. Violent confrontations between Gush Emunim and the IDF, took place during the withdrawal from Yamit in Sinai (spring 1982). After the completion of the withdrawal, however, all the institutions of the state and the World Zionist Organization cooperated with Gush Emunim agencies to establish dozens of settlements on the West Bank and in the Gaza Strip, which can be regarded as a complete victory for Gush Emunim.

Gush Emunim is not an institutionalized movement, and since 1981 has acted through the Jewish settlement organizations (YESHA) in the territories and with the settlement movement (AMANA), founded by members of Gush Emunim. The number of Gush Emunim activists has been estimated at a few thousand individuals willing to join in political demonstrations and assist in settlement activity. They aim to give the impression of following in the footsteps of the early pioneers and emulating their altruism on behalf of the Jewish people – a source of considerable political power. The slogans of Gush Emunim trade upon fear of an impending national catastrophe. They advocate harsh punishment (including the death sentence and exile) for Arabs engaging in unlawful activity or terrorism, express hatred of Arabs and maintain that there is no chance of achieving peace with them. Their combination of religious messianism, fears for national security, and hostility towards the Arabs has gained them considerable support among large segments of the Israeli population.

By 1985 the practical expression of Gush Emunim ideology was evident in the institutional bodies it established on the West Bank. Central to them is the Council of Jewish Settlements in Judea, Samaria, and Gaza (YESHA). Other sources of support are the LIKUD and the NRP, the Sephardi Tora Guardians Party, and Meir Kahane's KACH party.

Siah (Hebrew acronym: New Israeli Left)
Founded as an extra-parliamentary movement in 1969 following a protest letter sent to the prime minister by graduating high school students.

Its central argument was that a national liberation movement of the Palestinian people exists alongside Zionism, with an equal right to assert itself within the territory of Mandatory Palestine; hence the necessity of reaching a peace agreement with the Arabs on the basis of the June 4, 1967 borders.

During the 1973 election campaign, some members wished to limit themselves to extra-parliamentary activity while others were for taking part in the elections, resulting in a split: some Siah activists formed the "Blue-Red Movement," seeking to establish a socialist alternative to the State of Israel; others joined the "Ha'Olam Ha'Zeh – Koah Hadash" party. With these developments Siah effectively came to an end.

Peace Now

A mass protest movement established two months after Egyptian President Anwar Sadat's visit to Jerusalem during the negotiations between Israel and Egypt. Its first act was to send a letter from reserve officers to the prime minister in which they prevailed upon him to reach a peace agreement (March 7, 1978). Later, demonstrations and mass meetings were held. During the Camp David negotiations, most of the movement's activities were directed at achieving the peace agreements. After these were signed, the movement turned its attention to Gush Emunim and the settlements on the West Bank. It succeeded in freezing the establishment of five settlements and the removal of the Elon Moreh settlement (1980). After the outbreak of the war in Lebanon, Peace Now demanded Israeli withdrawal and was instrumental in the establishment of the Kahan Commission of Inquiry into responsibility for the massacres of Sabra and Shatilla ("The Demonstration of the 400,000"). A significant decline has taken place in the activities of Peace Now since the establishment of the national unity government in the summer of 1984. Some of the movement's leaders turned to political activity directed at unifying the Israeli left (the Massad movement).

The Movement for Greater Israel

An ideological movement founded after the Six Day War in 1967 which viewed the conquest of the West Bank and Gaza Strip as a historic turning point. The movement advocated the extension of Israeli sovereignty over the occupied territories. It regarded the biblical borders of the Land of Israel as the true borders, ensuring the strength and security of the state. The movement published a number of pamphlets, and its positions were published in **Zot Ha'Aretz** (This is the Land), a periodical first published April 26, 1968, on the establishment of the settlement in Hebron. From then on it protested against the West Bank settlement policies of the ALIGNMENT and against the peace agreement with Egypt. The movement's ideology is articulated today by the TEHIYA Party and GUSH EMUNIM.

ISRAELI LOCAL COUNCILS

Israeli urban settlements on the West Bank have the status of local councils. The status of those councils and their areas of control were determined by orders of the military government which are merely copies of the Israeli municipal ordinances, also including election laws for the local councils, city planning authority, taxation and licensing identical to those of the local government in Israel. There is no resemblance between them and the powers of local Palestinian authorities in the West Bank (See ISRAELI REGIONAL COUNCILS, COURTS, CREEPING ANNEXATION, PERSONAL STATUS OF ISRAELIS, MINISTRY OF HOUSING AND CONSTRUCTION, DEVELOPMENT CORPORATIONS). In September 1985, there were eight settlements on the West Bank with the status of local councils:

Name	Population (People)
Kiryat Arba	4,300
Efrat	1,350
Ma'aleh Adumim	12,400
Ma'aleh Ephraim	1,000
Ariel	4,950
Elkana	2,000
Givat Ze'ev	2,600
Emmanuel	3,800

See also DEMOGRAPHY (ISRAELI).

ISRAELI REGIONAL COUNCILS

These were established by military Order 783, issued March 20, 1979, and amended several times thereafter. According to the original order, four councils were established on the West Bank – JORDAN VALLEY, SAMARIA, MATEH BENYAMIN, and GUSH ETZION. Later two more councils were added – MT. HEBRON, and MEGILLOT. A similar order was issued in the Gaza Strip to establish Hof Gaza regional council. The bylaws of the regional council form appendices to the orders and specify the means by which the council is established, elected, its funtions, powers and responsibilities. These bylaws are almost identical to those of Israeli regional councils and were in fact copied from Israeli legislation. The council's bylaws have been amended several times. The most significant changes concern the establishment of a court for local affairs, the appointment of the councils as "local planning commissions" (See PHYSICAL PLANNING) and changes in their jurisdictional boundaries.

The jurisdictional boundaries were first defined as "the combination of all built-up areas belonging to each council" (and in some places also cultivated areas). In order to encompass all areas liable to be declared as state lands (See INTERFERENCE WITH PRIVATE LAND OWNERSHIP), the definition was changed (Order 848).

The West Bank has two types of councils (See also ISRAELI LOCAL COUNCILS):

1. Councils having jurisdiction over contiguous areas – their boundaries overlap territory defined as state land (declared or liable to be declared). These contiguous areas are in the Jordan Valley and the Dead Sea area (the Jordan Valley and Megillot councils).

2. Councils whose jurisdictional boundaries are not contiguous but rather composed of scattered state lands. The sub-districts of Nablus, Jenin, Tulkarm, Ramallah, Bethlehem, and Hebron are divided into four general areas (Samaria, Benyamin, Etzion, and Mt. Hebron). Patches of jurisdictional areas including state lands and Jewish settlements are scattered over these general areas. The total territory under the jurisdiction of the regional councils is about 2.15 million dunams, some 40 percent of the area of the West Bank. The size of the areas under each council is detailed below.

The division of the West Bank into general areas created, in essence, a Jewish administrative division unrelated to, and separate from the Arab sub-district administrative division, maintained by the military government. The system established is dual – one Arab (the sub-districts) and one Jewish (the regional councils).

The regional councils, whose jurisdictional boundaries are limited to patches of state lands, act and plan in the general areas, as though these were under their control, despite the fact that in these areas the Palestinian population outnumbers the Jewish settlers nine to one. With the approval of the military government they plan and construct roads and infrastructure, and control land use.

The councils are subordinate to the military government only in theory. In fact they function like Israeli councils directly under Israeli ministries and receive allocations directly from the state budget. In some areas the councils perform quasi-governmental functions and they wield considerable political clout.

Since they provide municipal services to settlements scattered over a large area and with tiny populations, the public outlay per person is higher than in Israel. Analysis of grants-in-aid allocated to the councils by the Ministry of the Interior shows that they enjoy priority over local and regional councils in Israel proper. Grants to West Bank (Israeli) councils per capita were (1983): Gush Etzion $230; Mateh Benyamin $245; Jordan Valley $408; and Samaria $357. By contrast grants to regional councils in

Israel were: Mateh Yehuda $86; Sha'ar Hanegev $126; Upper Galilee $97. The supply of services (such as busing pupils, garbage collection, street lighting, and engineering), paid for in full by the state and public authorities, enables the establishment of DEVELOPMENT CORPORATIONS. The combination of land ownership, planning authority and implementation capacity enable the councils to concentrate considerable economic and executive power in their hands. The councils are incorporated in a voluntary roof organization, YESHA.

For the personal status of Israeli residents, see PERSONAL STATUS OF ISRAELIS, COURTS (ISRAELI).

1. Mt. Hebron Regional Council

Established by Order 783 as amended. Its non-contiguous area spreads over the western and southern part of the Hebron sub-district. Twelve settlements fall within its limits. The total number of Jewish settlers 1985, does not exceed 850. According to the area development plan there will be 19 settlements housing 6,200 families (including a town of 2,500 homes on the Hebron-Beersheba road northeast of Shoket junction). One hundred thousand dunams of arable land and 60,000 dunams of pasture land were located in the area. The council supplies municipal services as in Israel, and serves also as a local planning committee.

2. Mateh Benyamin Regional Council

Established in 1979 by Order 783. Its non-contiguous area (made up of state land) is about 220,000 dunams in the Ramallah sub-district. The area of its planning region is about one million dunams, including 90 villages and five Arab towns, with a population of over 170,000.

Most of the area under its jurisdiction (some 150,000 dunams) is used for military and security purposes. Some 24,000 dunams directly serve the Israeli settlers, including 1,900 dunams of built-up area, 182 dunams of industrial area, and the rest for agriculture, pasture, roads, and forestry. The council incorporates 25 settlements (1985), housing 6,200 people, and one town, Givat Ze'ev (See ISRAELI LOCAL COUNCILS). Most of the Jewish settlers live in community settlements and a minority in agricultural settlements. The average percentage of commuters is 52 percent, mainly to Jerusalem, with some commuting to Tel Aviv.

The development plan of the regional council projects an increase in the number of settlements to 47 and a Jewish population of 125,000, by the year 2010. The target goal for 1986 is 22,000 people and 14 additional settlements. Commuters will continue to make up 50-60 percent of the work force. There are no plans for agriculture. The council delivers services (garbage collection, education, etc.), like its Israeli counterparts. A DEVELOPMENT CORPORATION is owned by the council.

3. Jordan Valley Regional Council

Established by Order 783 as amended, its contiguous jurisdictional area encompasses over one million dunams in the Jordan Valley. Five enclaves of Arab settlements (including the town of Jericho), totaling about 30,000 people were excluded from its territory. The council incorporates 25 civilian settlements with 2,950 residents (1985).

For the development of the area, see ALLON PLAN.

Some 70,000 dunams in the area have been set aside as suitable for cultivation (See AGRICULTURE (JEWISH)), of which less than half is currently (1985) under cultivation. Most of the settlements are moshavim; the remainder are kibbutzim and moshavim shitufiim. According to the development plan there will be 30 settlements containing 2,500 families – about 10,000 persons, not including the township of Ma'aleh Ephraim (See ISRAELI LOCAL COUNCILS). The major economic branch is agriculture, with some industry and tourism.

The council's educational system is based on transportation to Ma'aleh Ephraim, Hamra, and Masuah. The council operates municipal services, like its counterparts in Israel.

4. Samaria Regional Council

Established, 1979. Its non-contiguous area (made up of areas designated state land) is about 100,000 dunams, and is located in the Tulkarm, Jenin, and Nablus sub-districts (some 2.5 million dunams). The number of settlers (September 1985) is about 9,500. In addition, there are three urban settlements: Elkana, Ariel, and Emmanuel, with (September 1985) about 11,000 inhabitants (See ISRAELI LOCAL COUNCILS). The Jewish population in the region is approximately 20,000 Jews as against 377,000 Palestinians (127,000 in the Nablus sub-district, 140,000 in the Tulkarm sub-district, and 110,000 in the Jenin sub-district).

Thirty settlements are incorporated in the regional council, some of them still under construction. Of the existing ones, 20 are COMMUNITY SETTLEMENTS, four are urban, and two are MOSHAVIM. Their population breakdown is: under 15 families – five; 15-25 families – nine; 25-35 families – five; over 100 families – four. There are four settlements with rapid growth potential, excluding TOSHAVOT, all situated near the Tel Aviv metropolitan area The Samaria Regional Council operates municipal services, educational and health services, in accordance with Israeli practice and, also operates two educational centers for adults (for immigrants and for teacher training in Elon Moreh and a post-secondary college in Kedumim). The council has a large DEVELOPMENT CORPORATION and also functions as a local planning committee (See

PHYSICAL PLANNING).

5. Gush Etzion Regional Council

Established in 1979, its non-contiguous area spreads over the Bethlehem sub-district and the northwest part of the Hebron sub-district. Its planning area extends over 650,000 dunams, including 300,000 dunams of state land. The jurisdictional boundary of the council includes 80,000 dunams of fire zones, 100,000 dunams in the Judean Desert, 30-40,000 dunams on the mountain ridge (the expanded Etzion bloc), and 50,000 dunams on the western slopes of Mt. Hebron, up to the green line.

In the council's area are 13 Israeli civilian settlements and the local council of Efrat. The number of Jewish residents of the regions (excluding Efrat) is 3,500. The labor force is employed mainly (about 60 percent) in services, with the remainder in agriculture (See AGRICULTURE (JEWISH)), and industry. About 40 percent commute mainly to Jerusalem. Within the planning area of the council reside 230,000 Palestinians in five towns, 13 VILLAGE COUNCILS, and a large number of villages. According to the council's development plan, the Jewish population is expected to increase to 2,000 families, or about 10,000 persons (excluding Efrat).

The council supplies services, on the lines of local authorities in Israel, and serves as a local planning committee (See PHYSICAL PLANNING). The council also has a DEVELOPMENT CORPORATION.

6. Megillot Regional Council

Established by Order 783 as amended. Its contiguous area spreads over the eastern portion of the Bethlehem sub-district and mainly includes fire zones and the Judean Desert cliffs. There are four settlements, with a few hundred settlers. Although the council is nominally independent, its municipal services are provided in practice by the Tamar Regional Council, located within Israel on the southern Dead Sea coast.

JERUSALEM ZAKAH COMMITTEE (Lajnat Amual az-Zakah)

Az-Zakah is a religious charity tax required of Muslims. In countries under Islamic government, it is in effect a government tax, while elsewhere it is a religious obligation. Az-Zakah is 2.5 percent of a person's annual savings.

An 11-member committee was founded in Jerusalem in 1976, made up of Muslim religious personalities, and named the Zakah Funds Committee. Its purpose was to provide for the care and education of Muslim children according to religious principles. The committee has set up kindergartens and supports orphans, the needy, and the blind.

To date, the commiteee has opened six schools under the name "Riad Al-Aqsa." These schools give special attention to the Islamic education of their students.

EWISH NATIONAL FUND

Established in 1901, the Jewish National Fund (JNF) is an independent institution of the World Zionist Organization. Its major task since its inception has been the purchase of land, Jewish settlement, and land reclamation. The guiding principle of the JNF has been that ownership of these lands remains in the hands of the people and is leased to settlers on a 49–year lease.

After the establishment of the state, there no longer being a need for new land acquisition, land reclamation and afforestation became the JNF's major functions. It is now engaged in preparing land in Judea, Samaria, and the Gaza Strip for settlements, roads, afforestation, and pasture.

In 1981 it stepped up its land acquisition activities in Gush Katif (Gaza), Judea and Samaria. It also construct roads on the West Bank as a subcontractor to the government.

JNF Investments in the West Bank:

Year	Millions of Dollars
1974	0.47
1975	0.36
1976	0.29
1977	0.30
1978	1.20
1979	3.53
1980	3.10
1981	3.27
1982	1.94
1983	1.40

JEWISH RELIGIOUS COUNCILS

A Jewish religious council operates within every Israeli local and regional council, on the authority of a military government order. The orders, bylaws, structure and function of these councils are identical to those of their counterparts in Isrel. The West Bank religious councils sponsor a wide range of activities since the vast majority of the Israeli settlers (See DEMOGRAPHY (ISRAELI)) are religious and require their services.

This is reflected in the budgets of the West Bank religious councils from which several hundred people earn a livelihood (rabbis, ritual supervisors, clerks, ritual bath attendants, etc.).

JEWISH TERRORISM

The Jewish Underground

From the beginning of the occupation and especially since 1980, there have been several attempts to strike at Arabs on the West Bank and in East Jerusalem. These were perpetrated by covert Jewish organizations, at the center of which was a group of Gush Emunim leaders and activists known in the media as The Jewish Underground in the Territories, or The Jewish Terrorist Group. About 30 people were involved in these activities, practically all of them settlers from Kiryat Arba or other Gush Emunim settlements on the West Bank and in the Golan Heights. Personal assistance was offered by two senior officers in the civilian administration, and among the perpetrators were several IDF reserve officers and one career officer. Most of the activists occupied key positions in settler organizations in the territories and in Gush Emunim. Among them were a former chairman of the Kiryat Arba local council and his deputy, and the assistant editor of the settlement journal NEKUDA, four people who had served on the Gush Emunim secretariat in various capacities, the coordinator of regional projects in the Golan Heights, settlement secretaries, and committee chairmen in settlers' organizations.

Their most conspicuous operations were an attempt on the lives of leaders of the National Guidance Committee, in which the mayors of Nablus and Ramallah were injured (in retaliation against a Fatah attack on Hadassah House in Hebron in May,1980); an attack on the Islamic College in Hebron in which three students were killed in July 1983 (in response to the murder of yeshiva student Aharon Gross, a Hebron settler); a plot to blow up the Dome of the Rock on the Temple Mount in Jerusalem – in preparation for the rebuilding of the Temple (in the end they themselves decided against carrying out this plan); and an attempt to sabotage Arab buses in East Jerusalem (April, 1984). While the explosive charges were being set, in this latter operation, several of the organization's members were caught, and in the wake of their arrest the entire organization was uncovered.

The exposure of the Jewish terrorist organization set off a crisis and created a serious rift within Gush Emunim (See YESHA) and in the settlements. In July, 1985, members of the terrorist group were convicted. Some were sentenced to life imprisonment while others received fairly light sentences. There were some expressions of sympathy for the underground organization, headed by a lobby of more than 20 Knesset members (from the religious parties, Tehiya, and the Likud), who assisted the prisoners and their families. During 1985, some Jewish underground prisoners were pardoned and released.

The Lifta Group

A group of three Israelis that attempted to smuggle explosive material on to the Temple Mount in Jerusalem in order to inflict damage on the mosque in the winter of 1984. The three lived as drifters in the abandoned village of Lifta at the western entrance to Jerusalem and called themselves The Tribe of Judah. They succeeded in scaling the eastern wall of the Temple Mount and bringing a large quantity of explosives into the courtyard of the mosques. They were discovered during the night by Muslim guards and fled. The explosives and equipment they left behind led to their capture. Their motive was apparently mystical-extremist, and during their trial at the beginning of 1985 it was argued that they were emotionally unstable.

TNT

An underground Jewish, religious, chauvinistic organization. One of its objectives was to strike at Arab PLO supporters. Many of the members of this group are of American-Jewish origin with no military training, and hold extreme religious-nationalist views. Their actions include planting grenades in the Baptist Church in Jerusalem, in a church in the Ein Karem district of Jerusalem and in various mosques around the city, and opening fire on an Arab bus. The organization appears to have connections with KACH.

JOINT COMMITTEE (PLO-JORDAN)

Established in late 1978 by a decision of the Baghdad Summit as part of an attempt to institutionalize opposition to the Sadat initiative and the Camp David process. Its purpose was to subsidize investment and economic activities on the West Bank, to preserve the economic independence of the Palestinian sector, to create the infrastructure of an embryo state, develop existing institutions, provide assistance to individuals and organizations and, help them defend themselves against Israeli annexation policies.

For the budgets of the committee and its means of action, see SUMUD. The senior representative of the Jordanian government in the committee is the minister for occupied lands; representing the PLO is a member of the Executive Committee, Mohammed Milhem, though Abu Jihad,

Arafat's second-in-command, is the key figure on the Palestinian side.

JORDANIAN RED CRESCENT

Founded in 1950, it has branches in every city of the West Bank. Its purpose is to provide assistance to needy, sick people, to the families of political prisoners, and to further other humanitarian endeavors of such an organization. The organization has several physicians in villages and hospitals in the cities, such as the al-Hillal Women's Hospital in Jerusalem. The Red Crescent also runs old age homes, a school for retarded children, a center for physiotherapy, and a blood bank in cooperation with the al-Itihad Hospital in Nablus. The Red Crescent in Tulkarm was set up in 1950 and established a hospital, a mother-and-child center, a maternity hospital, and a girls' training center.

KACH (MEIR KAHANE)

An extremist, racist political movement headed by Meir Kahane, the former leader of the Jewish Defense League. Under his leadership, the latter group was active in the United States in the 1960s, claiming to provide physical protection for Jews fearing racial violence.

Kach was formally set up on September 29, 1972, with the intention of participating in the general elections. However, in election campaigns up till 1984, Kach failed to achieve the 1 percent of the poll necessary for representation in the Knesset. During those years it concentrated its activities on the distribution of extremist, racist literature, and on provocative actions designed to worsen relations between Arabs and Jews, particularly on the West Bank and Gaza (See JEWISH TERRORISM).

The movement advocates isolationism and xenophobia, based on an extremist interpretation of the religious doctrine regarding the chosen nature of the Jewish people.

The movement supports the establishment of Israeli sovereignty over the whole of Eretz Israel and immediate annexation of Judea, Samaria, and the Gaza Strip.

The movement sees the expulsion of Arabs from all areas of the country as the solution to the Arab problem. This derives from the assumption that Israel-Arab coexistence and a democratic Jewish state are an impossibility. For this reason it rejects the CAMP DAVID ACCORDS and the autonomy plan, and any other plan under which political or communal independence would be offered to the Arabs in Eretz Israel.

In the 1984 elections the movement won a seat in the Knesset. Public opinion polls in 1985 showed gains in popularity for Kach, especially among young, oriental Israelis.

KARP REPORT

Written by a panel of jurists headed by Yehudit Karp, representing the attorney-general, its task was to examine irregularities in the conduct of police investigation of charges against Israeli settlers on the West Bank, and their repercussions on relations between the settlers and the Arab residents of the area. The panel was appointed by the attorney-general on April 29, 1981, as a result of a letter from a group of Hebrew University and Tel Aviv University law lecturers, expressing concern for the rule of law in the territories and raising the issue of "private vigilante activities by settlers in Judea and Samaria." The panel included a representative of the police, the chief army prosecutor and the regional prosecutor. The report was completed on May 23, 1982, but its findings were not published until February 7, 1984.

The report looked into the activity of the investigative branch of the military police (Metsah) and advised a re-assessment of the instructions given to soldiers on when to open fire (See BEARERS OF ARMS). It also established that the division between police examination of civilians and military police handling of soldiers is detrimental to the results of their inquiries. The report examined 70 police investigations, 53 of which were not solved. In 15 files chosen at random the committee found police investigations inadequate. The cases included complaints by Arabs in Hebron of harassment by settlers, and complaints by the Arab residents of Kafr Kaddum that settlers had uprooted 300 olive trees.

In summary, the committee found that the large number of similar unsolved cases pointed to a failure on the part of the police to investigate incidents in Judea and Samaria in which Jewish settlers had been accused of harassing and intimidating the local populace. In doing so the committee justified the concern of the law lecturers who had called for the inquiry, for the rule of law in the territories (See PERSONAL STATUS OF ISRAELIS).

KIRIYA

A planned urban center for 3,000 to 5,000 families (12,000-15,000 people), serving also as a regional center. It is between 2,500 and 5,000 dunams in area. The designation of a settlement as a kiriya (town) is a temporary and non-binding matter. Certain COMMUNITY SETTLEMENTS (such as Kedumim) are classified on some lists as krayot (pl. of kiriya). Similar confusion exists in the classification of TOSHAVA and towns.

LAND ACQUISITION (ISRAELI)

In July 1967, the military government issued an order forbidding any land transaction without a written permit. At that time, the Israeli government sought to channel all Jewish land acquisition through the JEWISH NATIONAL FUND. In 1971, a "general permit" to "execute land transactions" was granted to Himanuta, a subsidiary of the JNF. In 1973, Moshe Dayan proposed that a general permit to purchase land be issued to private Israeli corporations and individuals. The Israeli government turned down his proposal.

In September 1979, the Israeli government (under the LIKUD) lifted the ban on private Jewish land purchase, precipitating a rush of land speculators. In the vicinity of Jewish settlements built in the metropolitan areas of Jerusalem and Tel Aviv, land values went up from $1,000-1,500 a dunam to $6,000-8,000. Some Arabs could not resist the temptation and despite local social ostracism and Jordan's imposition of the death penalty on anyone selling land to Israelis, tens of thousands of dunams were sold. It is estimated that the total area sold to the Israeli public and private bodies amounts to 125,000 dunams, out of which 25,000 were fraudulently acquired.

The sale of plots with dubious titles, attempts to force Arabs to sell land by intimidation and other shady operations, involving both Jewish and Arab speculators, became a national scandal. By summer 1985, hundreds of cases of fraudulent land purchase had been investigated by the police.

Land purchase irregularities were mainly due to the following causes:
1. Jewish land acquisition is perceived as a patriotic endeavor, therefore land speculators enjoy the close cooperation of the military government. When Arab sellers preferred to sell land confidentially, through irrevocable "power of attorney" given to straw men, the authorities extended the legal validity of such documents from five years to 15 years (orders 811, 847). When Arab courts attempted to "interfere" with the dubious transactions, the military government removed all matters concerning land on which a request for registration had been submitted from local COURTS, and vested them in REVIEW BOARDS. Some military government officials became land speculators after retiring from the service, using their connections and authority to advance their interests.
2. The MINISTERIAL COMMITTEE FOR SETTLEMENT decided, in April 1982, to approve private settlement ventures on the West Bank.

Consequently, land developers began to plan, purchase and sell land for private construction (See TOSHAVA). The authorities freely issued "permits" for toshava ventures. Speculators used these official permits to advertise offers for sale of private lots, before securing title deeds. As a result, hundreds of Israelis found themselves holding worthless scraps of paper.

LAND USE

Classification of land uses on the West Bank according to function (agriculture, built-up areas, nature reserves, roads, etc.) does not exhaust the subject, since land use is perceived only within the context of national control (Israeli and Palestinian). In the dual system prevailing on the West Bank, the test is not land use but the ethnic identity of the user. Land use has been mobilized into the national struggle for control of the region.

In the particular context of the West Bank, the classification "rocky land, unsuitable for cultivation" means "land which may be declared state land and transferred to Israeli use and ownership." Declaration of a "nature reserve," means taking it out of Arab hand and transferring it to the Nature Reserves Authority "to prevent uncontrolled Arab development." Designating an area as "essential military territory" means opening it up for the construction of Israeli settlements. The construction of Arab cooperative housing units "to improve housing conditions of Palestinians" is financed by SUMUD funds, in order to prevent confiscation by the Israeli authorities.

Land use classification on the West Bank is not determined by physical planners, but dictated by political considerations, translated *ex post facto* into the vocabulary of physical planning. The locations of many Israeli West Bank settlements were determined by the constraint of land availability rather than by planning or physical considerations. The widely-dispersed nature of Palestinian housing, which lacks all planning logic and hinders the creation of community services, is determined by the fear of expropriation. (See also PHYSICAL PLANNING.)

While the battle for control of the area is far from over, it is already possible to assess its results and sketch a map of land-use division between Israelis and Palestinians on the West Bank. Israel, employing a complex system of orders and laws (See INTERFERENCE WITH PRIVATE LAND OWNERSHIP) and the coercive power of the state, is coming closer to attaining its goal of controlling more than 50 percent of the West Bank, which will effectively remove all remaining restraints on settlement. The Palestinians will probably succeed in retaining control over some 2.7 million dunams (50 percent of the area), even though its use will be extremely restricted.

Existing and projected land use is described separately (See BUILT-UP AREAS (JEWISH), BUILT-UP AREAS (ARAB), AGRICULTURE, ROADS, PARKS and NATURE RESERVES).

LAW IN THE SERVICE OF MAN

A non-profit organization founded in 1980 by a group of Arab lawyers on the West Bank, its goal is to strengthen the principle of the supremacy of the law and defend human rights, according to international laws and treaties.

The organization carries out research and documentation and renders material assistance and advice to all who request it. It also disseminates information to the public. The organization carries out research on the legal situation on the West Bank and the extent to which it complies with international law. It publishes occasional papers reviewing orders issued by the military government. The library at the organization's headquarters contains material on legal and judicial topics on the West Bank. The organization is an affiliate of the International Commission of Jurists in Geneva.

LEAGUE OF UNIVERSITY GRADUATES (HEBRON) (Rabitat Al-Jama'in)

Founded in 1953 by a group of university graduates in Hebron with the aim of promoting university education in the Hebron area.

It opened a private high school and a library in Hebron. It also awarded loans to 650 university graduates and university students abroad.

The league has branches in Amman and Kuwait, which have a large Hebronite community.

LEGAL ADVISER (MILITARY GOVERNMENT)

Responsible among other things, for the following matters: legislation, legal advice and representation, prosecution and judgement in military courts. The major part of his work is the publication of SECURITY ENACTMENTS (Military Orders) and publication of secondary legislation (regulations issued on the authority of orders, and orders relating to local matters). The military government sees itself as filling the role of the sovereign authority in the territories, and the legal adviser is thus authorized to promulgate basic laws (security enactments). The military government holds this legislation to be the equivalent of the existing laws on the West Bank (the local law). The legal adviser uses this principle in revising local law in accordance with Israeli law. These legislative acts (more than 1,100) are not subject to any parliamentary review whatsoever. HIGH COURT OF JUSTICE rulings have allowed changes in local laws and the court has confirmed most of the military government orders. As a result, the legislative system on the West Bank is entirely lacking in checks and balances (See CREEPING ANNEXATION).

LIKUD (PARTY)
A bloc made up of three parties: the Herut movement, the Liberal Party, and La'am.

The bloc was founded in 1973, before the elections to the eighth Knesset. In the elections to the ninth Knesset the Likud won enough Knesset seats to form a government for the first time. It maintained its lead in 1981. In 1984 the Likud formed a national unity government with the Labor Party.

Major Points Concerning the West Bank and Gaza Strip in the Likud Platform
1. Judea, Samaria and Gaza will not be handed over to foreign rule and Israeli sovereignty will be established in the entire area of western Eretz Israel, i.e., the territory between the Jordan River and the Mediterranean; Jewish settlement will be permitted in any part of Eretz Israel. The Arabs of Eretz Israel may become Israeli citizens with full civil rights, if they so wish.
2. The Likud opposes the establishment of a Palestinian state, since this would endanger Israel's existence and impede any chance of peace in the region.
3. The autonomy arrangements agreed upon at the Camp David conference constitute the solution to the Palestinian problem and guarantee that no Palestinian state will be established and that there will be no partition. The Arab nation has been given self-determination in 21 sovereign Arab states.
4. The Likud will act to renew negotiations on the agreement to grant full autonomy to the Arab residents of Judea, Samaria, and Gaza.

MAPAM (THE UNITED WORKERS' PARTY)
A Zionist, socialist, pioneering party founded in 1948 with the unification of the following parties: Ahdut Ha'Avoda, Poalei Zion, Hashomer Hatsair. After a while Ahdut Ha'Avoda left Mapam and another faction, led by Moshe Sneh, split and joined Maki (the Israel Communist Party).

In 1969 Mapam joined the ALIGNMENT with the Labor Party, leaving in 1984 with the establishment of the national unity government.

142

Mapam favors peace agreements with Arab states based on territorial compromise and recognition of the right of all the states in the region to exist, the solution of the Palestinian problem through the establishment of a Jordanian-Palestinian state on the East Bank and in the evacuated areas of the West Bank. It favors only military strongholds and condemns settlements on the West Bank. Mapam supports the Yariv Shem-Tov formula which states that Israel should enter into negotiations with any Palestinian group willing to recognize Israel and condemn terror.

MATSAD (PARTY)

(See MORASHA).

MERCAZ ICHLUS (SETTLEMENT TYPE)

A temporary location for settlers intending to establish a new settlement. Different from a COMMUNITY SETTLEMENT in that construction is under the supervision of the MINISTRY OF HOUSING AND CONSTRUCTION and not under the settlement department of the WORLD ZIONIST ORGANIZATION. The allocation of housing is supervised by the ministry in conjunction with the settlers and it varies with the character of the group.

MILITARY GOVERNMENT

The legal basis for the operation of the administrative and judicial systems in Judea and Samaria is the proclamation on law and administration (No. 2) issued June 7, 1967. According to the proclamation, the commander of the IDF forces on the West Bank assumed "any power of government, legislation, appointive, or administrative".

From the inception of the military government, the entire system was built on military personnel (both regular and reserves), who carried out the task of preserving security and the civilian tasks of government. The system was designed as a double chain of command: the local commander (the district military commander) was responsible to two parallel systems, with two aspects – military and civilian. He dealt with day-to-day security and also with civilian activities in his district. In his military capacity he was subordinate to the military commander of the area and through him to the chief of staff. In his civilian capacity, he was responsible to the West Bank governor (who dealt with civilian matters) and through him to the coordinator of activities in the territories, who was himself directly responsible to the minister of defense (and not the chief of staff).

These two chains of command came together only in the office of the defense minister. The first phase of military government (1968-1974), concurrent with Moshe Dayan's term as minister of defense, was notable for its complete centralization. The military and civilian arms of the administration worked as one, and there were no serious disagreements between them. This was largely due to the personal involvement of Moshe Dayan in decision-making in both spheres and at all levels, including local. Even so, a civilian bureaucracy began emerging at the staff officer level and while they were theoretically subordinate to the West Bank governor, they acted in tandem with the Israeli ministries. In 1968 the government had already decided that civilian operations in the territories should be carried out not by military officers but by civilian representatives of the various ministries, who would be "coordinated" by the military governor (See STAFF OFFICERS). Increased political agitation in the territories, which began before the Yom Kippur War (1973), as well as Moshe Dayan's resignation from the Defense Ministry, brought about structural changes in the military government. The military arm was made directly subordinate to the regional commander, who until then had dealt only with civilian affairs. This centralization at the local level was seen as an appropriate response to political extremism on the West Bank, and an effective tool for opposing radical forces in the region. The result was that civilian matters, which had previously had the full attention of the regional commander, became of secondary importance, the staff officers were left without any central coordinating authority and matters in their areas of jurisdiction were neglected.

With the election of radical mayors on the West Bank (1976) (See ELECTIONS, MUNICIPALITIES) and especially after the Likud assumed power (1977), there began a period of open confrontation between the military government and the municipalities. During Ezer Weizman's term as minister of defense (1977-1980), the degree of confrontation was relatively moderate. After his resignation however, when Prime Minister Menachem Begin took over his post, Chief of Staff Rafael Eitan became directly responsible for the military government.

The coordinator of operations in the territories was made directly responsible to the chief of staff, making the civilian branch completely subordinate to the military branch. In November 1981, the CIVILIAN ADMINISTRATION was established in the territories. Order 947 created a complete separation between the two branches of the military government and established separate bureaucracies, one military (on the local and regional level) and the second civilian. Civilians were appointed as coordinator of activities in the territories and head of the civilian administration. The two systems, operating in an uncoordinated fashion, created duplication, compounded yet further by personal disputes. In February 1982, Minister of Defense Ariel Sharon approved a new definition of the system of military government in the territories, with regard to its civilian functions:

A. The coordinator of activities in Judea, Samaria and the Gaza Strip is directly responsible to the minister of defense.

B. The role of the coordinator of activities in Judea, Samaria and the Gaza Strip is to instruct, guide, advise, coordinate and supervise, in the name of the minister of defense, the activities of all government ministries, the civilian administration, state institutions, the various public authorities and private bodies in all matters concerning their activities in Judea, Samaria, and the Gaza Strip.

C. The coordination of civilian operations between the Israeli ministries and the civilian administration in Judea, Samaria, and the Gaza Strip will be carried out by the coordinator *inter alia* through the DIRECTORS-GENERAL COMMITTEE.

D. The chain of authority for dealing with the affairs of the CIVILIAN ADMINISTRATION will be:

1. Head of the civilian administration, responsible to the coordinator of activities who is in turn responsible to the minister of defense.

2. All civilian matters that, according to current organizational structure, have been submitted for approval to the minister of defense through the coordinator of activities will continue to be passed on to the minister of defense for approval in the same way.

3. The head of the civilian administration will refer his problems to the coordinator.

4. The ongoing links and working arrangements of the staff officers of the various government ministries and the ministries themselves, will remain in effect (See STAFF OFFICERS).

For the structure of the civilian administration, its powers and tasks, see CIVILIAN Administration MINISTERIAL Responsibility.

MILITARY GOVERNMENT BUDGET

Divided into a regular and a development budget. In 1983/4 the military government regular budget was $105 million and in 1984/85 some $70 million. In 1977 the share intended for public capital investment (See PUBLIC CONSUMPTION AND INVESTMENT) was 11 percent of the total budget, in 1981 it was 9.7 percent, and in 1984, 19.3 percent. No substantial change has taken place over the years regarding the composition of the regular budget: about two-thirds is allocated to salaries and 30 percent to activities, 45 percent to education, 16 percent to health, 4.5 percent to public works, and 4.5 percent to welfare.

The number of civil servants has remained quite stable, growing by about 1,000 from 10,607 in 1976 to 11,614 in 1985. In 1976 the number of Israeli officials in the territories was about 400, and in 1984 about 325. The overwhelming majority of local (Arab) employees of the military government work in education (75 percent) and 13 percent work in the health services. There has been an absolute decline in the number of agricultural advisers and workers in the judicial system. Israeli officials are concentrated in the offices of customs and taxation, the treasury, and in offices dealing with government property. Apparently the administration cannot count on local workers in those areas, thus Israeli officials are a majority, in contrast to the community service branches where the Israelis are an insignificant minority.

The salaries of Israeli officials are far higher than those of the local employees. In 1977 the salaries of local workers were 46 percent of those of the Israelis; in 1982, 40 percent; and in 1984, 46 percent. The inequality is even more conspicuous in expense accounts and car allowances. For the proportion of the budget of the military government in the total expenses of the Israeli government (regular and development budgets) in the territories (including investment in the Israeli sector of the West Bank), see MINISTERIAL RESPONSIBILITY, FISCAL BURDEN, TAXATION.

MINISTERIAL COMMITTEE FOR ARAB REFUGEES

Committee established on August 1, 1982, following the initiative of former cabinet minister Mordechai Ben-Porat to formulate principles and methods for solving the problem of the refugees on the West Bank and in the Gaza Strip through resettlement. The committee, headed by Ben-Porat, included David Levy, then vice premier and minister of housing and construction, Moshe Arens, then minister of defense, Yitzhak Shamir, then minister of foreign affairs, and others.

The basic conception guiding the committee was to avoid dealing with the political aspect of the refugee problem: the political problem would be solved through the Camp David accords and other peace agreements between Israel and the Arab countries. Israel would insist that the refugees be absorbed in their countries of residence, in exchange for the absorption of Jews from Arab countries in Israel. The committee was intended to deal with the social and economic aspect of the refugee problem in areas under Israeli control. The refugee camps were the main target of the committee. According to the rehabilitation program, new neighborhoods were to be built for the occupants of the camps. They would be attached to existing municipalities or else become independent local authorities.

The rehabilitation plan was based on the one carried out in the Gaza Strip, where the overcrowded refugee camps were thinned out and new neighborhoods established near the cities, offering improved housing conditions and quality of life. The housing units in Gaza were three to four times larger than those owned by the refugees in the UNRWA camps. Some of the housing units and the land were transferred to the ownership of the residents.

The plan was intended to change the image of the refugee and transform him into a city dweller. His dependence on UNRWA would decrease, and his ties with the local authorities would be strengthened. The plan for the West Bank was to take five years with a budget of two billion dollars. The financing was to come from the refugees, the residents of the West Bank, and international bodies.

UNWRA is categorically opposed to the rehabilitation plan and the transfer of refugees from the camps. The plan was buried in 1984 with the fall of the Likud government.

MINISTERIAL COMMITTEE FOR SETTLEMENT

Activities regarding settlement on the West Bank are based on the decisions of a joint settlement committee of the government and the WORLD ZIONIST ORGANIZATION (WZO). In accordance with a convention between the government of Israel and the WZO, the settlement committee is empowered to decide on settlement activity throughout the Land of Israel, and its decisions become government decisions if no minister objects at a cabinet meeting. The head of the settlement committee is the minister of agriculture, seven of its members are cabinet ministers, and the other seven are representatives of the WZO executive.

In addition to the members who take part in the meetings, there are also professional representatives from the government ministries, from the WZO, and from the Jewish Agency, government institutions and corporations, the IDF, and settlement bodies, depending on the subject under discussion. The main function of those representatives is to prepare the subjects under discussion and give expert opinions regarding the planning and establishment of settlements.

Since 1977 particular emphasis has been placed on decisions affecting the settlement and development of the West Bank. The decisions set basic guidelines for each settlement, including: its location and character; its projected size in the short and long term; employment trends in the settlement; the body responsible for establishing it; and the government's financial allocation for land, infrastructure and construction.

The decisions did not generally relate to the budgetary requirements such as construction of housing, infrastructure, public institutions, and investment to provide jobs. These remained to be discussed and dealt with by the several ministries in their areas of jurisdiction. In some cases decisions were made subject to legal inquiry by the attorney-general's office regarding land ownership.

The settlement committee set rules and made decisions regarding settlement activity on the West Bank, the main ones being:

1. Approval of the development plan for Jewish settlement in various areas of the West Bank.

2. The granting of favorable terms for leasing government lands – the collection of 5 percent of the value of the land as rent if the settler committed himself to living in his home for five successive years after the completion of construction.

3. Approval of the principle that private developers would be included in the establishment of settlements on the West Bank, especially on the basis of independent financial resources (Decision of April 25, 1982).

Difficulties arose in the activities of private developers in establishing settlements. Consequently in April, 1983, the settlement committee charged the Ministry of Housing and Construction with the task of undertaking a professional evaluation of each proposed settlement to determine whether it fit into the local fabric and the necessary social services could be assured for the settlers.

Since August 8, 1982, the committee has decided to establish and develop 48 settlements: eight in the Samarian Hills, six in Western Samaria, seven in the Jordan Valley, five in the Jerusalem, Gush Etzion area, two in the Hebron hills, nine in the Yatir (south Hebron) region, and three in the Gaza area. The committee also approved the conversion of eight military outposts (See NAHAL) into civilian settlements.

In the summer of 1984, with the establishment of the national unity government, it was announced that 27 settlements which had been authorized by the committee had not yet been established or populated. The settlement committee has not been convened since the end of 1984. According to the coalition agreement between the Labor Alignment and the Likud, seven settlements were to be established during the first year of the national unity government. In January 1985, it was decided to establish the agreed settlements. Five are within the Alignment settlement map (See ALLON PLAN) and two are on the mountain ridge. The first settlement was completed in December 1985.

MINISTERIAL RESPONSIBILITY

The military administration constitutes the legislative, administrative, and judicial authority on the West Bank, according to INTERNATIONAL LAW. It follows that the minister of defense, charged with the military forces under Israeli law, holds ministerial and parliamentary responsibility for the occupied territories. This responsibility is both territorial and functional. In fact, this is how the defense minister's role has been understood by politicians, the military, and the media. It may appear that all actions on the West Bank, in every area of activity, are carried out in the name and on the authority of the military government, directly subordinate to the Ministry of Defense (See MILITARY GOVERNMENT, CIVILIAN ADMINISTRATION). In reality, however, the defense minister has never singlehandedly controlled everything carried out in the occupied territories, and different Israeli agencies have operated there, each in its own sphere of competence. One may discern a continuous process of relinquishment of administrative powers by the military and their assumption by Israeli civil authorities. This process began as far back as the incumbency of the first defense minister after the Six Day War (Moshe Dayan) and continued during the incumbency of Defense Minister Shimon Peres (1974-77). The process gathered momentum after the first Likud government came to power, and in particular after the signing of the peace treaty with Egypt and during the autonomy talks (See AUTONOMY PLAN (ISRAELI)). From 1980 on, the policy has been to transfer direct responsibility for a number of administrative sectors from the military government to Israeli civilian bodies.

With the formation of the national unity government (1984), the sole authority remaining in the hands of Defense Minister Yitzhak Rabin (and the civilian administration) was responsibility for the Arab population (security and administration), with all other areas of Israeli civilian activity controlled by other authorities. While these activities are ostensibly carried out in the name of the administration, this is no more than a nod to the demands of international law. The actual administrative responsibility for natural resources – water and land – rests with the ministers of agriculture and justice. The water resources on the West Bank are managed by the national water company, Mekorot; management of land expropriation, through the device of declaring it state land rests in the hands of the attorney-general (Ministry of Justice). The situation with regard to land management can serve as an example of the constraints on the defense minister's authority even in an area directly connected to the local population. The official responsible for approving

149

declarations of state land, a senior employee in the Ministry of Justice, is currently the final arbiter of such declarations.

The incumbent acts according to her own priorities, and the minister of defense may not intervene even if, in his judgement, declaring a certain area state land (in the heart of Hebron or Nablus for instance) is likely to cause security problems. Although signing such declarations is the responsibility of a staff officer subordinate to the minister of defense, this officer is actually a regular employee of the Israeli Lands Authority, which reports to the minister of agriculture. Israeli activity in the territories – settlements, industry, infrastructure – has been officially taken out of the Defense Ministry's hands. Construction and road maintenance are the responsibility of the minister of Housing and Construction, and supervision of Israeli settlements rests with the Ministry of the Interior. Rural settlement is the responsibility of the World Zionist Organization, industry, of the minister of Industry and Trade, and so on. Each of these is directly responsible to the Knesset since their ministry's budget includes their activities on the West Bank.

In 1983, for example, the extent of the financial activity of the various civilian government offices on the West Bank came to some $280 million; of this sum, $220 million was investment in Israeli settlements. In the same year, the entire budget of the military government was $105 million. In other words, the minister of defense is responsible for a budget that comes to only a quarter of total Israeli government outlay on the West Bank. The budget of the Ministry of Housing and Construction alone is equal to the military government's entire civilian budget. Although coordinating bodies exist, such as the Committee of Directors-General and the Ministerial Committee for Settlement, the defense minister and those responsible to him enjoy no special status. While a coordinator of activities in the territories functions on behalf of the defense minister, and STAFF OFFICERS deal with infrastructure, settlement and so on in the territories, this coordinating system lacks the power of veto. The process by which the military government relinquished authority on the West Bank and focused on the security aspects of controlling the Arab population, resembles the process which developed in Israel after the 1948 war in the areas under military rule in the Galilee and the Triangle. The difference is that in Israel, Israeli law and administration were officially applied to these areas. On the West Bank the minister of defense continues to be the formal source of power, legislative, juridical and administrative.

In this situation, the lack of comprehensive ministerial authority and clear parliamentary responsibility invites violations both of the rule of law

150

and orderly administration.

MINISTRY OF AGRICULTURE

Involved in settlement on the West Bank through the Israel Lands Authority (the staff officer in charge of government and abandoned property, see INTERFERENCE WITH PRIVATE LAND OWNERSHIP); Mekorot, the Israeli national water company; the NATURE RESERVES AUTHORITY (See PARKS AND NATURE RESERVES); and the settlement department of the WZO, whose budget is part of the ministry's and whose actions are directed by the Joint Settlement Committee of the government and the WZO (See DROBLESS PLAN).

The Ministry of Agriculture is therefore only indirectly involved on the West Bank through independent bodies.

In the second Likud government (1981-84) the ministry, especially Assistant Minister Michael Dekel, sought direct involvement in the establishment of settlements. Since that function was divided between the Ministry of Housing and Construction and the Settlement Department and was defined according to the form of settlement, the assistant minister introduced a new form of settlement, the TOSHAVA. Settlements of that type were to be established by private individuals and entrepreneurs based on independent financial resources. In April, 1982 the Ministry of Agriculture's initiative was approved. However, within a short time it became evident that the "private entrepreneurs" had been promised generous budget allocations, that the use of public funds for development was not based on uniform criteria, and that the entrepreneurs had published prospectuses for the purchase of lots in areas which had not been authorized or had not been thoroughly planned. As a result, in April 1983, the MINISTERIAL COMMITTEE FOR SETTLEMENT decided that the Ministry of Housing and Construction should submit the plans for the TOSHAVOT to professional scrutiny and place them within the overall settlement plan, thus effectively ending the direct involvement of the Ministry of Agriculture in settling the West Bank. (See also LAND ACQUISITION.)

MINISTRY OF HOUSING AND CONSTRUCTION

The major factor in Israeli settlements and infrastructure in the territories, the ministry acts through three branches: The Authority for Rural Construction, the Urban Construction Offices in the ministry (Jerusalem and Central Districts) and the Public Works Department. The Authority for Rural Construction is responsible for building settlements defined as "non-urban." That definition is a bureaucratic rather than a professional planning term. Until 1982 three settlements were defined as "urban" (Ma'aleh Adumim, Kiryat Arba, and Givat Ze'ev). Since then six other settlements have been transferred from the supervision of the Authority for Rural Construction to that of the Urban Construction Offices. The Rural Construction Authority deals with 81 settlements, 59 in Judea and Samaria (the hill regions and the western slopes) and 22 settlements in the Jordan Valley. In these settlements the authority is responsible for developing construction sites, the erection of housing units, assisting individual construction (See BUILD YOUR OWN HOME), and in linking the settlements to the national infrastructure grids. In 1982 it was decided that the World Zionist Organization would no longer erect temporary structures in the settlements under its supervision, and the Ministry of Housing would be responsible for construction and infrastructure. In the non-urban settlements there were about 5,300 units in 1983 and in 1985 there were about 6,200. Seventy-five percent of the additional construction in 1983-85 was subsidized, self-built construction.

The Urban Construction Offices were responsible for nine urban settlements in 1985. In those settlements the number of housing units (completed or under construction) reached 9,200. In 1983, 4,283 units were occupied and 3,428 were under construction. During 1984 some 2,000 additional units were occupied, and about 3,200 were in various stages of construction. In 1984 a program for the construction of 1,977 units was planned, but in fact only 1,000 units were begun because of a marked decline in demand. The construction program for 1985 was 1,400 units and in 1986, less than 500 units. In 1983 the construction program of the ministry amounted to 25% of total public construction in Israel. Since then, the proportion of West Bank (Israeli) construction rose to 27% in 1984, and 30% in 1985. In 1985, the breakdown of building starts was: Galilee 6.8%; Haifa 7.2%; Central Israel 25.6%; Negev 7.9%; Jerusalem 23.1%; West Bank 29.4%. At the end of 1985 the stock of apartments in various stages of construction totalled 4,583, which permits the same rate of settlements in 1986-7 as was achieved in 1984-5. The construction is carried out by private contractors. The involvement of the Ministry of Housing is in programmatic planning, allocation of land, development of building sites, infrastructure, construction of public institutions, interim financing, and obligation to purchase some of the units. That obligation frees the contractors of the risk of being left with unsaleable apartments. The ministry undertakes in advance to purchase 50 percent of the project if the apartments are not sold on the market. In 1983 the ministry undertook to purchase 1,007 units in projects built on the West Bank. That year the number of apartments which the ministry undertook to purchase throughout the country was 3,741. In 1984 there was a reduction in the number of units to which that undertaking applied.

The involvement of the Ministry of Housing in urban construction is multi-tiered. The ministry supplies the infrastructure (roads, water, electricity, and sewerage) to the site, determines the level of assistance to the developers and the degree of involvement in the development of the infrastructure within the settlements. The ministry also assists in purchase, rental and self-built construction, determines the level of assistance in erecting public institutions and commercial centers, or it subsidizes them completely (through its Shikun Upituah company). According to one estimate the total annual budget of the Ministry of Housing (in direct activities connected with building housing units) is $100 million. The ministry's ability to maneuver among the various annual building programs approved in various fiscal years ("permission to undertake obligations"), to manipulate aid and repayments of interim assistance loans to contractors, and to use the funds of the Shikun Upituah company, makes the Ministry of Housing an independent agent in the system. The considerations of the minister heading it are therefore critical in determining the pace of development of settlements on the West Bank.

The third branch of the ministry dealing with the West Bank is the Public Works Department. That department is responsible for the paving of access and arterial roads on the West Bank (See ROADS), and thus it makes a critical contribution to the development of satellite cities in the Jerusalem and Tel Aviv areas. In 1984-85 over half of total outlay for roads transferred from the ministry's budget to the Public Works Department was invested in the West Bank.

MORASHA

A parliamentary caucus composed of POALEI AGUDAT ISRAEL and Matsad, which ran for the 1984 Knesset elections, winning two seats. It also has one cabinet member. Matsad, a group headed by Knesset member Rabbi Haim Druckman, left the National Religious Tenth party during the Knesset session (1981-84) on the basis of an uncompromising stand regarding the vital political and religious importance of retaining the West Bank and Gaza.

MOSHAVIM MOVEMENT (SETTLEMENTS)

Founded in 1921 when Nahalal, the first moshav, was established. Today it is the largest moshav movement, comprising 270 settlements. It regards itself as an ideological movement. Its settlements are mainly based on agriculture with some industry. Its view of settlement on the West Bank is that of the ALIGNMENT, i.e., supporting settlements in the Jordan Valley and in areas not heavily populated by Arabs. As of September 1985, it had the following settlements on the West Bank:

Petzael (est. 1972), 211 people
Netiv Hagedud (est. 1975), 126 people
Tomer (est. 1978), 166 people
Khinanit (est. 1980), 100 people
Na'ama, 42 people

MUKHTARS

Individuals chosen by the hamula (extended family) to represent it before the authorities. In small villages, the mukhtars constitute the only municipal authority and are personally appointed by the administration. In towns and large villages they represent the interest of the hamula, and effectively serve as the eyes and ears of the authorities in that hamula. They receive small salaries from the administration, but their major source of income is from fees in exchange for services to individuals (certification of documents, licenses, etc.). The mukhtars are called on to assist the authorities in security matters when it becomes necessary to identify or arrest suspects. The mukhtar is present during house searches in order to testify that there are no irregularities.

The mukhtars represent refugee camp residents before UNRWA. They pass on the demands and requests of the refugee camp residents to UNRWA and vice versa. The mukhtars' role, status and power occasionally cause friction with camp directors and the village and city councils. The position of mukhtar, rooted in tradition, is regarded as apolitical, hence mukhtars are not considered collaborators with the occupation forces.

MUNICIPALITIES (PALESTINIAN)

West Bank towns are the centers of political, economic, social, and cultural activity for the Palestinian community. The total population of the cities and metropolitan areas of the West Bank (according to our estimates, not including East Jerusalem) is about 370,000. The West Bank contains 25 settlements classified as towns, listed below with the estimated number of inhabitants in 1984.

Concerning the difficulty in estimating population, see DEMOGRAPHY.

1. Jenin	20,000	14. Hebron	66,000
2. Nablus	90,000	15. Ya'abad	5,500
3. Ramallah	24,000	16. Arrabah	4,900
4. al-Bira	29,000	17. Tubas	6,800
5. Bethlehem	24,000	18. Anabta	4,200
6. Beit Sahur	8,500	19. Kalkilya	12,000
7. Beit Jala	8,000	20. Salfit	3,800
8. Jericho	9,000	21. Bir-Zeit	3,000
9. Silwad	3,400	22. Beituniya	2,600
10. Deir Dibwan	3,700	23. Halhul	8,500
11. Yatta	10,000	24. Dura	7,500
12. Bani-Zayd	3,000	25. Kabatiya	7,000
13. Tulkarm	26,000		

It must be pointed out that the municipal status of these towns does not necessarily indicate that they are larger. Some towns such as Silwad, Beituniya, and Salfit are smaller than certain VILLAGE COUNCILS. For the occupational and industrial composition of the cities, see INDUSTRY. The legal basis for the activity of the municipalities on the West Bank is the Jordanian Law of Municipalities (No. 29, 1955). According to that law, the municipalities are empowered to act in such distinctly municipal areas as water and electricity supply, the establishment of public markets and butcheries, schools and other institutions. The municipalities may issue bylaws (subject to the approval of the Council of Ministers).

For the financial aspect of the municipalities, see TAXATION AND REVENUES, and PUBLIC CONSUMPTION AND INVESTMENT.

See also PHYSICAL PLANNING & ELECTIONS (PALESTINIAN).

Even during the Jordanian period, the municipalities, particularly the city councils and the mayors, were politicized, dealing with issues beyond the scope of the authorities granted to them by law. The Jordanian central government often intervened to suppress their activities, discharging elected mayors and replacing them with its own appointees. The Israeli occupation increased the political involvement of the municipalities, as (see below) they became the only independent Palestinian bodies whose activities were permitted. Similarly the residents' dependence on the municipalities increased as they represented the community to the authorities and served as liaison between the Israeli military government and the Jordanians.

During the first phase of the occupation, Moshe Dayan instructed the military governors to refrain from intervening in the activities of the municipalities and to give them authority over and above the provision of standard municipal services (See MILITARY GOVERNMENT). The mayors who had been elected (or appointed) by the Jordanian government were loyal to the Hashemite regime. They represented the wealthy families and were essentially pragmatic and moderate. They were interested in maintaining correct relations with the Israeli administration, which in any case scarcely intervened in their affairs, and also in maintaining ties with the Jordanian government, which placed substantial financial aid at their disposal. The Israelis, Jordanians, and the moderate mayors joined together to block radical supporters of FATAH who threatened to create an alternative leadership in the cities. As a result, the municipal elections held in 1972 (See ELECTIONS (PALESTINIAN)) saw the moderate mayors re-elected.

This relatively tranquil period ended with the Yom Kippur War. The radicalization of the Palestinian community, which reached a peak in 1974 after the Rabat conference, also found expression in the municipal sphere. Despite signs that Palestinian nationalism was increasing in the cities, Israel permitted the holding of elections in 1976. As a result six radical mayors were elected and the relations of the administration with local government on the West Bank assumed a confrontational character. The mayors regarded themselves as political representatives aspiring to political power primarily in order to engage in the struggle against the Israeli regime. For its part the latter began viewing the mayors as PLO representatives, instigators and violators of public order. The massive land expropriations and the large-scale settlement activities initiated by the Likud government after 1977, and especially after the CAMP DAVID ACCORDS brought the confrontation to a peak. Israel launched a campaign of intimidation calculated to humiliate the mayors, which actually increased their prestige in the Palestinian community. The deportation of certain of the mayors and the assassination attempt on others (1981) created a wall of alienation between the Israeli administration and the municipalities on the West Bank.

When the CIVILIAN ADMINISTRATION was established in 1981, it was boycotted by the municipalities. The administration reacted by deposing nine mayors, and in response most of the municipalities on the West Bank suspended operations. Israeli officers were appointed in place of the ousted mayors and thus autonomous Palestinian municipal authority on the West Bank was effectively abolished. That action, in fact a response to the steps taken by the Palestinian mayors, was later presented as a premeditated policy designed to destroy the centers of PLO power in the territories. The policy was closely connected with the efforts to foster the VILLAGE LEAGUES. The appointment of Israeli officers as mayors of Arab towns facilitated settlement activity and increased economic integration and land seizures.

The Hebron municipality offers an excellent example of that byproduct of Israeli policy. The firing of the Palestinian mayor (who had replaced the previously ousted elected mayor) permitted expansion of the Israeli presence within the municipal area of Hebron, in the Jewish quarter. Since 1983 there have been signs of gradual change in the attitudes of the Civilian Administration towards the few municipalities which still remain in office (Bethlehem, Tulkarm, and others).

Negotiations between the authorities, the Jordanians and Palestinians, over the reinstitution of Arab mayors bore fruit in Nablus, where Zafer al-Masri was appointed mayor in November, 1985. Before negotiations regarding appointment of other mayors had been concluded, Zafer al-Masri was assassinated (March 1986).

An appropriate political climate for renewing the autonomous activities of West Bank towns has not been created. The Palestinian community remains disenfrenchised, even at the local level, and devoid of any autonomous authority.

MUSLIM CHARITABLE ASSOCIATION IN JERUSALEM

(Jamiyat al-Maqassed al Hayriyah al Islamiyah)

An organization established in 1956, its name was taken from a similar organization active in Beirut at that time. The founders were active in the Arab Nationalist Movement (al Qaoumiyun al-Arab) who believed that they could reach the masses by means of direct contact through clinics, charity and other activities.

In the mid-1960s a conflict arose between the founders and the Jordanian government, which purged the association of all its political elements. Today it functions as a non-political charitable organization, administering a large hospital (360 beds) on the Mount of Olives in East Jerusalem as well as seven clinics in Jerusalem and the surrounding villages, which treat patients free and take a token payment for medicines. In 1984 the association had more than 4,500 members.

NAHAL

A unit of the IDF in which, as part of their military service, soldiers, mostly members of pioneering youth movements, work on kibbutzim and settlements considered sensitive from the security point of view. In recent years Nahal soldiers have been sent to occupy outposts on the West Bank and in the Gaza Strip for the purpose of opening them up for later civilian settlements. These outposts aroused bitter controversy among the kibbutz movements, whose settlement plans rejected settlement in areas of dense Arab population (See ALLON PLAN). In October 1983, the minister of defense decided to cease using Nahal soldiers to man new outposts in Judea and Samaria.

List of Nahal camps as of February 1985:

Name	Area	Year of Establishment
Ginat	Samaria	1983
Irit	”	1984
Migdalim	”	1984
Almog	Jordan Valley	1983
Mul Nevo	” ”	1983
Beit Arava	” ”	1983
Nahal Tsvi	” ”	1983
Bitronot	Samaria	1983
Elisha	Jordan Valley	1983
Brosh	” ”	1983
Anhil	Judea	1982
Dorit	”	1983
Eshkolot	”	1983
Negohot	Hebron Mts.	1982
Tsalaf	”	1984
Ma'aleh Levona	Samaria	1984

NATIONAL ACCOUNTS

For statistical purposes, the West Bank and Gaza Strip are treated as units independent of Israel. Economic activity there is investigated and reported by the national accounts system – in short, as though they constituted a national economy in every respect. A special chapter in the statistical yearbook and a series of special publications detail, among other things, the Gross National Product (GNP), Gross Domestic Product (GDP), import and exports, and a balance of payments for the West Bank and Gaza Strip. The links with Israel are defined as those of a "common market," a definition which implies the existence of two separate entities. In accordance with this model, Israeli goods marketed on the West Bank and in the Gaza Strip appear as exports, and wages to residents of the territories working in Israel as unilateral transfer payments.

This system of accounting began immediately after the occupation and emanated from the assumption that the economy of the territories would remain separate and independent – an assumption resulting from fear that they might become a burden on the Israeli economy (See ECONOMIC POLICY). The method persisted even though the assumption of economic separation was quickly invalidated by objective conditions and as a consequence of the economic integration policy pursued by all Israeli governments. Economic accounting and analysis according to the "national economy" model gradually became irrelevant and inaccurate.

The daily, complex, economic interactions over the non-existent green line, the movement of tens of thousands of workers, the transfer of goods and services worth hundreds of millions of dollars, lacking any effective monitoring and control – all these call the reliability of the statistics into question. At the end of the 1970s the "national economy" model for the West Bank and Gaza Strip also lost its territorial basis. None of the activity in the Jewish settlements, nor the infrastructure investments of the Jewish Agency, were included in the national accounts of the territories. Israeli activity was included in Israel's account. The economic interactions between, for example, Hebron and Kiryat Arba, Ariel and Tulkarm, appear in reports as connections between separate economic entities. At the beginning of the 1980s the national accounts of the territories became merely instruments for reporting the economic activity of the Palestinian population, completely integrated into the Israeli system, but effectively isolated from it, in such a way as to serve Israel's own political and economic interests (See ECONOMIC POLICY, FOREIGN TRADE, INDUSTRY, AGRICULTURE, FISCAL BURDEN, EMPLOYMENT).

NATIONAL GUIDANCE COMMITTEE (PALESTINIAN)
Established in 1978 as a supervisory committee to follow up decisions of a meeting of public leaders on the West Bank, held in opposition to the Camp David agreements. The supervisory committee continued functioning and became a political body named The National Guidance Committee. It played an active part in leading opposition to the Camp David agreements and Israeli occupation and became a target of both the Israeli administration and the settlers. Three of its members, Mayors Basam Shak'a of Nablus, Karim Halaf of Ramallah, and Ibrahim a-Tawil of al-Bira, were the targets of an assassination attempt in 1980. The first two lost their legs. Two other members, the mayors of Hebron, Fahd Kawasme and of Halhul, Muhammad Milhem, were expelled to Jordan. Other members were subject to house arrest. These harassments have totally paralyzed the committee. Fahd Kawasme was murdered in Amman at the end of 1984.

NATIONAL RELIGIOUS PARTY

A religious political party, the NRP was established in 1956 with the merger of Hamizrahi and Hapoel Hamizrahi movements. In issues of security, foreign affairs and the economy its positions are similar to other Zionist parties, but it sees its particular role as the struggle for the religious character of the state.

The principles of the NRP regarding the West Bank are as follows:

1. Israel must have sole sovereignty over the area between the Jordan and the Mediterranean, the capital of which is united Jerusalem.

2. No Jewish settlement whatsoever must be removed, and Jewish settlement must continue in the cities, towns, and agricultural villages (See HAPOEL HAMIZRAHI), in obedience to the divine commandment that the Jewish people return and settle its land for all eternity.

3. Parts of the Land of Israel may not be transferred to foreign control or sovereignty.

4. Legislation shall continue to be enacted applying Israeli law and administration to the Jewish settlers of the West Bank and the Gaza Strip, who are Israeli citizens.

5. Responsibility for the security of Judea, Samaria, and Gaza lies in the hands of the government alone.

In the 1984 elections there was a decline in support for the NRP, especially on the West Bank and in the Gaza Strip, although most of the Jewish settlers there are products of the religious-national education system founded by the NRP. It has fallen from 12 seats in the ninth Knesset to four seats in the eleventh Knesset. At the same time there has been a rise in the power of the TEHIYA and MORASHA parties, whose positions on the West Bank are more extreme.

NEKUDA (JOURNAL)

A monthly published by The Association for the Advancement of Population and Absorption in Judea, Samaria, Gaza, and the Jordan Valley, the ideological organ of the settlements, mainly expressing the positions of GUSH EMUNIM.

The first issue was published on December 28, 1979 and by February, 1985 84 issues had been published. The circulation of **Nekuda** is 10,000, sent to subscribers both on the West Bank and in the Gaza Strip and on the other side of the green line, including libraries, public institutions, professionals and academics. The magazine sometimes appears in the form of an ideological pamphlet, when its circulation reaches 50,000 copies. The editorial board consists of the heads of the Israeli local councils in the territories and its editor is the chairman of YESHA.

OPEN BRIDGES

The term used for the network of ties which has arisen between the West Bank, Israel and Jordan which functions by way of two bridges over the Jordan River: Allenby and Damia. The system grew out of the circumstances created when hostilities ceased in 1967. It began with Israel looking the other way while agricultural produce was dispatched over the bridges. Over the years this became institutionalized, and is now the major factor permitting the continuation of quasi-normal life on the West Bank. The possibility of crossing the Jordan River and returning, prevented the Palestinian community on the West Bank (and to a certain extent in Gaza) from being cut off from the rest of the Palestinian community and separated from relatives living in other Arab countries.

The number of people crossing the bridges each year is evidence of the durability of this connection. The number of residents crossing the bridges was approximately 300,000 in 1976-78, and reached 380,000 in 1982. In addition, more than 100,000 visitors cross the bridges into the West Bank every year. The number of visitors increases during the summer months, with the arrival of tens of thousands of West Bankers who work abroad.

The economic ties between the West Bank and the Arab world are important to the territories but have made no real contribution to the growth of the Palestinian sector of the West Bank (See AGRICULTURE, INDUSTRY).

The Israeli and Jordanian authorities, which have collaborated in institutionalizing the open bridges, have changed the terms of their relationship from time to time. The Israeli administration, knowing how important the ties are to the Palestinians, has frequently prohibited the transfer of goods and people over the bridges, as a means of collective punishment. The ban has been imposed on age groups (young people), on entire areas, on towns and villages. Hoping to encourage young people to emigrate, the military government ruled that West Bank residents in their twenties and thirties who exit by way of the bridges, may not return home until nine months from their date of departure. A person not returning within three years loses his right to residency on the West Bank. A blacklist prevents the entry of "undesirables." Packaged goods may not be imported in case explosives are smuggled in. Jordan also forbids the entry of "undesirables" to its territory and between 1983-85 restricted visits of young West Bank residents to one month, in order to counter the emigration of young people from the territory. Agricultural and industrial exports to Jordan are restricted (See AGRICULTURE, INDUSTRY). The open bridges have both advantages and disadvantages for Jordan and Israel, and from time to time there are calls on both sides to close them. It is, however, unlikely that the ties over the Jordan will be severed, as they are a product of necessity for all concerned.

PALESTINIAN CHARITABLE ORGANIZATIONS

On the eve of the Israeli occupation (1967) there were 89 charitable organizations on the West Bank registered according to Jordanian law. In 1983 there were 166, here grouped by administrative district:

District	Number of Organizations	Number of Institutions	Number of Beneficiaries
Hebron	33	127	24,792
Bethlehem	42	89	9,977
Jericho	4	–	–
Ramallah	35	56	9,570
Nablus	20	46	15,262
Jenin	18	65	5,580
Tulkarm	14	45	3,244
Total	166	428	68,425

The areas in which these organizations are active are as follows: rehabilitation and vocational education for women, services for the handicapped, educational services, health services, community services, kindergartens, ambulances, a blood bank.

A STAFF OFFICER supervises the activities of the charitable organizations and authorizes the establishment of new ones. Since 1981 the policy of the CIVILIAN ADMINISTRATION has been to reduce the establishment of new charities as much as possible, as some are viewed as fronts for subversive activities. The contribution of the civilian administration to these organizations, some of which provide elementary services such as a blood bank, ambulances, and nursery schools, is minimal. In 1983-84 only 2.7 percent of the administration budget was allocated to support the charitable organizations. The total budget of these organizations is five times greater than the administration's total welfare budget, and it is financed by contributions and grants from the Arab world and from religious and secular charitable institutions abroad. (The major Palestinian institutions and associations are listed by name in this handbook.)

PALESTINIAN LAWYERS, DOCTORS, & PHARMACISTS ASSOCIATION

1. Pharmacists Association

Founded in 1952, membership (1984): 225 (including East Jerusalem). The association has local committees in West Bank cities, and a central committee in Jerusalem subordinate to the association directorate in Amman. The head of the association represents it in the directors' council of the General Association of Jordanian Pharmacists in Amman.

Among its functions, the Jerusalem committee oversees and coordinates pharmaceutical factories on the West Bank. It pays half a salary to unemployed pharmacists and helps find them work. It plans to establish field pharmacies to serve the villages.

2. Dentists Association

Founded in 1953, membership, in Jerusalem and the West Bank (1984): 150. The association has branches in all West Bank cities and its center is in Jerusalem. It has representatives on the Council of Directors of the Jordanian Dentists Association headquartered in Amman.

The association examines qualifying doctors and licenses them to practice after meeting the conditions laid down in Jordanian law.

3. Lawyers Association

According to Jordanian law, foreign attorneys were forbidden to appear before West Bank courts. In 1967 the Israeli military administration issued an order canceling this restriction and authorized Israeli attorneys to represent clients in the occupied territories. In 1968 a petition was submitted to the appeals court in Ramallah challenging this revision.

The plaintiff argued that the Israeli administration lacked the authority to change Jordanian law in this instance, but the Ramallah court rejected this argument and ruled that it lacked the power to annul orders of the military government. The court also ruled that change was necessary in light of the continuing strike of local West Bank lawyers.

The Association of Lawyers in Jordan was founded in 1950. After the Six Day War it began a general strike in protest against the transfer of the appeals court from Jerusalem to Ramallah and the application of Israeli law on Jerusalem. After a short period, some lawyers returned to work, while others have continued their strike to the present. About 300 lawyers are still striking though 150 have broken the strike. The latter formed a committee and applied for formal registration as a union, which was denied them by the military government and they have since applied to the High Court of Justice. In the meantime they were expelled from the Jordanian union for breaking the strike.

PALESTINIAN TRADE UNIONS

Two types of trade unions are active on the West Bank – branches of unions based in Amman and independent unions.

The first group mainly comprises professional associations of doctors, dentists, pharmacists, and engineers. The second group is mostly made up of blue-collar workers: carpenters, metalworkers, employees in tourism, the food industries and so on.

Jordanian law specifies the activities of the trade unions and lays down election practices, membership in the General Federation of Jordanian Trade Unions and the government apparatus which supervises them. Some of the unions, interested in Jordanian government assistance, act in accordance with the above-mentioned law, but others, in particular those wishing to preserve their Palestinian identity, have no links with the general federation in Amman. The trade unions on the West Bank are divided between those identified as Communist, those identified as nationalist and controlled by FATAH, and those controlled by the REJECTION FRONT.

The Israeli administration permits union activity within strict limits. For instance, unions are not allowed to operate in East Jerusalem, which has been annexed to Israel. The Israeli GENERAL FEDERATION OF LABOR operates there instead. The administration intervenes in the activities of the trade unions at the general West Bank level, as they are viewed as a cover for political activity. In the years 1982-83 dozens of union activists were arrested, union halls and offices were closed and a general congress of West Bank trade unions was banned (December 1982). Some 140 Palestinian trade union branches have not been approved by Israeli authorities (1985).

List of unions and membership (according to "The Arab Thought Forum" (1981):

Name:	Membership 1967	1980
Union of Workers of the Jenin Municipality and Public Institutions	–	513
Union of Workers of the Tulkarm Mun.	15	1,248
Un. of Print Workers, Nablus	163	84
Un. of Bakery Workers, Nablus	–	112
Un. of Sanitation Workers, Nablus	4	411
Un. of Needle Workers, Nablus	11	723
Un. of Leather and Rubber Industry Workers, Nablus	5	207
Un. of Construction Workers, Nablus	17	2,236

Name:	Membership	
	1967	1980
Un. of Drivers and Garage Workers, Nablus	–	47
Un. of Workers of Nablus Municipality and Public Institutions	154	724
Un. of Workers of Ramallah Municipality and Public Institutions	72	3,858
Un. of Pharmaceutical Workers, Ramallah	–	142
Un. of Workers of Bethlehem Municipality and Public Institutions	3	864
Un. of Wood Workers, Hebron	–	344
Un. of Needle Workers, Hebron	–	86
Un. of Shoe Industry Workers, Hebron	–	313
Un. of Textile Workers, Hebron	–	165
Un. of Hotel and Restaurant Workers, Jerusalem	–	1,284
Un. of Electric Company Workers, Jerusalem	–	412
Un. of Construction Workers, Jerusalem	–	366
Un. of Workers of Augusta Victoria Hospital, Jerusalem	–	154
Un. of Shoe Workers, Jerusalem	–	100
Un. of Workers of Al-Makasad Hospital, Jerusalem		264
Un. of Print Workers, Jerusalem	–	92
Total:		14,749

PARKS AND NATURE RESERVES

As of 1984, there were four archeological sites with national park status on the West Bank: Herodion, Qumran, Hisham's Palace, and Sebastiya. Tel Jericho (Tel a-Sultan) is also to be opened as a park. The number of visitors to the national parks on the West Bank has fallen steadily since the beginning of the 1980s, indicating that few Israeli and foreign tourists visit the West Bank. Some 250,000 dunams have been declared nature reserves, and an additional 90,000 dunams are being prepared for nature reserve status. The declaration on nature reserves (signed March 1, 1983) was issued by decision of the MINISTERIAL COMMITTEE FOR SETTLEMENT in the framework of "a plan for land acquisition," in other words, declaration of a nature reserve signifies the transfer of the area to Israeli control. Nature reserve inspectors (the Green Patrol) also engage in "preventing shepherds from trespassing on state lands," and in enforcing orders prohibiting the harvest of herbal plants (mainly za'atar)

– thyme – which has caused considerable indignation in the Palestinian population.

The reserves are slated for development as tourist sites, and will serve as an economic base for the settlements in the area.

PERSONAL STATUS OF ISRAELIS

Israeli settlers on the West Bank carry with them their Israeli personal and communal status even though they have, in a legal sense, settled outside the borders of Israel and are subject to West Bank law (Jordanian law and SECURITY ENACTMENTS) like any other resident. In effect, however, Israeli legal, judicial and administrative norms apply to them. A tangled system of Israeli laws, military government orders, *ad hoc* regulations and extralegal arrangements (See CREEPING ANNEXATION) ensure that Israeli residents in the territories (or new Jewish immigrants from abroad) are equal in status with Israelis resident in Israel proper. They enjoy immunity from local law and its executive organs (police, army). In the relations between Israeli settlers and the local population, the Israelis also enjoy a clear judicial preference, since disputes between an Israeli and a Palestinian may not be heard before a local Arab court. Instructions of the attorney-general state that a local policeman may not report a crime committed by an Israeli resident. This dual system, and the double standard on which it is based, causes great damage to the principles of the rule of law and equality before the law (See KARP COMMISSION).

The special status of Israeli authorities in the territories (See ISRAELI LOCAL and REGIONAL COUNCILS), which enjoy all the privileges of their Israeli counterparts yet are free of state control (See CIVILIAN ADMINISTRATION), is transforming them into a state within a state.

PHYSICAL PLANNING

Physical planning on the West Bank is based on procedures set out in the Jordanian City and Village Planning Law of 1966, as amended (and in effect made meaningless) by the SECURITY ENACTMENTS. In the first years of Israeli rule, procedures for physical planning and building permits were completely uncontrolled and unregulated. When the government realized the political and physical importance of the planning process, it issued Order 393 (1970). This order authorized the military commander to forbid, halt or set conditions for construction. Order 418 (March 1971) made far-reaching changes in the Jordanian law. The hierarchical system of local, district, and national planning committees (customary in Israel and Jordan) was eliminated and their customary composition was altered. Instead, all planning powers were transferred to a high planning committee made up entirely of Israeli government representatives. District committees were eliminated and the licensing powers of the village councils transferred to the military government. The powers of the local planning committees, with responsibility within municipal boundaries, were drastically reduced. The high planning committee was authorized to amend, revoke or place conditions on any license issued by a municipality, to issue licenses itself or grant exemptions and even assume the powers of local committees.

The involvement of local residents in the planning process became minimal and theoretical. The government's involvement was also limited at first since it lacked means of enforcement. To all intents and purposes its efforts were limited to preventing Arab construction in sensitive military areas and in areas slated for Jewish settlement by the ALLON PLAN.

In 1977, when the Likud came into office, military government policy regarding physical planning was revised. The whole planning process underwent considerable development. Physical planning became a central instrument in carrying out settlement policy and in the creation of physical facts. While the planning process for Jewish settlement was devolved, with the participation of all Israeli planning authorities including representatives of ISRAELI REGIONAL and LOCAL COUNCILS, severe restrictions were placed on physical planning for the Palestinian population.

During the years 1982-84 plans for the densely populated areas were completed. Some of them (the Greater Jerusalem plan and Road Master Plan No. 50) were "deposited" through the procedure specified in Jordanian legislation. A petition against the road master plan was rejected by the Israeli HIGH COURT OF JUSTICE. The comprehensive regional plans for Judea and Samaria were not "deposited" legally but the planning authorities act in accordance with them as though they have been approved. The physical planning process reflects Israeli interests exclusively, while the needs and interests of the Palestinian population are treated as constraints to be overcome (See LAND USE). Once sufficient land for unlimited Jewish settlement was assured, statutory planning became the main method of controlling the areas remained in Palestinian possession.

While the professional planning office (which operates under the high planning committee) carried out regional plans for the Arab population, the Jewish regional councils draw up their own development plans for the same areas. Although the law forbids issuing a building permit without a town planning scheme, which in turn must be based on a district master plan, most of the Jewish settlements were built without proper planning procedures. In effect, Jewish settlements do not have to go through any formal planning procedure. The State Comptroller's report of 1984 determined that "according to the findings, the settlements in Judea and Samaria were established without due attention to the required planning procedures." By the end of 1985, the high planning committee had processed 191 plans for Jewish built-up areas. The total area involved covers tens of thousands of dunams, and is intended for accommodating over 500,000 settlers.

PLO POLITICAL PLANS

Excerpts from PNC (Palestine National Council) resolutions, and other official PLO statements concerning the occupied territories.

1974 (PNC, June)

1) Reaffirm the PLO position on Security Council Resolution 242. PNC "refuses to have anything to do with this resolution at any level, Arab or international, including the Geneva Conference."

2) PLO "will employ all means, and first and foremost armed struggle, to liberate Palestinian territory and to establish the independent, combatant national authority for the people on every part of Palestinian territory that is liberated."

3) PLO "will struggle against any proposal for a Palestinian entity the price of which is recognition [of Israel], peace, secure frontiers, renunciations of national rights – the return and the right to self-determination."

4) Once it is established, the Palestinian national authority will strive to achieve a union of confrontation countries.

1977(Palestinian Six-Point Program)

1) "We reaffirm our rejection of Security Council Resolutions 242 and 338," and " our rejection of all international conferences based on these two resolutions, including the Geneva Conference."

2) "[We] strive for the realization of the Palestinian people's rights to return and self-determination within the context of an independent Palestinian national state on any part of Palestinian land, without reconciliation, recognition or negotiations as an interim aim of the Palestinian revolution."

1982 (December 14, Joint Palestinian-Jordanian Communique)

(See REAGAN INITIATIVE)

1) Agreement to develop a special and distinguished relationship between Jordan and liberated Palestine.

168

2) Agreement "to continue joint political moves on all levels and in conformity with the FEZ SUMMIT RESOLUTIONS."

1983 (February, PNC, Algiers)
1) Affirms "the need to develop and intensify armed struggle against the Zionist enemy."
2) "The PLO is the sole legitimate representative of the Palestinian people **inside** and **outside** the country."
3) Affirms "the need to double efforts to strengthen the steadfastness (SUMUD) of our people inside the occupied homeland – to put an end to enforced emigration and to preserve the land and develop the national economy."
4) Rejects "all plans aimed at encroaching upon the right of the PLO as sole legitimate representative in any form such as power of attorney or agent…"
5) "Considers the resolution of the FEZ SUMMIT as the minimum for political action… which must be complemented by military action in all that it entails;" affirms, "that its understanding of these resolutions does not contradict commitment to the political program of the PNC resolutions."
6) "The PNC sees future relations with Jordan developing on the basis of a confederation between two independent states."
7) Supports the BREZHNEV PLAN, rejects the Reagan plan.

PNC resolution (November 1984) stressed PLO willingness to join the diplomatic process, in close cooperation with Jordan, with an immediate objective to change the United States commitment not to negotiate with the PLO (See HUSSEIN-ARAFAT AGREEMENT). The formulas used (FEZ resolutions, special and distinguished relations with Jordan, confederation) are in accordance with previous PNC resolutions (see above). PLO wished to demonstrate that "diplomatic action does not rule out armed struggle," therefore it initiated in the summer of 1985 naval and other acts of terrorism. In February 1986 the PLO refused to accept Security Council Resolutions 242 and 338; King Hussein suspended "coordination" with chairman Arafat.

POALEI AGUDAT ISRAEL (SETTLEMENTS)

Poalei Agudat Israel is a religious workers movement which broke away from Agudat Israel, but remains associated with it through the Council of Torah Sages. Founded in 1922, it commenced activity in 1925. Its major principles with regard to the West Bank are:
A. Rural and urban settlement throughout the Land of Israel, especially Judea and Samaria. This stems from a desire for full Israeli sovereignty

over all parts of Eretz Israel under Israeli control. The State of Israel itself is perceived as a national expression of the commandment to settle the land.

B. Areas of Eretz Israel currently under Israeli control – Judea and Samaria, the Jordan Valley, and the Gaza Strip – shall not be handed over to foreign rule. The settlements founded there shall not be dismantled and there shall be no halt in the momentum of settling the land.

C. While the commandment of settling the land demands that no other national entity be given any status, non-Jews living there are not to be expelled or dispossessed.

D. A real peace agreement between Israel and its neighbors will not be achieved through weakness, but through internal strength. Only in this way can a real peace be established, recognizing that Israel must continue to remain in control of all parts of Eretz Israel.

Poalei Agudat Israel Settlements in the West Bank (1985):

Mevo Horon	moshav shitufi	258 persons
Matityahu	moshav shitufi	120 persons
Nahliel	moshav shitufi	50 persons

POLICE

Empowered to act in the territories by Order No. 52 of 1967, which places the police under the orders of the military government of the area. It enjoys the authority given to soldiers according to the SECURITY ENACTMENTS and the authorities granted to the police by the Jordanian law in force in the area. In theory the police force is under the orders of the military government, in fact, it acts independently, subject to its own chain of command, according to the Israeli police ordinances (See CREEPING ANNEXATION). The budget for police and Border Police units in the occupied areas comes from the Ministry of Defense. The KARP REPORT reveals the problematics of police action in the complex juridical situation in which various contradictory legal systems are applied. The local courts judge the Arab residents according to Jordanian law; the military courts try the residents according to military law in security offenses; the military courts deal with IDF soldiers; and Israeli courts hear the cases of Israelis accused of criminal acts (See COURTS (LOCAL AND MILITARY)).

Because the police are subject to two different command hierarchies, duplication, contradictions and ambiguous situations are created. The police are unable to act effectively because responsibility for enforcing the law, on the authority of military orders, is incumbent on the military government not the police force. This both prevents the police from acting freely and relieves it of full responsibility for enforcing the law in the territories as it does within the green line. Additional problems in the functioning of the police derive from the disproportion between its structure and requirements. The location and number of police stations laid down in 1968 have not changed despite the increase in crime and the establishment of new Israeli settlements. The police force in Israel has been enlarged by 50 percent since 1968, as has the Border Police, but in the occupied territories the police force has not been augmented. For example, the number of police detectives in the Judea district is one-third the number in Jerusalem, where the population is similar in size. The number of policemen serving on the West Bank is as follows:

Year	Local Policemen	Israeli Policemen
1980	391	211
1981	391	211
1982	404	214
1983	415	210

POLITICAL INSURANCE

Israeli financial institutions have refused to grant development loans to Israeli businesses in the territories without government guarantees of repayment in the event of withdrawal from the territories. It was necessary, according to the existing law, to bring all such requests before the Finance Committee of the Knesset for approval. As Israeli economic activity in the territories increased, the process became increasingly drawn-out and complicated. For this reason, a special government insurance company was founded in April 1971, named Yanai (and later Inbal). It insures loans and investments against the following risks:

1. A change in territorial status which would require abandonment of businesses.

2. A change in the administration's policy, which would prevent proper functioning, including curfews.

3. Commercial damage resulting from a political boycott.

In addition, Israeli businesses were insured against the risks covered in Israel by the Property Tax Law and Compensation Fund (for damages from enemy action). At the end of 1972, a Jewish Agency request that its loans for agricultural settlements in the territories be insured by Yanai was also approved. At the end of 1973, Yanai's guarantees were expanded to include the property and investments of public and private contractors, and the property of every Israeli settling in the territories. All Israeli settlements, without regard to their political position on the future of the territories, are concerned to insure their property against the risk of a "change in territorial status."

POST AND TELECOMMUNICATIONS

The mail and telecommunications system on the West Bank is characterized by nearly complete physical integration with the Israeli system, with a functional separation between services to Israeli residents and those supplied to the Palestinian population. The mail service for Palestinians is based on 37 local post offices and 250 village mailmen who also operate more than 100 manual telephone exchanges, including 27 which are manned 24 hours a day in the villages and towns.

The mail service for Israelis is based on six mobile mail routes serving only the Jewish settlements and bypassing the Arab settlements along the way. In addition, post offices and postal agents operate in the large Israeli settlements.

The telephone network on the West Bank is connected to the Israeli network and its dialing areas, with the Jerusalem region taking in most of the West Bank, from its southern border to Nablus. The Tulkarm and Kalkilya exchanges have been closed down and transferred to the Israeli exchange on the other side of the green line. The Hebron exchange was also closed down and transferred to Kiryat Arba. The number of Arab subscribers, proportionate to the population, is very low. In Hebron, with a population of 70,000, there were only 900 outside telephone lines in 1984. In the entire Hebron sub-district (not including the town itself), there were some 350 telephones in 1984 (in 18 manual exchanges), serving 80,000 people. Some 680 telephones were installed for the Arab population in 1982, and 1,580 in 1983.

In the Jewish settlements, telephones are installed on request. In the settlements of Shiloh, Givon, and Beit Horon (about 250 families in 1984), there were 300 outside lines. In Psagot (50 families) there were 90 outside lines (including those of the regional council). The first digital telephone exchange in Israel was installed in Ariel.

PRESS (ARAB)

Up till 1966 three daily newspapers were published in East Jerusalem: **Fi'lastin** (founded in Jaffa, 1911), **a-Dif'aa** (founded in Jaffa, 1934), and **al-Jihad** (founded in Jerusalem, 1953). Only **al-Manar** was published in Amman. In March 1967, a new Jordanian press law restricted the number of papers to three. The main purpose of that measure was to transfer two Jerusalem papers to Amman and merge them as **a-Dustur**. The other Jerusalem newspapers were intended to merge as **al-Quds**. This measure was implemented shortly before the 1967 war. The publication of **al-Quds** ceased as a result of the war and resumed in December 1968, with a license from the Israeli Ministry of the Interior.

In June 1972, **al-Fajr** and **a-Sha'ab**, as well as bi-weeklies and monthlies, were published. Since 1980 **al-Fajr** has published an English edition (a Hebrew edition was suspended after a brief period). Under Israeli administration the Arab press has seen unprecedented growth. Today three daily papers, five weeklies, four bi-weeklies, monthlies, and other journals are published. **Al-Quds** has a circulation of 10-15,000, **al-Fajr**, 3-5,000, and **a-Sha'ab**, 2-3,000. The papers are circulated on the West Bank, in East Jerusalem and in Gaza. The total staff employed by the newspapers is about 125. Some of their funding comes from Jordanian and PLO sources (See JOINT COMMITTEE, DEMOCRATIC FRONT, COMMUNIST PARTY).

All the Arab publications are produced in East Jerusalem because Israeli press laws, despite their severity, are preferable to the draconian measures of the MILITARY GOVERNMENT (See CENSORSHIP). The Arab press views itself as "mobilized" and in the vanguard of the national struggle against occupation. This is expressed in the main topics aired in its press: self-determination, the fostering of Palestinian identity, and steadfastness (SUMUD) under Israeli occupation. Sixty percent of the articles and editorials deal with the West Bank and the Gaza Strip, 30 percent with Israeli internal matters, and only 10 percent with international news. All sections of the Arab press are geared to the central political issue: the Palestinian problem.

I. Weekly and Monthly Publications
al-Mitaq (The Covenant)
A weekly which first appeared on February 2, 1980. Edited by Mahmud al-Hatib. The publication claims to represent the position of the REJECTION FRONT in the Palestinian camp and supported the rebels against FATAH in 1983. It began appearing as a daily in August, 1984.

al-Taliah (The Pioneer)
A weekly which first appeared on February 27, 1978. Acknowledged as the organ of the COMMUNIST PARTY on the West Bank. Its editor is Bashir Barghuti, a prominent West Bank party leader. The military government forbids the circulation of **al-Taliah** in the occupied territories, and readers must obtain it in Jerusalem. A monthly supplement on socialism and liberation movements throughout the world is also published.

al-Shira'a (The Sail)
A weekly first published on May 1, 1978. Its editor was Marwan al-'Asali, a prominent Palestinian journalist who died in 1980. After his death, the newspaper increased its political involvement and was considered one of

the most radical publications on the West Bank. In the summer of 1983 the newspaper was shut down by the minister of the interior, who claimed that it belonged to the REJECTION FRONT. Its owners denied the claim and appealed to the HIGH COURT OF JUSTICE. Their appeal was rejected, the court accepting the opinion of the Israel defense establishment.

al-Bayader (The Threshing Floor)

A monthly publication which preceded the weekly **al-Bayader a-Sayassi**. The journal, which first appeared in March 1976, is devoted to literature – particularly Palestinian literature – and culture.

On April 1, 1981, editor Jack Hasmo began publishing the political weekly, **al-Bayader a-Sayassi**, identified with the mainstream of the PLO and supporting the leadership of Yassir Arafat. It is thought to have the largest circulation of any weekly on the West Bank.

al-Kateb (The Author)

A literary publication which started publication on November 1, 1978, edited by As'ad al-'As'ad (a poet well known on the West Bank). It was published after a legal battle by al-'As'ad against the Ministry of the Interior, which originally refused him a license to publish. It is considered a communist literary organ.

al-Wahadah (Unity)

First published as a weekly on February 20, 1982, but ceased publication after a number of months because of financial difficulties. Its editor has since died, and its license was subsequently revoked by the authorities.

al-Fajr al-'Arabi (A Weekly in Hebrew)

First published as an independent newspaper in September 1980, edited by Ziad abu Zayyad, who was also editor of the daily Arabic newspaper of that name. It was a bi-weekly intended to promote dialogue between Jews and Arabs on the basis of common recognition of the need to find a political solution to the Arab-Israeli conflict and involving the partition of the country into two states. The newspaper's staff included Israeli writers (both Jews and Arabs) and residents of the occupied territories. The newspaper offered the Israeli reader extensive reports on events in the territories and on political developments in the Palestinian nationalist movement, which received little coverage in the Israeli press.

In November 1983, publisher Paul 'Ajluni decided to close the newspaper as it was not making a profit. It has not appeared since.

al-Sharuq (The Sunrise)

First published in Gaza several years ago, edited by Muhamad Has. It has appeared irregularly and recently it has taken the form of a local paper concerned with the problems of the Gaza Strip. It is not circulated on the West Bank.

al-Fajr al-Adabi

A monthly literary supplement which first appeared on September 1, 1980, published by **al-Fajr**. Since March 1982, it has been published in soft cover, edited by poet 'Ali al-Khalili of Nablus.

al-Tauratu Wa-al-Mugatam'a (Tradition and Culture)

A quarterly which began publication on April 1, 1974, by the COMMITTEE FOR FAMILY IMPROVEMENT. The publication is concerned with Palestinian folklore and culture but appears irregularly, due to intervention by the censor.

al-Awdah

A bi-weekly in Arabic which first appeared November, 1982. Its publishers are Raymonda Tawil and Ibrahim Qura'in. Its circulation in the West Bank and Gaza is banned. By the end of 1985 the publishers brought out an English version with the same name, identified with the mainstream of the PLO.

II. Daily Newspapers

al-Quds (Jerusalem)

The first Arab newspaper to appear in East Jerusalem after the occupation in 1967. Its first issue was published on November 8, 1968, and it aroused sharp controversy as to whether newspapers should be published under the occupation or whether the press should go underground.

It began in a six-page, letterpress format. Today it has doubled in size and is printed in a modern offset plant. The editor and owner of the newspaper is Mahmud Abu al-Zuluf, a native of Jaffa. The newspaper is unaffiliated politically, and its owners view it as an economic enterprise. It can be considered the mouthpiece of the Hashemite monarchy.

al-Fajr (The Dawn) (Arabic Edition)

First published as a weekly on April 7, 1972, edited by Yussef Nasser and owned by Paul 'Ajluni, a Palestinian who emigrated to the United States in 1947 and became an American citizen. The editor, Yussef Nasser, was abducted for political reasons in February 1974, and there has been no trace of him since. After the kidnapping the newspaper continued appearing, gradually coming out as a daily paper. It claims to represent the Fatah position within the PLO.

a-Sha'ab (The People)

A daily paper appearing since July 21, 1972, ranking third in circulation after **al-Quds** and **al-Fajr**. Its editor is veteran journalist Mahmud Ya'ish, formerly an editor of the Jordanian paper **a-Difa'a** (before the merger) and later of **al-Quds** (on the eve of the 1967 war).

al-Fajr (English Edition)
First published on April 23, 1980, as a weekly supplement to the Arabic daily. In 1983, it received a separate permit. Intended for English readers in Israel and hundreds of subscribers abroad, it is the only Palestinian organ appearing in English in the occupied territories.

PRISONS
West Bank prisons come under the authority of the Israel Prison Services. They function as an integral part of the Israeli system.

The central prisons for security offenders from the territories are Nablus (Jneid), Jenin, Fara'ah, Ramle, Hebron, Tulkarm, Beersheba, Gaza, Ashkelon, and Nafha. Prisoners sentenced to up to five years are held in West Bank jails and those sentenced to five years or more are transferred to prisons in Beersheba, Nafha, and Ramle. In some cases these prisoners may be placed in other jails. A new detention center for young offenders was founded in 1982 in Fara'ah (Samaria).

The concentration of thousands of security offenders in the jails turns imprisonment into a sort of training ground for the struggle against Israeli occupation. "Graduates" of Israeli prisons are accorded honored status by their peers and gain easier terms for West Bank university admission and for university examinations. After their release, the prisoners are entered on the security forces blacklist, and they are the first to be detained in the event of preventive arrests.

Several complaints have been submitted about treatment in the prisons, for the most part dealing with overcrowding and brutality (See DETENTION AND INTERROGATION). From time to time sit-down and hunger strikes break out among security prisoners. These strikes usually spread to West Bank towns, accompanied by demonstrations and violent clashes with the security forces. In 1984, 675 criminals, 2,182 security prisoners, 120 detained on criminal charges, and 473 detained on security offenses, all from the territories, were in prison. In 1985, 1,150 security prisoners were released, in exchange for three Israeli prisoners of the Lebanon War, held by a splinter group of the PFLP.

PRO-HASHEMITE GROUPS
Loyalty to Jordan on the West Bank and to a lesser extent in the Gaza Strip, is based on the traditional establishment and its administrative, economic and commercial links to the Jordanian government.

176

Dependence on Jordan in matters of local government, education, health, housing, passports, religious affairs, banking, etc., gives the Jordanians considerable clout.

A wide range of employees and officials have, since 1967, received their salaries from the Jordanian government, whether or not they have continued to work for the civilian administration. Thousands of pensioners also continued to receive their pensions from the Jordanian government.

The various institutions with bureaucratic machinery on the West Bank have practical working ties with the Jordanian ministries. This goes for the Muslim religious establishment, the education system, health, charitable and other organizations.

In addition to the government apparatus, links with Jordan are also maintained through the following bodies: the CHAMBERS OF COMMERCE in Arab towns, which issue permits for import and export over the Jordan River bridges; the Examination Committee (See EDUCATION), which administers the Jordanian examinations given in West Bank schools; agricultural associations (See COOPERATIVES); MUNICIPALITIES; and VILLAGE COUNCILS, which have ties with the Jordanian ministries in budgetary & supervisory matters; the WAQF institution through its East Jerusalem office, which deals with religious affairs, educational institutions, and health and welfare associations. Charitable organizations in East Jerusalem and heads of distinguished families, mukhtars and sheikhs remain close to Jordanian officials in Amman in order to further local and family interests.

The West Bank is officially represented in the Jordanian senate, parliament, and cabinet, although most of these delegates actually live in Amman. A few do reside in the West Bank, traveling frequently to Jordan. The most prominent is Hikmat al-Masri of Nablus, an acting chairman of the Jordanian senate. West Bankers who held key positions in the Jordanian government in 1984 were Tahr al-Masri, foreign minister, resident in Nablus, and 'Adnan Abu-'Odah (also from Nablus), known as the Palestinian closest to King Hussein. By 1985 the position of West Bankers in the Jordanian government had become even stronger.

The power of the Jordanian loyalists on the West Bank and in Gaza is dependent on administrative support (such as the issuing of passports) and on cash transfers from the JOINT COMMITTEE PLO-JORDAN, channeled mainly through Jordanian banks. This financial support reaches various institutions, companies, and private individuals who mostly use it for housing. The Jordanian line is reflected in the daily **al-Quds**, largest of the West Bank newspapers.

In Gaza, most Jordanian financial support is channeled through the Association for Aiding the People of the Gaza Strip, whose director is Gaza's former mayor, Rashad a-Shawah. The association arranges passage over the bridges for agricultural produce, passports and financial assistance. In Gaza the connection with Jordan is mediated only through the association under a-Shawah's control, while on the West Bank it is spread over dozens of institutions and bodies.

PUBLIC CONSUMPTION AND INVESTMENT

Public (or government) expenditure is the total operating expenditure of the military government (for civilian purposes) and of the Arab local authorities. Its level (in relation to local use of resources) and the changes in it from year to year, express in momentary terms the level of services provided to the inhabitants. For the physical and quantitative measures of the level of services, see EDUCATION, HEALTH, etc.

Public investment in fixed assets is the total development budget expended by the military government and the expenditure of Arab local authorities directed at the creation of a physical infrastructure, and other fixed assets (roads, public buildings, sewerage, mechanical equipment, electricity, water, etc.). These budgets do not include investments in the Jewish sector in the territories (See INVESTMENT IN SETTLEMENTS). The share of investment in local uses, and the seasonal changes in it, express development trends in the economic and public infrastructure. For the fiscal burden on Israel as a result of its expenditures on the West Bank, see FISCAL BURDEN.

Public Expenditure

In examining the data on public consumption on the West Bank, it should be taken into account that the West Bank is not a "national economy" except for the purpose of Israel's accounts (See NATIONAL ACCOUNTS). The structure of local uses is not comparable with true national economies, since it has no defense and foreign relations expenditure, and no capital market. Hence, the proportion of public consumption on the West Bank is less than that of sovereign states. In 1979, for instance, the share of public expenditure on the West Bank was only 6 percent of the use of local resources, as opposed to 23 percent in Israel, 19 percent in Jordan and 18 percent in Syria. If, however, defense expenditure is deducted, the ratio changes to 6 percent in the West Bank, 12 percent in Israel and 10 percent in Jordan. In an underdeveloped economy in need of rapid growth, ongoing consumption expenditure should be relatively high for investment in human capital (education, health, etc.). The rate of public consumption on the West

178

Bank does not meet the growth demands of the economy and indicates a very low level of services. More importantly, public expenditure rates have not only shown no growth but have actually dropped since 1968. In 1965 (towards the end of Jordanian rule) the level was 13 percent, while under Israeli rule the proportion of public consumption in local uses fell from 12 percent at the beginning of the 1970s to 8 percent at mid-decade, and 6 percent by 1979. In 1981-82, the share was 6.7 percent and in 1983 it went up to 7.6 percent of local uses.

In absolute terms, total public expenditure (military government and municipalities) in 1983 was 421 million shekels, as against 240 million shekels in 1968 (at 1980 prices), a growth of 75 percent. Since 1980 public expenditure has maintained a fixed absolute rate (except in 1983 when it increased by 4 percent in real terms). Given population growth, expenditure per capita has dropped.

In 1982 public expenditure per capita in the West Bank was $120 as against $800 ($2,000 including defense expenditure) in Israel, a proportion of 1:6.6. Expenditure on health per capita, for instance, was 8 percent of Israel's. Education expenditure came to 12-15 percent of Israel's. In addition to the above figures, public consumption of services provided by voluntary organizations (See UNRWA, FOREIGN AID) must be taken into account. According to estimates, total average annual transfers in 1982 came to about $14.5 million, 80 percent for operating budgets. Inclusion of this sum increases public expenditure per capita by 50 percent, up to $180. Fairly efficient use was made of funds available to the public sector (See HEALTH, EDUCATION, etc.). This in itself, however, is unsatisfactory and clearly insufficient to ensure economic growth. Moreover, an analysis of the FISCAL BURDEN shows that monies collected from residents of the territories, which could have been used to improve the public sector, were not distributed in the territories but transferred to public consumption in Israel.

Public Investment
If the situation in public consumption is discouraging, the state of public investment is graver still. Public investment was 1.8 percent of the local uses in 1981, 2.4 percent in 1982, and 2.8 percent in 1983. The proportion of public investment in fixed assets fell from 16 percent in 1974/75 to 9 percent in 1977/78, then increased to 12.3 percent in 1981, 14.6 percent in 1982 and 18.1 percent in 1983. Israeli funding of public investment dropped off during these years. In 1971/72 it reached 53 percent of total public investment, and after continuous decline reached 11 percent in 1980. It rose again to 54 percent in 1982, and 48 percent in 1983.

According to estimates, total public capital formation (including municipalities) in the West Bank (1968-1983) reached some $350 million or $15-20 million per year. The development budget of the military government in 1981 was $10 million, in 1982/83 some $14 million, in 1983/84 $19 million, and in 1984/85 $13.5 million. In 1984/85, 12 percent was invested in water works, 10 percent in electricity, 14.5 percent in road construction, 4.7 percent in schools, 12 percent in telephone grids and 9.5 percent in health. Some $4 million were given to municipalities as loans and grants. Investment in the development of regional infrastructure in areas beyond the limits of the cities and the larger villages was particularly low. Public investment in regional infrastructure amounts to no more than a quarter of total public investment. An examination of public investment items indicates that most of it goes towards improving services with only a small part going to economic development.

In the absence of a central economic authority, there is no promotion of investment in regional infrastructure aimed at encouraging growth. This is only one example of the deliberate freeze characterizing government policy as regards the Arab productive sector (See ECONOMIC POLICY, FOREIGN AID).

Public investment in improvement of services is reflected in the quantitative statistics on construction of public buildings (See PUBLIC CONSTRUCTION) and the decline in the number of hospital beds (See HEALTH). It is instructive to compare public investment in the Arab and Jewish sectors on the West Bank. Between 1968 and 1985 some $2.0 billion was invested in settlements and in civilian infrastructure for Jewish settlements in the West Bank (See INVESTMENT IN SETTLEMENTS), or an average of about $100 million per year. The sum invested in 1980-82 to develop Israeli settlements was equal to the entire public investment in the Arab sector over 17 years.

Public investment is divided between the military government and the Arab local authorities (in addition to voluntary organizations). During the occupation their relative contributions have undergone changes. In 1968-1973, the local authorities' share in public expenditure (including investment) was 15 percent. By 1980 this had risen to 30 percent as the result of a decrease in military government expenditure. During the years 1981-84 the Arab municipalities' share came to about a quarter of total outlay. The participation of the municipalities in investments of the public sector in the territories was as follows: 1975 – 22.8 percent; 1977 – 33.9 percent; 1978 – 57.3 percent; 1981 – 54 percent; 1982 – 22.3 percent; 1983 – 17.7 percent. The significant change in the absolute rate of total military government investment in fixed assets, relative to the stability of the public consumption budgets, indicates that the government has no clear investment program nor development priorities. Investment and financing are used as political tools, aimed at encouraging collaborators and penalizing opponents.

While the government was engaged in promoting the VILLAGE LEAGUES, its investment in the rural sector rose, and its investment decreased significantly in the municipal sector. In 1978 the civilian administration contributed 34 percent of funding for rural projects. In 1982 its share rose to 80 percent of total outlay. In 1981/82, when the political struggle between the civilian administration and the municipalities was at its height (See CIVILIAN ADMINISTRATION, MUNICIPALITIES), government contribution to municipal projects reached $400,000. After the Palestinian mayors were dismissed and replaced by Israeli officers, the government's contribution to municipal projects rose tenfold.

Changes in Arab municipal investment are affected not only by reduction in the military government's share, but also, and perhaps principally, by the transfer of development funds from Jordan and other Arab countries (See SUMUD). These transfers increased from 1977 onwards and reached their peak in 1978, when they came to approximately $25 million (to the municipalities alone). It is difficult to obtain reliable figures for total Sumud transfers for public investment (a considerable portion is classified as private consumption and in particular as investment in housing (See CONSTRUCTION). Some 60 percent of the investment funds in projects initiated by voluntary organizations (See FOREIGN AID), and classified as "local participation," are in actual fact Sumud funds transferred through Jordanian banks and cooperatives.

In 1982, the transfer of Sumud funds without prior approval was banned. As a result, municipal development budgets fell by 42 percent and investment in projects by 58 percent – an indication of the overwhelming weight of this source of funding in West Bank public investment. In 1983/84 funding for projects from outside sources was only 20 percent of its level prior to the ban and the share of the Israeli government in their funding rose accordingly (though the actual extent of this investment was small). At the end of 1984 a decision was taken to ease the restrictions, and unilateral transfer soared.

REAGAN INITIATIVE

Raised in a televised address by President Reagan on September 1, 1982, at the completion of the evacuation of the PLO from Beirut. In addition to the public speech, its principles were communicated to governments in the Middle East.

Summary of the initiative (sometimes termed "Plan"):

A. The United States will maintain its commitment to the CAMP DAVID process.

B. The U.S. will maintain its commitment to the conditions required for recognition of and negotiation with the PLO (acceptance of Res. 242, 338, and cessation of terrorism).

C. The objective of the transitional period (See CAMP DAVID) is transfer of authority from Israel to the Palestinian inhabitants.

D. Full autonomy for the Palestinians means giving the Palestinians real authority over themselves, the land and its resources, subject to fair safeguards on water.

E. Participation of Palestinian inhabitants of East Jerusalem in the election of the Self Governing Authority.

F. Progressive Palestinian responsibility for internal security based on capability and performance.

G. Real freeze of Israeli settlement activity in the territories, but opposition to dismantling existing settlements. The Palestinian problem cannot be resolved through Israeli sovereignty or control over the West Bank.

H. The U.S. will not support the formation of a Palestinian state but rather a final status of the territories based on association with Jordan.

I. The Palestinians must take the leading role in determining their own future through the provisions of the CAMP DAVID ACCORDS.

J. The status of East Jerusalem must be determined through negotiations.

K. The status of Israeli settlements must be determined in the course of negotiations on the final status of the territories. The U.S. will not support their existence as extraterritorial outposts.

The Israeli government rejected the initiative *in toto,* on September 2, 1982. In its decision, the following points were emphasized:

A. Rejection of U.S. position on participation of East Jerusalem residents in elections to the AUTONOMY authority, for its implication is partition of the city.

B. Israel must remain responsible for internal and external security, which are inseparable.

C. There is no mention in the CAMP DAVID ACCORDS of a freeze on settlements. Israel will continue to establish them in accordance with Israel's natural right.

D. Israel rejects the U.S. interpretation of full autonomy as giving the Palestinians authority over land and water. The autonomy applies not to the territory but to the inhabitants.

E. There is nothing in the CAMP DAVID ACCORDS that precludes the application of Israeli sovereignty over Judea, Samaria, and the Gaza district following the transitional period (of AUTONOMY).

The U.S. informed King Hussein of the Reagan Initiative and his reaction was "that the proposals are serious and that he is giving them serious attention." The Jordanians conditioned public acceptance on an agreement with Yassir Arafat. In the winter of 1982, consultations were held in Algiers and in Amman on a joint Jordanian-PLO position, with participation of U.S. officials. They culminated in a draft statement which included, apparently, the following paragraph: "Due to the importance of the time element, there is no escape but to engage in diplomatic action based on the FEZ resolution and on other Arab and international resolutions, including the Reagan Initiative." It was agreed to include PLO representatives, not necessarily members of the Palestine National Council (PNC), in a joint Jordanian-PLO delegation. Arafat, however, failed to gain a majority in the PLO for that move. Consequently King Hussein did not publicly endorse the initiative. (Compare HUSSEIN-ARAFAT AGREEMENT.) The joint Palestinian-Jordanian communique issued at the end of these negotiations (December 14, 1982), mentioned only that "the two sides agree to act in conformity with the FEZ resolution and within the framework of joint Arab moves." The initiative was not mentioned. The PNC congress in Algiers (February 1983) stated: "The Reagan Plan in form and content does not fulfill the inalienable national rights of the Palestinian people... For these reasons, the PNC declares its refusal to consider the plan as a proper basis for a lasting and just solution to the Palestinian cause and the Zionist-Arab conflict." (See PLO POLITICAL PLANS.)

President Reagan has often reiterated his commitment to his 1982 initiative. King Hussein's initiative of spring 1985, and U.S. Assistant Secretary of State Richard Murphy's missions were attempts to reactivate the initiative. Arafat's refusal in February 1986 to accept Security Council Resolutions 242 and 338 resulted in the suspension of these renewed efforts.

RED CROSS

An international agency with headquarters in Geneva, Switzerland, the International Red Cross is composed of three bodies: the International Red Cross, the League of Red Cross and Red Crescent organizations, and recognized national Red Cross and Red Crescent societies. The governing body of the organization is the Council of Representatives. The IRC is the founding body of the Red Cross, an executive body acting as a neutral intermediary in armed conflicts and violent uprisings. The

Red Cross acts upon its initiative and under the authority of the GENEVA CONVENTION to provide health care and assistance to victims of war and states in civil war.

The Red Cross is active on the West Bank through the Geneva Convention regarding the protection of civilians, especially Article 49. Representatives of the Red Cross have intervened with the Israeli authorities to lift curfews from cities, they have protested against the destruction of houses, the seizure of lands, and the establishment of settlements. The chief activity of the Red Cross is the protection of prisoners and political detainees (See DETENTION AND INTERROGATION).

Representatives of the Red Cross made 126 prison visits in 1984, speaking without witnesses to 3,800 detainees. Representatives of the Red Cross are present at trials in military courts, they give material aid to the families of prisoners and they have also provided special medical equipment for the prisoners themselves. The Red Cross also provides free transportation to families of prisoners. In 1983 the Red Cross agency for locating relatives transferred more than 57,000 messages from thousands of families in the territories occupied by Israel to relatives in Arab countries. The Red Cross acts through a head office in Tel Aviv, subsidiary offices in Jerusalem and Gaza, and local offices in Hebron, Bethlehem, Ramallah, Nablus, Jenin, Jericho, and Tulkarm.

REFUGEE CAMPS

1. Balata Camp

Established in 1980 within the municipal boundaries of Nablus. Most camp residents are from 65 villages and towns in the Jaffa, Ramle, and Lod areas. Among them are Bedouin from the same areas, from the Arab Abu Qishaq, al-Qur'an, al-Hashashin, a-Sawlmah, al-Ka'abnah, and al-Jamusin tribes. The camp covers 252 dunams. The number of inhabitants in May 1967, was 9,820, or 1,727 families. In January 1984, there were 10,284 residents or 1,684 families. A vocational training center, four schools, and a youth activity center are located in the camp. In 1984 the total number of school pupils was 2,792.

2. Deir Amar Camp

Located near Deir Amar village in the Ramallah area, started in 1949 as a tent camp. In 1951 construction of permanent concrete structures with asbestos roofs was begun, and was completed in 1957.

The camp covers 145 dunams. In 1949 it had about 3,000 inhabitants. Between 1949 and 1967 some 1,000 people left the camp and moved to nearby areas. On the eve of the 1967 war, the number of residents was 2,000, of whom 1,000 abandoned the camp during and after the war. The 1983 UNRWA census cites 1,053 residents.

The camp has two schools for boys and girls, with a total of 447 pupils.

3. Askar Camp
Set up in 1950 within the municipal boundaries of Nablus, on the main road to the Damia Bridge. The vast majority of the camp's residents lived in 25 villages in the Jaffa and Haifa areas before 1948. There are also Bedouin from the Jaffa and Beersheba areas. The camp covers 209 dunams. In May 1967, it housed 5,671 people or 994 families; in January 1984, there were 7,704 people or 1,387 families.

The camp has a youth center and four schools serving 2,097 pupils.

4. Camp No. 1
Established in 1950 in the western section of Nablus on the main road to Tulkarm and Jenin, within the jurisdiction of the Nablus municipality. The majority of the camp's residents lived in 20 villages and towns in the Jaffa, Haifa, and Acre areas before 1948. The camp covers 45 dunams. In May, 1967, the number of inhabitants was 2,853 or 519 families; in January, 1984, there were 3,535 inhabitants or 669 families.

The camp has two schools serving about a thousand students, and a youth center.

5. Al-Far'aa Camp
Set up in 1949 on a rocky hill by the al-Far'aa spring, about 17 kilometers north of Nablus (on the Nablus-Tubas road). The majority of its residents lived in 61 villages and towns in the Haifa, Jaffa, and Beersheba areas before 1948. The camp area is 225 dunams. In 1967 it had 6,340 inhabitants (1,074 families); in January 1984, there were 4,119 inhabitants (832 families). The camp has three schools for boys and girls serving about a thousand pupils, and a youth center.

6. Kalandiya Camp
Set up in 1949 as a tent camp. In the years 1951-57 the tents were replaced by permanent concrete structures with asbestos roofs. The camp area is 353 dunams and it is located on the main Jerusalem-Ramallah road next to Atarot (Kalandiya) airport. In 1949 it had 3,000 inhabitants originating from 39 villages in the Jerusalem area. On the eve of the 1967 war there were 4,800 inhabitants, but about half of them abandoned the camp during or after the war. The 1983 census cites 4,224 residents (637 families). There are four elementary and secondary schools for boys and girls, serving 1,781 pupils. There is a youth activities center (closed indefinitely by the military government) and a vocational training center.

7. Al-Ama'ari Camp

Set up as a tent camp in 1949. By 1957 the tents had been replaced by concrete structures with asbestos roofs. The camp is situated within the municipal boundaries of al-Bira. In 1949 there were about 2,000 inhabitants in a 94 dunam area. On the eve of the 1967 war there were 3,938 residents, about 700 of whom abandoned the camp during or after the war. In April 1983 the number of residents according to the UNRWA census, was 4,164. There are four elementary and secondary schools for boys and girls. The total number of pupils in 1983 was 2,244. The camp also has a youth activities center.

8. Shuafat Camp

The last camp to be set up on the West Bank. Construction began in 1965 and was completed in 1966. It absorbed thousands of Palestinians who had been living in the ruins of the Jewish Quarter of the Old City of Jerusalem since 1948. In 1966 the camp housed 3,000 residents in an area of 203 dunams.

On the eve of the 1967 war the camp had 3,870 residents. About 300 abandoned the camp during or after the war. In April 1983, there were 5,171 inhabitants comprising 706 families, according to the UNRWA census. The camp has four elementary and secondary schools for boys and girls, serving 1,458 pupils. There is also a youth activities center. It is situated within the expanded municipal area of Jerusalem (See EAST JERUSALEM).

9. Jalazun Camp

Set up in 1948, 10 kilometers from Ramallah on the Nablus road. It covers 254 dunams. The camp began with about 3,500 inhabitants. The number grew to 4,974 by 1967. During and after the war 1,700 abandoned the camp. The last (1983) UNRWA census cited 4,730 inhabitants.

10. Nur Shams Camp

Set up in 1952 on the slopes of a rocky hill three kilometers east of Tulkarm. It is divided into northern and southern sections by the Nablus-Tulkarm road. During the British Mandatory period, the site was used as a hard-labor prison.

The vast majority of the inhabitants lived in 25 villages in the Haifa and Galilee areas before 1948. The camp covers 226 dunams. There were 3,895 inhabitants (683 families) in May 1967, and 4,235 inhabitants (654 families) in January 1984. The camp has two schools serving 1,050 inhabitants, and a youth center.

11. Tulkarm Camp

Set up in 1950 in the eastern section of Tulkarm, within the municipal boundaries. The vast majority of the camp's residents lived in some 85 villages and towns in the Haifa and Jaffa areas before 1948. The camp also houses Bedouin from the Arab al-Hawaret, al-Balunah, al-Huweitat, al-Fuqra, and al-Barah tribes. The camp area is 165 dunams. In May 1967 there were 8,327 residents (1,400 families); in January 1984 there were 9,387 residents (1,667 families). The camp has five schools serving 2,450 pupils, and a youth center.

12. Jenin Camp
Set up in 1953 west of Jenin, within its municipal boundaries. During the British Mandate, the location served as a British military camp and railway station. The vast majority of the inhabitants lived in 25 villages and towns in the Haifa area in 1948. The camp covers 370 dunams. In May 1967 there were 7,290 inhabitants (1,223 families); in January 1984 there were 8,085 people (1,537 families). There are five schools serving 2,185 pupils, and a youth center.

13. Other Camps
Jericho area – Aqbat Jaber: 27,700 residents (1967), 2,290 (1975), 2,924 (1984). Ain Sultan: 18,900 residents (1967), 570 (1975), 702 (1984). Nu'eimah: 5,350 residents (1967), empty (1975). Karameh: 20,120 residents (1967), empty (1975).

Hebron area – Fawar: 4,930 residents (1967), 2,990 (1975), 3,299 (1984). Arrub: 2,870 residents (1967), 4,230 (1975), 4,702 (1984). Dehaishe: 7,630 residents (1967), 5,380 (1975), 6,165 (1984). Aidah: 1,930 residents (1967), 1,680 (1975), 2,211 (1984). Beit Jibrin: 1,290 residents (1967), 840 (1975), 1,080 (1984).

Refugee Camp Staff
Heading each camp is a director appointed by UNRWA, serving as liaison between the agency and the camp. The director, himself a former refugee, lives in the camp. He oversees food and welfare distribution and registration of beneficiaries, authorizes settlement in the camp and directs students into higher education. Camp residents fill the lower-level jobs, such as sanitation work. Middle-level employees, such as doctors and teachers, are generally outsiders.

Refugee Camp Development
The refugee camps grew from tent camps set up as temporary shelter into permanent camps and neighborhoods. Most of them developed into homogeneous neighborhoods with urban characteristics. Camp residents have a relatively high level of services, provided by UNRWA, including water supply, medical facilities, mother-and-child-care centers, nutrition centers, sanitation services, educational facilities, religious centers and

commerce.

Location of Refugee Camps
Two major factors determined the location of most of the refugee camps: available area and proximity to a town. Most of the refugee camps on the mountain ridge in Judea and Samaria are built near towns.

There are three types of refugee camps:
1. Official camps with non-uniform buildings;
2. Official camps with uniform buildings;
3. Unofficial concentrations of refugees, with non-uniform buildings.

Official Refugee Camps with non-uniform buildings
These originated as tent camps and gradually turned into permanent camps, with houses built individually by each family. The building process was gradual and in some cases tents remained alongside the buildings, which caused overcrowding.

Official Refugee Camps with uniform buildings
These were also tent camps in which tents were replaced by standard construction financed by UNRWA. In these camps, UNRWA supplied regular services, and distributed housing free to the refugees, so that ownership of the camps remained in its hands. These camps are also overcrowded.

Concentrations of Refugee Camps with non-uniform buildings
These are not "refugee camps" in the official sense, but rather concentrations of destitute families who are often not registered as refugees with UNRWA. They live in poor conditions, without UNRWA services, mainly near the larger towns on the West Bank. Large concentrations are found in Nablus and Ramallah. There is a "refugee neighborhood" in Bethlehem.

REFUGEES

Refugees (Jordan)
The number of Palestinian refugees who moved to the West Bank and Jordan and registered with UNRWA as needing aid was 465,500 in 1950. Twenty percent of the total was in Jordan, with the rest, some 373,000, on the West Bank. In the 1967 war, 150,000 of the refugees living on the West Bank fled to Jordan. The great majority of the refugees on the West Bank and Jordan are from Israel's central region, the agricultural areas around the coastal plain, the Judean and Samarian foothills, and west Jerusalem. After 1967, the number of Palestinian refugees in Trans-Jordan reached 650,000, the result both of the absorption of 150,000 refugees from the West Bank and of natural increase. According to the

UNRWA figures, their numbers reached 799,700 in 1984. Of these, 31 percent live in refugee camps and the rest are scattered in different urban and rural areas in Jordan. There are 10 camps: six were set up immediately after the 1948 war and four more after June 1967. They are: Irbid, al-Husn, Suf, Jarash, a-Zarqa, al-Baq'a, Marqa, Jabal al-Hussein, a-Talbiyah, and al-Wahdat. The last three have become neighborhoods of Amman.

Refugees (West Bank)
The number of refugees registered in 1950 with UNRWA as needing aid was 373,000. In 1984 the number registered was 357,000.

In 1984 there were 20 refugee camps on the West Bank housing 91,000 people. The other 266,000 live in the cities and villages of the West Bank (See REFUGEE CAMPS).

All these camps were founded after the 1948 war, with the exception of Shuafat, established in June 1966, for 3,000 refugees who had lived until then in the Jewish Quarter of the Old City of Jerusalem.

Refugees (Gaza Strip)
UNRWA began its work in the Gaza Strip in 1950. At that time, 200,000 people were registered as in need of aid. (The original number of Gaza Strip residents was about 80,000.) As a result of natural increase this number reached 428,000 in 1984 (38,000 left the Gaza Strip for Jordan after the June 1967 war). The refugees who fled to the Gaza Strip in 1948 were from the southern region of Israel and in particular from villages and towns in the Beersheba, Ashkelon, and Jaffa areas. They concentrated in a narrow region between six and 10 kilometers wide and some 45 kilometers in length. As a result of the lack of work and the large numbers of refugees in the Strip by comparison with the number of native residents, the economy was chronically depressed. This explains why a much higher proportion of Gaza Strip refugees continued living in refugee camps than in any of the other locations where UNRWA operated. Of the registered refugees in the Gaza Strip, 56 percent lived in the area's eight camps, as opposed to an average of 35 percent elsewhere (Jordan, Syria, the West Bank, and Lebanon). The eight camps are: Jabaliya, a-Shati, Nuseirat, al-Burj, al-Ma'azi, Deir al-Balah, Khan Yunis, Rafah.

REHOVOT GROUP; PROFESSORS GROUP
This group of academics, scientists, and leading figures in the economy met periodically at the Weizmann Institute in Rehovot from 1968 to 1973 with the aim of influencing Israeli policy in the territories. At the group's initiative and with the help of Prime Minister Levi Eshkol, a number of

professors carried out various surveys of the population of the territories (refugee camps, UNRWA, and some economic studies).

The group's initiative helped establish the Erez industrial park at the northern end of the Gaza Strip, and Atarot northeast of Jerusalem, which were experiments in integrating Israeli capital, know-how, and management, with Arab labor from the areas bordering Israel and the territories.

REJECTION FRONT

A collective term for Arab countries and Palestinian organizations opposing the use of diplomacy in the struggle against Israel. The multiplicity of the groups active on the West Bank and in the Gaza Strip reflects the divergencies of opinion within the Arab world and among the Palestinian organizations. The Rejection Front or the "Democratic Alliance" includes the following organizations: the Communists; the Popular Front for the Liberation of Palestine; and the Democratic Front.

The Democratic Alliance
Founded subsequent to the Lebanese War and comprising the Popular Front (George Habash), the Democratic Front (Naif Hawatmah), the COMMUNIST PARTY and the Liberation Front (under Iraqi sponsorship). The Democratic Alliance opposes the course taken by Yassir Arafat after 1982, based on alliance with moderate Arab countries and Jordan, and the pursuance of the national struggle by diplomatic means.

Supporters of the Democratic Alliance are considered a large minority on the West Bank and in Gaza (approximately 20 percent of the population). The strongest group in the alliance on the West Bank is the Communist Party, followed by the supporters of Hawatmah, with the Habash group in third place. The Iraqi-affiliated organization has negligible influence.

The Popular Front for the Liberation of Palestine (George Habash)
Operates military-terrorist cells in the territories, and engages in political and propaganda activity. "Volunteer Committees" in the cities and villages (once known as "1976 Committees") and the East Jerusalem **al-Shira'a** (See PRESS (ARAB)) have been known for the past few years as the organs of Habash's supporters. An underground pamphlet by the name of **Raiyat a-Sha'ab** is distributed occasionally on the West Bank, with a position close to that of the front. Similar views are expressed in the newspaper **al-Mitaq** and the organ **a-Ahad**, published in Jerusalem.

Habash's front enjoys a relatively strong position in the Arab universities and in particular at the Catholic University in Bethlehem, where its supporters control the student council.

The Democratic Front (Naif Hawatmah)
Maintains political and propaganda activity in the territories along with military-terrorist cells.

The Democratic Front has "Voluntary Committees" along the lines of those run by other organizations, and its supporters express their views in the newspaper **al-Mitaq** and the publication **al-Ahad** in East Jerusalem. The Democratic Front is thought to enjoy a relatively strong position on the NATIONAL GUIDANCE COMMITTEE, where about a third (eight) of the 24 members (the number of members has varied) have supported it. In elections to student councils it generally joins forces with the other organizations in the Democratic Alliance. Until the convening of the 17th council in Amman (at the end of 1984) its members cooperated with FATAH supporters.

RELIGIOUS COMMUNITIES

On the basis of a survey made in 1967 in the occupied territories by the IDF and the Central Bureau of Statistics, the Muslim population on the West Bank was about 531,500. The Christian population was about 31,900. In the Gaza Strip there were 187,500 Muslims out of a total population of 190,300 adults. Since 1967 no further survey has been made in the territories, but it would appear that the relation of 95 percent Muslims and 5 percent Christians persists.

Most of the Muslim population is Sunni, and the affairs of the community are run by the SUPREME MUSLIM COUNCIL in Jerusalem. This body is still subordinate to the Jordanian Ministry of Religions and works in close coordination with it. The Supreme Muslim Council appoints, dismisses, and pays the salaries of the religious bureaucracy and takes care of the Islamic holy places, clearly acting according to directives from Amman.

The significance of this situation is that the religious establishment in fact enjoys virtual autonomy in its actions throughout the West Bank, with limited intervention from the military government. The reason for this is the OPEN BRIDGES policy, on the one hand, and the failure of the military government to impose its will on the Supreme Muslim Council, on the other.

The influence of Palestinian nationalism on the policies of the Supreme Muslim Council is also limited. The preachers in the mosques, who wield enormous influence on public opinion in the West Bank, are generally careful not to be drawn into giving extremist nationalist sermons. On the other hand, the members of the Supreme Muslim Council emphatically refrain from any contact with members of the CIVILIAN ADMINISTRATION. They are willing to meet only with military personnel, claiming that if they did not maintain contact with the latter, their lives would be endangered.

The situation in the Gaza Strip is otherwise. Because of its isolation from the Muslim religious establishment in Egypt, the Muslim council there is forced to maintain stable links with the civilian administration of the Gaza Strip.

The Christian minority is divided among a large number of churches. The church with the highest membership is the Greek Orthodox, with the Latins following in second place. The other churches are numerically small: the Greek Catholics, Armenians, Syrian Catholics, Ethiopians, Anglicans, Lutherans, and Copts. Patriarch Theodorus I, the head of the Greek Orthodox Church in Jerusalem, is also head of the church in Jordan. Within the community there is tension between the senior priesthood, largely Greek, and their faithful, who are mostly Arabs. The Arabs seek a greater say in administration of the church, communal affairs, and education and are dissatisfied with the minor role accorded to them. Most of the holy places on the West Bank belong to the Greek Orthodox Church. Its predominance is based on possession of most of the space within the principal holy places such as the Church of the Holy Sepulchre.

The head of the Roman Catholic Church is the Latin Patriarch Beltritti. Since a large number of Arabs occupy important positions in the church, there is less internal tension. The Anglican and Lutheran Churches have solved the leadership problem differently. An Arab bishop was placed at the head of the Arab Lutheran Church and the Anglican Church.

The Christian community is concentrated in the Jerusalem area, in Nablus, around Bethlehem, in Ramallah and in the Jenin area. A large number have migrated, particularly to South America but also to Western Europe.

The relation of the Christian religious establishment to Israel is not uniform, but in general it is not hostile. In contrast with the Latins, who tend to be more involved with the national problem, the Greek Orthodox are careful to avoid political involvement.

The total world population of Samaritans is around 550, half living in Nablus, the other half in Holon, in Israel. The former are Jordanian citizens; their children study in the public elementary schools in Nablus, though they have separate religion classes. A high priest functions as their spiritual head and their civil affairs are handled through various committees.

REVIEW BOARDS

In November 1967, the regional commander issued Order 172 according to which one or more review boards were established to hear appeals of decisions made by the military or civilian administration. According to INTERNATIONAL LAW, civilian courts do not have authority over a military government. International law also stipulates that a military administration is required to compensate the inhabitants for damages caused to them only on the signing of agreements terminating the occupation.

Nevertheless, the review boards were established in order to enable the inhabitants to sue the administration. They are manned by military personnel, chaired by a lawyer, and the order states: "The members of the board are subject to no authority except that of the law or the SECURITY ENACTMENTS, and they are not subject to the authority of a commanding officer." The powers delegated to the review boards cover absentee lands, government lands, and matters of taxation and bureaucracy. They also have the power to review decisions regarding compulsory purchase of land for public use and the expropriation of water rights. Since 1980 the review boards have also heard most of the appeals of the residents of the territories against seizure of land for Jewish settlement. The procedures constitute a violation of due process of law: the stronger party, the military government, is represented by military attorneys who are provided with maps and aerial photographs. The civilian plaintiff lacks documents attesting to his ownership of the land. He is called upon to prove that it is all either cultivated or arable, otherwise part of it may be expropriated. Finally, even if the board does grant the appeal, its decision merely has the status of a recommendation.

The review boards have not helped the residents of the territories. They have become a tool in the hands of the military government for attaining their goals in expropriating land. The residents of the West Bank would appear to have another judicial recourse, the HIGH COURT OF JUSTICE. However, that body has limited itself to considering the procedures of the review boards and does not generally review the facts of the cases. Therefore some argue that the review boards were established to bar the inhabitants from appealing to the High Court of Justice.

ROADS

In 1976, the total length of the West Bank road system was 1,400 kilometers, 93 percent of them paved. The system resembled a fish skeleton – the watershed road serving as the major axis, with access roads branching off it to the east and west. After the 1948 war the branch roads leading from the coastal plain fell into disrepair, having become dead ends.

The Jordanians engaged in local road construction for the use of Jordanian army roads, and repaved the Jerusalem – Jordan bridges – Amman roads. In the 1950s the Jordanians realigned the road system on the East Bank into a north-south axis (Aqaba-Amman–Irbid-Damascus), in place of the east-west axis from the Palestinian coastal cities. As a result the local nature of the West Bank roads became even more pronounced.

Under Israeli rule, West Bank road alignment changed in conformity with the geostrategic conceptions of the different governments.

In the years 1967-77, when the conceptions of the Labor Party prevailed, roads were planned on a north-south axis (See ALLON PLAN, DEFENSE STRATEGY). Labor did not plan east-west roads crossing the West Bank, not wishing to create a complete integration with the Israeli system. This period saw the completion of the Jordan Valley, Dead Sea and Allon roads.

By the mid-1970s planning began on the Trans-Samarian road mainly for military purposes – to facilitate rapid travel from the coastal plan to the defensive line on the Jordan Valley. With the Likud in power, the linear orientation (north-south) was abandoned, and was replaced by a system based on east-west axes. Its goal was to bring about a complete integration of the West Bank and Israeli systems and promote Jewish settlement in all parts of the West Bank.

A new road master plan (1983-84) established priorities for paving of roads defined as follows: "development of high-demand areas by creating accessibility to settlement areas, bypassing Arab settlements, and development of new settlement areas."

Special emphasis was placed on paving convenient roads from new settlements located in the metropolitan areas of Jerusalem and Tel Aviv to the city centers. This was because commuting, on which most of these bedroom communities are predicated, calls for rapid access to places of work and entertainment in the cities.

The Road Master Plan (No. 50) calls for construction of 1,000 kilometers of roads necessitating land expropriation on a very large scale. This road system is not intended to serve Arab settlements and, indeed, is characterized by its avoidance of them. In practice, two parallel road systems have been created on the West Bank, one for Israeli use and other other, in existence prior to 1967, and with certain improvements, for Palestinian use.

ROGERS PLAN

An American plan for peace in the Middle East, first presented by Secretary of State William Rogers on December 9, 1969. Much of it refers to the international situation prevailing at the end of the 1960s and Israeli-Egyptian relations and thus is no longer relevant. Regarding the West Bank and East Jerusalem the plan states that changes in the 1949 armistice line need not reflect the Israeli occupation after 1967 and must be limited to minor rectifications as required for mutual security. It further states that lasting peace cannot be achieved without a solution of the problem of the Palestinian refugees who became homeless after the wars of 1948 and 1967. A just solution must consider the hopes and aspirations of the refugees as well as the legitimate problems of the states of the region. The United States will not agree to unilateral action regarding Jerusalem. Any solution to the problem of Jerusalem must be reached through negotiations and agreement between the parties, especially between Jordan and Israel, while considering the interests of other states and the international community.

The plan was viewed in Israel as hostile and was rejected by the Israeli government. The attitude of the United States towards Jerusalem spurred the government of Israel to begin expropriating lands and building large neighborhoods across the green line (1970): Gilo, Ramot, and East Talpiot.

SECURITY ENACTMENTS

The term security enactments refers to the military government's legislation in the occupied territory. Over the years, this legislation has expanded beyond security matters into economic and social spheres. According to international law, the commander of the area replaces the sovereign authority in the region, and the orders issued by him have equal legal standing with primary legislation (such as Jordanian laws). In an order issued in 1967 shortly after the occupation began, it was declared that "security enactments take precedence over all law, even if they do not explicitly repeal it," and that "all legislative powers will reside exclusively with the military government."

Regulation 43 of the HAGUE Convention forbids a government to alter existing legislation in occupied territories unless it is "absolutely impossible" to abide by it. The Israeli High Court of Justice has, however, recognized the economic constraints of a protracted occupation, and ruled that the necessity of maintaining "normal life" (and not only security needs) may also justify changes in existing law through legislation by the military government.

In this way, the High Court provided a legal basis for fundamental change in every aspect of West Bank legislation (See CREEPING ANNEXATION).

The military governor is the executive, legislative, and judicial authority. International law sanctions this power, but sees it as a temporary measure for a short period of occupation. When a government has this kind of autocratic power, in contravention of the rule of law and accepted standards of justice, and exercises it over a long period, the situation soon becomes intolerable.

Moreover, the security enactments, which encompass all facets of life on the West Bank and in the Gaza Strip, are not subject to public review other than that of the minister of defense. Even the High Court's powers of judicial review are extremely limited. As a result, the military governor may enact primary and secondary legislation without checks and balances, carry it out by virtue of his executive authority, and even subject it to his own judicial review, since judicial powers also lie in his hands. In the absence of any binding norms (since the GENEVA CONVENTION is not recognized by Israel), the rule of law in the territories becomes rule by decree. The absolute powers of the military governor allow him to turn the security enactments, by definition temporary, into permanent legislation, side by side with the previously existing law in the region (Jordanian or previous legislation).

During the years the military government has been in existence, more than 1,500 orders and amendments have been issued, divided by subject as follows: agriculture – 29; banks – 14, business – 66; commerce – 48; currency – 55; education – 26; censorship and freedom of expression – 14; health – 20; institutions (including Israeli institutions and municipalities) – 173; insurance – 16; judiciary – 197; land – 97, legislation – 24; public order – 239; security – 304; taxes – 85; traffic – 96; a total of 1,503 legislative acts (including repeals).

SPORTS AND CULTURAL CLUBS (ARAB)

Numerous youth clubs primarily concerned with sports and cultural activity operate on the West Bank. Soccer is the most popular of the sports offered. The clubs also sponsor various social activities. Since 1967, a new phenomenon has been in evidence – emphasis on Palestinian national identity through annual exhibitions of materials with political themes, including paintings, books, posters, embroidery, and other handicrafts. The League of Clubs on the West Bank coordinates and supervises the activities of the clubs.

The following is a listing of West Bank clubs:

Jerusalem Area

Name of Club	Year Founded	Number of Members
Ahli Silwan	1978	200
Al-Muwazafin (The Clerks)	1955	1,558
Jabal al-Mukkabir	1976	876
Sur Bahir	1978	319
al-Katolik	1934	250
al-Itihad al-Ortodoks al-Arabi	1942	400
Silwan Sports Club	1965	600
al-Hillal al-Maqdisi	1972	1,000
al-Kharijin al-'Arab	1966	570
Ahli Shu'afat	1973	1,400

Nablus Area

Kashafat Hattin	1959	250
Salfit a-Riadi	1974	225

Tulkarm Area

Tulkarm al-Riadi al-Thaqafi	1970	616
Kalkilya al-Ahli	1977	241

Hebron Area

Young Women of Hebron	1980	720
Ahli al-Halil	1974	270
Tareq ben Zayd	1977	400
Shabab al-Khalil	1943	1,200
Shabab ad-Dahariya	1974	1,080

Bethlehem-Jericho Area

Hillal Ariha	1974	500
al-Ortodoksi al-'Arab/Beit Sahur	1963	642
a-Shabab a-Thaqafi/Beit Sahur	1949	200
a-Siriani al-Ortodoksi/Bethlehem	1949	365
al-Salami a-Riadi	1965	250

Jenin Area

Jenin a-Riadi	1972	235

STAFF OFFICERS

"Civilian staff officer" is a generic term for a group of Israeli civil servants "on loan" to the MILITARY GOVERNMENT and its CIVILIAN ADMINISTRATION, who carry out professional tasks for the civilian authorities. Staff officers work in their own area of expertise, under the authority of their ministries. The military government has appointed more than 30 staff officers to the following areas: interior, justice, electricity, telecommunications, religious affairs, mail, water, health, education, welfare, housing, abandoned and government properties, surveying, assessment, road construction, archeology, national parks, nature reserves, land registry, agriculture, finance, legal counsel, administration, comptroller's office, spokesman's office, transportation, duties and taxation, employment, statistics, fuel, and insurance.

The staff officers operate in the territories under authority granted them by order of the military government. These powers are both legislative and executive according to both Jordanian law and the SECURITY ENACTMENTS. The staff officers exercise the authority of the Jordanian crown, cabinet, judicial system, statutory authorities, and have supervisory authority over statutory and other bodies, including the power to enact by-laws. In Israeli usage, the staff officers are described as holding the same status as directors-general in their respective branches, similar to heads of Israeli ministries. While they may appear to derive their authority from the military government and operate independently of the Israeli system, staff officers are, in fact, directly subordinate to their ministries and receive instructions straight from ministry heads, including political directives from the ministers themselves. The basis for this unmediated connection to the Israeli system may be found in a government decision of October 1968, according to which "civilian activity in the occupied area will be carried out by the appropriate government ministries, each in its own area of authority and fiscal responsibility. Representatives of the ministries (the staff officers) will act in coordination with the commander of the IDF forces in the area, with regard to the local population." The double chain of command both from the military government and the Israeli government system, and the fact that staff officers act on the authority of specific ministries, creates confusion regarding authorization of their activities. The institution of staff officers and the way it works can only be interpreted as *de facto* annexation (See CREEPING ANNEXATION).

STANDARD OF LIVING

Standard of living, as measured by the Gross National Product per capita, private consumption per capita, or other measures such as nutritional value of diet, ownership of appliances, motorization rate, density of housing, or quality of services, all showed marked improvement until 1981.

The GNP per capita grew at an annual rate of 12 percent until the mid 1970s, and at 5 percent until the beginning of the 1980s. In 1982, GNP per capita was $1,400, triple the rate in 1968, and private consumption per capita on the West Bank was $1,200. Since then private consumption per capita has shown no change. The standard of living of Palestinians in the West Bank remained relatively high, but at the same time lower than the Israeli standard of living by a ratio of 1:4.

Other indicators have shown the same trend. The caloric value of the West bank diet was 2,861 (per capita/diem) in 1984; 2,854 in 1983; in 1970, it was 2,344 calories. The caloric value of the West Bank diet is higher than in Jordan and Syria, and lower than in Israel (3,069 calories per capita per diem, 197 grams of protein, and 119 grams of fats in 1982).

Ownership of appliances on the West Bank in 1985 was as follows: in urban areas, 94 percent of families owned an electric refrigerator; 97 percent, a television set; 75 percent, a washing machine; 63 percent, a solar water heater. In rural areas, 55 percent owned an electric refrigerator; 23 percent, a washing machine; 72 percent, a television; and 35 percent, a solar water heater. In 1967, 5 percent of all households owned a refrigerator and 2 percent, a television. By 1972, 14 percent owned a refrigerator and 10 percent, a television. The number of private cars has grown from 1,626 in 1970 to 29,787 in 1984. The percentage of urban families with private cars has reached 18 percent.

For housing density, see CONSTRUCTION, also EDUCATION, ELECTRICITY, WATER.

The rise in the standard of living was made possible for the most part by the employment of West Bank workers in Israel, and to a lesser extent by unilateral transfers of savings by West Bank workers in Arab countries – indicated by the rapid growth in GNP (triple) as against the more moderate growth in the Gross Domestic Product (See NATIONAL ACCOUNTS). The relative prosperity attained is based on total dependence on external factors, over which West Bankers have no control.

STUDENT COUNCILS (PALESTINIAN)

Elected annually in each university. Three main blocs participate: FATAH, leftist organizations, and the Muslim fundamentalists. Supporters of Jordan do not take part in the elections for the student councils. In most cases in recent years (1980-84), FATAH supporters have formed coalitions with leftist organizations. These coalitions later disintegrated during the internal struggle within P.L.O. preceding the seventh congress in Amman (late 1984). Towards the beginning of the 1984-85 academic year elections in most of the Arab universities were postponed except in Hebron, where the Muslim bloc won, owing to the split between the FATAH and leftist opposition which had controlled the Hebron student council in 1984.

In both Bir-Zeit and an-Najah the student councils were led by a coalition of FATAH and the left in 1984. In Bethlehem the students were led by leftists (supporters of George Habash, Naif Hawatmah, and the Communists).

The results of student councils elections in 1985 were: Bir Zeit, FATAH 38%, Left (REJECTION FRONT) 36%, FUNDAMENTALISTS 26%; al Najah, Fatah 50%, Left 13%, Fundamentalists 37%; Hebron, Fatah 50%, Left 7%, Fundamentalists 44%; Bethlehem, Fatah 44%, Left 44%, Fundamentalists 12%.

SUMUD

Sumud is the Arabic term denoting steadfast clinging to the soil of the homeland. At the Palestine National Council congress in Algiers in February 1983, it was resolved that "the council affirms the need to redouble the efforts of the residents of the territories to become closer to the land, in order to bring forced emigration to an end and to protect the land and the national economy." The PLO and Jordan realized that Israeli settlements, constraints on productive elements on the West Bank, the lack of credit, scarcity of housing, and military government repression could lead to mass emigration from the territories. In order to combat annexation, the Arab summit conference in Baghdad set up a JOINT COMMITTEE (JORDAN-PLO), charged with the management and transfer of aid funds to the residents of the West Bank and Gaza Strip. In 1983 it was also decided to make available to "the Palestinians in the conquered territories" – i.e. Israeli Arabs – "all the means with which to continue their national struggle." The annual budget granted to the Joint Committee for the "Steadfastness Aid Fund" was $150 million.

The Joint Committee distributes funds to local authorities, trade unions, private citizens, universities, newspapers, and cooperatives. Unemployment allowances are paid to university graduates, government workers, lawyers, and the retired. Large sums are set aside for housing aid. Every landowner in possession of a building permit (Israeli in Jerusalem, municipal-Arab or military government in the West Bank) is entitled to an interest-free loan of 7,000 dinars. In addition, promoters of industrial and commercial concerns receive investment aid. The pattern of Sumud fund distribution has aroused criticism in the West Bank.

The Israeli government did not interfere with the transfer of funds until 1982, though it was clear that Jordan and the PLO were acquiring considerable political influence on the West Bank. This hands-off attitude was partly the result of economic considerations. Cessation of transfers would have meant loss of foreign currency revenues and would have required the military government to come up with alternative development funds. In 1982, with the establishment of the civilian administration and the battle against PLO influence, an order was issued banning the transfer of Sumud funds to the region, and another order established a development fund. According to these orders, transfer of funds from abroad without permit was banned. The transfer of "enemy funds"– i.e. funds of the Joint Committee – was permitted only through the "Regional Development Fund" managed by the military government.

As a result of these measures the transfer of funds to institutions and bodies under governmental supervision diminished considerably, and the government was forced to provide development funds from its own budget (See PUBLIC CONSUMPTION AND INVESTMENT.) Housing aid funds and employment allowances, however, continued to reach the territories through other channels.

In 1984, with the change in MILITARY GOVERNMENT policy, there was a liberalization of the attitude to the transfer of Sumud funds. In the meantime, however, the grants of the "Steadfastness Aid Fund" had diminished following the failure of several Arab oil-producing countries to meet their obligations.

Official sources in Amman disclosed (September 1985) that $435 million were distributed since 1980 on the West Bank and Gaza by the joint fund, or $87 million a year.

SUPREME MUSLIM COUNCIL

The body which managed Muslim affairs in Mandatory Palestine. It was founded in 1922, and Haj Amin al-Husseini, the Mufti of Jerusalem, was placed at its head. In the prevailing circumstances, the council assumed the political leadership of the Palestinian Arabs. Opposition to the council was centered around the Nashashibi family and the two camps were called al-Majlisin (supporters of the council – the Majlis) led by the al-Husseini family and al-Mu'arada (the opposition), led by the Nashashibis. The British disbanded the Muslim Council in 1937 and dismissed its members, holding it responsible for the Arab Revolt of 1936-37. From 1937-1948, the council was made up of appointees and ceased being a political body. After the Jordanian occupation, the council was dissolved and its authority transferred to the Waqf ministry in Amman.

With Israeli occupation the council was re-activated and now, in addition to its religious functions, provides a framework for various political forces on the West Bank and Jerusalem, including members known for their Communist party sympathies.

The council is responsible for managing the WAQF and for the Shar'i court system (See COURTS (MUSLIM RELIGIOUS)) in Jerusalem and on the West Bank.

The council is not officially recognized by the Israeli authorities; nevertheless, it functions without interference (See also RELIGIOUS COMMUNITIES).

TAXATION AND REVENUES

Both direct and indirect taxes are levied on the West Bank. The indirect taxes are: import duties, excises on local products, supplementary excises (VAT), levies on goods in inventory, fuel, and stamp taxes on documents and exit permits. All the indirect taxes, with the exception of stamp tax, are imposed and collected according to Israeli laws and regulations applied in the territories by military orders. The indirect taxes on local production are identical to Israeli purchase and value added taxes. The rates vary by order of the military government simultaneously with rates changes in Israel. Only stamp tax is collected according to Jordanian practice.

Revenues and income from indirect taxes in 1983 were as follows:

Supplementary excise tax (VAT)	40.2 percent
Excise tax	26.2 percent
Import duties	6.2 percent
Stamp tax	27.4 percent
	100.00 percent

The direct taxes are: income tax, municipal property tax, business tax, and rural property tax. These taxes are based on Jordanian legislation, with some revisions in the rates. Prime importance is attached to income tax since these monies go directly to the military government while property tax goes, for the most part, to the municipalities. Priority given to income tax is also evident in the fact that all West Bank tax collection offices are managed by Israelis, under whom are Palestinian employees. A considerable portion of West Bank income from tax revenues is collected from MILITARY GOVERNMENT employees, for whom the tax is deducted at source. This amounted to some 40 percent of the total income tax collected in 1983, an indication of a high rate of tax avoidance. According to an estimate by the STAFF OFFICER for taxes, tax collection from the self-employed on the West Bank stood at about 15 percent of its real potential in 1983.

In 1983 revenues from direct taxation were distributed as follows: income tax – 74 percent; municipal property tax – 22 percent; business tax – 2.9 percent; village property tax – 1 percent. The relative importance of direct and indirect taxation on the West Bank has changed during the occupation, as shown in the following table:

Taxes and Revenues on the West Bank, selected years:

Type	1966	1972	1983
Direct Taxes	12.8	8.2	28.0
Indirect Taxes	78.6	81.3	72.0
Other	8.6	10.5	–
Total	100.0	100.0	100.0

In 1982 total taxes and levies collected on the West Bank came to $62.5 million ($58.3 million by the military government and the rest by the local authorities). In 1982, taxation came to 7.3 percent of the Gross Domestic Product, and in 1983 to 7.6 percent as against 9.3 percent in 1972. The local tax burden has therefore not increased. In calculating taxes, however, it must be taken into account that in 1982, laborers from the territories working in Israel paid income tax and national insurance amounting to $31.2 million, including employers' contributions. West Bank residents also paid import duties and taxes on goods brought into Israel (See FISCAL BURDEN).

TAXATION OF ISRAELIS

Amendments to Israeli income tax law (1978, 1980) state that the income of an Israeli citizen (originating from or received in the territories) is considered as if its source were in Israel or as if received in Israel. A portion of the profits of a company based in the territories with Israeli citizens among its shareholders is liable to Israeli income tax in an amount proportionate to the number of Israeli citizens among its shareholders. Tax paid by an Israeli citizen to the authorities in the territories is credited to his Israeli income tax. Israeli citizens resident in the territories are entitled to a 7 percent reduction in income tax by definition as residents of a development town. In addition, there is no purchase tax on apartments on the West Bank. Legally, the territories cannot serve as a tax shelter for Israeli citizens, neither for the self-employed, nor for corporations (even if the corporation is registered and operates in the territories), nor for wage-earners.

Despite this, the West Bank functions as a convenient tax haven. A business controlled and managed in the territories by non-citizens of Israel is not liable for Israeli income tax. In other words, tourists, temporary and "permanent" residents who do not have citizenship are not required to pay taxes. Wage-earners resident in the territories but not Israeli citizens are not liable for taxes on income received for work in the territories. An Israeli employing residents of the territories who are not Israeli citizens does not have to deduct tax at source on the income they receive from him, since they are not required to pay Israeli income tax. Employing local workers in West Bank Israeli factories is considerably cheaper than employing Israelis since there is no need to pay payroll taxes or national insurance. Companies registered and operating in the territories, not controlled by Israelis and whose shareholders are not Israeli citizens, are not liable for Israeli income tax.

There is some doubt as to whether a dividend paid to an Israeli resident by a local company is liable for Israeli income tax if paid abroad. If paid in the territories, it is taxed at a maximum rate of 25 percent, while if paid in Israel, it is taxed at a maximum rate of 45 percent.

No clear definition lays down when a company is to be considered "resident in the region," but it is quite likely that the income of an Israeli citizen from a company registered abroad, under foreign control, and operating in the territories, is not liable for taxes since the company's income is not liable. The major tax haven lies, however, in the inability of the tax authorities to gather information on the economic activity of Israeli residents of the territories. It is doubtful whether they can even require Israeli citizens living on the West Bank to submit annual tax returns. It is therefore hardly surprising that dozens of Israeli companies have registered with the registrar of companies on the West Bank.

TEHIYA PARTY

A political movement founded in 1979 following the CAMP DAVID ACCORDS, on the initiative of Knesset members Geula Cohen and Moshe Shamir, who had split from the Likud. Before the 1984 elections, Rafael Eitan's Tsomet movement joined, forming the Tehiya-Tsomet movement. Its platform is as follows:

– The Israeli nation has an eternal and inalienable right to all of Eretz Israel.

– This right should be exercised by the establishment of Israeli sovereignty over Judea, Samaria, and the Gaza Strip, and all the historic sites in Jerusalem (i.e., the Temple Mount).

– The Arab minority on the West Bank, living under Israeli sovereignty, and holding Jordanian citizenship, will be given the option of being permanent residents of the State of Israel with equal rights and responsibilities other than military service and the right to vote. They will remain Jordanian citizens with the right to vote in their country's elections.

– To actualize Israeli sovereignty, there must be widespread settlement, especially in Judea and Samaria, in order to block the establishment of a Palestinian state.

TERRITORIAL DEFENSE

Most West Bank settlements are defined as "border settlements" (or in army nomenclature, "confrontation settlements"). As such, they are organized within the framework of the Territorial Defense Unit of the IDF. That framework is not limited to the self-defense of isolated and distant settlements. As the network of settlements became increasingly dense, the emphasis was transferred from the perimeter of the individual settlement to cultivated fields, communications between settlements, and the guarding of economic and community facilities. The settlements are clustered into "forward sections" with a combined command in the rear.

The units of the Territorial Defense are supposed to delay the potential enemy until the arrival of army units (either regular forces or reserve forces) from further away. Every settlement has an allotted number of fit combatants including two officers. The combatants come from infantry, armored, artillery or combat engineering units, but do not have other specialized military occupations. The soldiers of the Territorial Defense Units in the "confrontation settlements" are considered to be quality reserve forces who know the combat area well and are highly motivated to defend their own homes. These soldiers and their officers frequently object to being transferred from their old units to Territorial Defense Units. In disagreements between those officers and the commander of the Territorial Defense in the IDF (who is also responsible for civil defense), the chief of staff has found it necessary to make a final decision. During Rafael Eitan's term as chief of staff, preference was given to the Territorial Defense.

The units of the Territorial Defense are organized in regional "hedgehogs" which defend strategic areas and possible avenues of attack. Most of the forces of the Regional Defense from each settlement are concentrated in the "hedgehogs," while within the borders of the settlement, for contiguous defense and to allow for the maintenance of economic activities, an officer and a small number of soldiers are stationed. Every unit of the Territorial Defense has a mobile force equipped with armored personnel carriers. The mobile force is composed of combatants assembled from three settlements in order not to bring together the residents of a single settlement in a framework in which serious casualties could destroy an entire settlement.

Reserve soldiers within the Territorial Defense are prepared for mobilization at very short notice, including by telephone, and for rapid access to their posts, weapons and ammunition. They keep their personal weapons with them (like all reserve officers and many soldiers, if they so wish) – while in the settlement armories heavier arms are stored for use on the platoon level.

Settlements in the area which are located in the midst of hostile populations are also organized in the Territorial Defense, but urban settlements whose residents work (and frequently sleep) outside the borders of the settlement find it more difficult to allocate the necessary military manpower and call up reserve soldiers in the case of a sudden alert. In these settlements, as in the agricultural settlements, the weapons are intended for defense of those to whom they are issued, not to protect their presence on the West Bank.

In settlements where few members have done national service, the burden of guard duty falls on reserve soldiers brought to the settlements for that purpose. Since there are considerable numbers of small settlements (see DEMOGRAPHY (ISRAELI)), the added security burden they present far outweighs any strategic advantage.

The extreme ideological outlook shared by the settlers and their relative independence, subject to their own local military commanders, have led to excesses. Groups of settlers have retaliated violently or gone on the rampage following Palestinian terrorist attacks. The infrastructure and material at their disposal have served them in several illegal operations including some directed against official government decisions. The findings of the KARP COMMITTEE and the emergence of the Jewish underground should be seen in this context.

TOPOGRAPHY, FLORA

The inclusive area of the West Bank is 5.8 million square kilometers (about one-quarter of Mandatory Palestine), including 5.5 million dunams of land area and 300,000 dunams of the Dead Sea surface. This region divides into a number of sub-areas. The major ones are as follows:

Mt. Hebron – an elongated mountainous bloc, length about 45 kilometers and width about 20 kilometers. The mountain plateau is moderately inclined; its width expands from Bethlehem in the north (four kilometers) to Hebron in the south (20 kilometers). South of Hebron the plateau bifurcates eastwards (Yata area) and westwards (Dahariya area). The elevation of the Hebron mountains is between 700 and 1,000 meters, but high points do not tower over their surroundings. The Mt. Hebron bloc is bounded on the east by the desert threshold and the Judean Desert, and its eastern slopes descend precipitously to the Syrian-African rift. To the west extends the Judean high foothills (shephela), 300-600 meters above sea level.

Jerusalem mountains – from north of the Mt. Hebron-Bethlehem bloc extends a saddle whose western part is lower and its eastern (the Mt. of Olives-Mt. Scopus ridge) higher. Its spine is narrow and from it descend deep, dry wadis westwards and eastwards. A moderately inclined plateau extends northwards, and beyond it the Beit-El-Ba'al Hatsor anticline, more than 1,000 meters above sea level, marking the border between Judea and Samaria.

Mt. Samaria – is composed of hills divided by a number of wide valleys running in both east-west and north-south directions. Its central section, the Nablus mountains, is high (800 meters above sea level) and its northern part – the Jenin hills – lower and hilly (300-400 meters). Mt. Samaria descends gradually westwards to the coastal plain and northwards to the Ta'anakh valley.

In the eastern West Bank, the Jordan and Dead Sea Valleys extend north and south, forming part of the Syrian-African rift. In the northern West Bank this valley is 200 meters below sea level and in the south, at the Dead Sea's edge, it is 400 meters below sea level.

The West Bank's land may be classified in four categories, according to quality. Some 1.5 million dunams are desert and rocky ground, unfit for cultivation. Some 1.75 million dunams are suitable for grazing. About 250,000 dunams are natural forest and two million dunams are suitable for cultivation. This arable area divides into four main types: 1. deep soil with a gradient of 4-15 percent, about 150,000 dunams; 2. deep soil with a gradient of up to 45 percent, about half a million dunams; 3. soil of moderate depth, with a gradient of more than 15 percent and with high pebble content, about 450,000 dunams; 4. mountainous areas with thin topsoil and high rock content, suitable for olive groves and vineyards, about 900,000 dunams. Most land suitable for intensive cultivation (types 1-3) is in the north and central region. West Bank rainfall varies between 600-800 millimeters on the massif, 500-600 mm on the western slopes, 250-400 mm on the desert threshold in the east, and 200 mm in the Jordan Valley. The natural flora are the remnants of the natural forest, mostly low-lying, though with a small percentage of taller trees. The typical components of the forest are the common oak and the Palestinian terebinth, but the carob and gum terebinth are also common. Where the forest has been destroyed, Mediterranean undergrowth, mostly *sarcopoterium spinosum, calycotome villosa* and *salvia* has replaced it. In the Jerusalem-Ramallah area, the Jerusalem pine is also common. The area is very rich in natural and landscape assets.

From the point of view of administration (See ISRAELI REGIONAL COUNCILS), the West Bank is divided into seven administrative sub-districts: Hebron (1,050 square kilometers); Bethlehem (850 square kilometers); Ramallah (770 square kilometers); Nablus (1,590 square kilometers); Tulkarm (330 square kilometers); Jenin (330 square kilometers); and the Jordan sub-district (340 square kilometers).

TOSHAVA (SETTLEMENT TYPE)

A suburban settlement serving as a "bedroom community" for its residents. Though it provides few services it is close – within 30 minutes' traveling time – to a major metropolitan area (Tel Aviv or Jerusalem). Its planned population varies from 500 to 2,000 families or 2,500-8,000 residents and it occupies 2,000-5,000 dunams.

The settlements are constructed under the BUILD YOUR OWN HOME scheme. The government contributes to infrastructure, investment, mortgages and INCENTIVES, and the settlements are built by private developers. The term itself is without significance, since on different lists the same settlement appears as KIRIYA, town or toshava. See also LAND ACQUISITION.

UNITED KIBBUTZ MOVEMENT (TAKAM)

A movement created by the merger of the two largest kibbutz movements, Ha'Kibbutz Ha'Meuhad and Ihud Ha'Kvutsot veHa'Kibbutzim in 1979. The movement regards itself as independent and formulates its own political line.

The kibbutz movement's view of settlement on the West Bank is as follows: settlements must be in the barren security zones of the Jordan Valley, the Etzion bloc, the Judean Desert, and the Gaza Strip. The movement supports the implementation of autonomy in Judea, Samaria, and Gaza, except for the aforementioned security zones, on condition that Israel has full control of those zones and the settlement areas in them, and that they have territorial contiguity with Israel.

The movement considers that a solution to the Palestinian problem will be achieved through a peace agreement with Jordan, through which a Jordanian-Palestinian state will be created. The movement rejects in principle the Gush Emunim policy of settlement in densely populated areas. The kibbutz movement has affiliations to the following youth movements: Mahanot Ha'Olim, Hanoar Ha'Oved veHaLomed and the Scouts.

Takam Settlements on the West Bank:

Name (year of founding)	Region	No. of People (Sept. 1985)
Gilgal (1973)	Jordan Valley	142
Yitav (1976)	Jordan Valley	42
Almog (1981)	Jordan Valley	103
Na'aran (1975)	Jordan Valley	143
Har Musa (in formation)	Hebron Hills	
Mitzpeh Shalem (1977)	Jordan Valley	118
Kalya (1968)	Jordan Valley	122

UNIVERSITIES

There are five accredited degree-granting universities on the West Bank: an-Najah University in Nablus, Bir-Zeit University, Bethlehem University, the Islamic College in Hebron (Hebron University) and Jerusalem University (comprising three separate colleges – the Abu-Dis College of Science, the Nursing College in al-Bira, and the Religious College in Beit Hanina). There are also seven teachers' colleges: two run by UNRWA, a men's college in Ramallah and a women's in a-Tira; and three under government management, Kaduri Teachers' College in Tulkarm, a men's college in al-Arub and a women's college in Ramallah. In addition, there are two commercial colleges, a-Rawda in Nablus, and the Modern College in Ramallah; the Polytechnic Institute in Hebron (offering civil, structural, construction, and electrical engineering); the Shar'ai Institute in Kalkilya, and a further 10 junior and teachers' colleges.

The senior university Bir-Zeit was founded as a two-year teachers' college and incorporated as a university in 1972 (the first degrees were granted in 1973). Student body (1984) – approximately 2,500. Instructors – 193, in the faculties of humanities, economics, sciences, and engineering. Owned by a "charitable organization" run by a 10-member board of trustees. Tuition – 150 dinars for undergraduates, 200 dinars for the masters program. Research institutes operate in association with the university. Degrees granted – B.A., M.A., diploma in education.

The largest university (in terms of its student body) is an-Najah University in Nablus. Founded in 1945 as a high school, in 1963 it became a commercial college and teachers' college, and in 1977 a university. Student body (1984) – 3,450. Instructors – 197. Faculties – humanities, natural sciences, economics and business, engineering, education. Degrees granted – B.A. and teaching certificate. Managed by a 12-member board of trustees.Tuition (1984) – 161 dinars.

Bethlehem University was founded in 1973. Student body (1984) – 1,500. Instructors – 24.Faculties – humanities, business, administration, nursing, and post-secondary courses in hotel management, early childhood education, and sanitary inspection. The university is owned by the La Salle Brothers order and managed by a A14-member board of trustees. Degrees granted – B.A. and diplomas in the post-secondary courses. Tuition – 120 dinars (1984).

Hebron University was founded in 1971 as an Islamic seminary, becoming a university in 1980. Student body (1984) – 1,725. Instructors – 60. Faculties – Islamic studies and humanities.Run by a nine-member board of trustees. Degrees granted – B.A. Tuition (1984) – 120 dinars.

Jerusalem University: The Abu-Dis College of Science, opened in 1982. Student body (1984) – 300. Instructors – 69.Faculties – sciences, mathematics, physics and chemistry, sociology, and computers. Managed by an 18-member board of trustees.Degrees granted – B.A. Tuition – 25 dinars per semester.

The religious college in Beit Hanina, opened in 1978. Student body (1984) – 310. Instructors – 16. Faculties – Islamic law and Arabic language. Managed by a seven-member board of trustees. Degrees granted – B.A. Tuition – 25 dinars first year, 20 dinars second and third years.

The School of Nursing in al-Bira, founded in 1979. Student body – 140. Instructors – 30. Faculties – public health and nursing. Degrees granted – B.A. Tuition – free.

The universities on the West Bank (and in the Gaza Strip) established a Council of Higher Education, charged with coordinating the activities of the universities to prevent unnecessary duplication and establishing criteria for academic accreditation and degree-granting authority. The council is not recognized by the Israeli administration and its activities are frequently disrupted by infighting and conflicts of interest.

Up till the Six Day War, there were no academic institutions in the territories of any kind. The military government approved the establishment of the universities, although Jordanian Education Law No. 16 (1964) does not apply to universities. Relations between the military government and the universities were tense from the start. This stemmed from the military government view of the universities as hotbeds of subversion in academic guise. The universities, particularly the students, regard their purpose as the training of a cadre of leaders and intelligentsia for the Palestinian state of the future. The Israeli view of all forms of political expression as subversive activity aimed at the destruction of Israel, and the Palestinian view of Israel as an occupying power and illegitimate ruler, made the clash inevitable. The military government's reaction to political activity and "disturbance of the peace" in the universities, was to close them down. The closures were executed in accordance with the SECURITY ENACTMENTS in two ways: instructing the university administration to cease all teaching and research activity, and declaring the university campus a "closed area." with a ban on entry and exit. Since 1979 some of the universities have been closed for lengthy periods(an-Najah University for four months, Bir-Zeit for three months) and their campuses declared closed areas.

Until 1980 the military government lacked a legal framework for dealing with the universities. At the end of 1980 Order 854 was issued. This granted wide and exceptional authority to the "responsible authority" particularly in the following areas: licensing of academic institutions, licensing of staff in academic institutions, supervision of curriculum and textbooks in academic institutions. In addition, it gave the military government the authority to revoke or refuse to grant a teaching permit to persons convicted of a breach of security regulations, or those who had been in administrative detention. One of the factors taken into account in granting a permit for an academic institution is "considerations of public order." The paragraph in Jordanian Education Law No. 16, according to which teachers are prohibited from joining political parties, allowed the military government, on one occasion, to demand that teachers from outside the territories sign a declaration renouncing political activity. The lecturers refused to sign the declaration, and the military government responded by refusing them entry to the West Bank. After a lengthy period of confrontation, the military government backed down.

The military government has not fully exploited the powers it granted itself and, in point of fact, they were unnecessary. The security enactments and defense regulations from the Mandatory period give it the power to censor texts, prevent teaching and research and prevent students from pursuing their studies.

The use of stringent enforcement measures, coming in response to acts of sedition and expressions of nationalist sentiment, served only to heighten frustration and resistance, inviting, in turn, yet harsher reprisals.

A committee of faculty members from the Hebrew University has sharply criticized the administration's violation of academic freedom, which went well beyond security considerations. The committee recommended abrogating Order 854, refraining from closing the universities as a collective punishment, and giving the universities permission to acquire books and periodicals without censorship. To date, there has been no improvement in the relations between the administration and the universities, and violations of academic freedom continue (See UNIVERSITY GRADUATES, STUDENT COUNCILS).

A survey (1984) of Hebrew and Israeli studies at West Bank universities showed the following:

Bethlehem University: Two courses in Hebrew, for beginners and advanced students (electives), Judaism taught in the framework of religious studies (philosophy department). Zionism is taught in the political science department (including analysis of texts).

Bir-Zeit: Three courses, all of them undergraduate: two in Hebrew language (beginners and advanced) and one (elective) in the sociology of Israel.

an-Najah: Two courses in the political science department: a one-semester course on the Israeli political system, and a course on the history of Zionism and the modern history of Israel, as part of a course in Palestinian history. Courses in Hebrew language (at all levels); course on the Israeli economy; Israel studies center in the process of formation.

UNIVERSITY GRADUATES (PALESTINIAN)

The number of high school graduates receiving the Arab League matriculation certificate (Tawejihi) has risen rapidly since 1967. In 1969, 2,132 students successfully completed the matriculation examinations; in 1981/82, this rose to 8,518. The number of university students also increased rapidly. In 1967 there were no universities on the West Bank (other than small post-secondary colleges). In 1984 seven institutions with university status were functioning in the area (See UNIVERSITIES). The number of students rose from 1,086 in 1975/76 to 7,478 in 1981/82. In 1984/85 the number stood at about 10,000. In addition, in1982, 9,000 students were studying abroad, and 7,800 in 1983.

212

The number of university graduates each year is estimated at 1,500 with a further 1,000 completing their studies abroad (most graduating from universities in Arab countries but also in the United States, Europe, and the Communist bloc), about two-thirds of them in the humanities and social sciences.

Over and above this, there are an estimated 7,000 with 13 or more years of education who are seeking employment annually. There is a very limited supply of jobs on the West Bank suited to these graduates. Workers in the government sector whose job requires post-secondary education number approximately 7,500. The vast majority are in education. The number of doctors, veterinarians, judges, social workers, school principals, directors of welfare institutions, and agricultural instructors has hardly changed over the past 10 years. The total number of vacancies in the civil service filled by employees with post-secondary education does not exceed 400 (including teachers) annually. In 1983 only 120 employees with post-secondary education were employed in the West Bank's industrial sector. The total number of jobs suitable for workers with more than a secondary education is an estimated 14,000 – two work places per job-seeker (compared to 14 places for each job-seeker with a post-secondary education in Israel). In 1981, 11,700 professionals were in employment, and in 1983, 12,000, about 8 percent of the total West Bankers employed. According to estimates, only 15 percent of post-secondary graduates find work in their professions. Employment for graduates of higher education is therefore particularly scarce. It is claimed that some 10,000 university graduates were unemployed in 1984, though a survey conducted by the military government in the same year indicates that only 4,000 graduates are unemployed. This survey, however, does not specify where the 29,000 working academics it mentions are employed. It is estimated that more than half of those employed are not working in their professions.

The Jordanian government and the PLO, aware of the problem, grant 20 dinars a month to humanities and social science graduates, 30 dinars a month to engineers, and 50 dinars to doctors. The total budget for this purpose is one million dinars.

The payments are made via the Association of University Graduates, headquartered in Jerusalem. Until 1981/82 most degree-holders from the West Bank sought employment outside the area. Since 1983, this option has ceased to exist, as a result of the worsening economic situation in the oil-producing countries, and of emigration regulations issued by the Jordanian government (See DEMOGRAPHY). As a result, employment for university graduates has become a major issue on the

West Bank. Lack of development in the West Bank's economic sector, cutbacks in the Israeli administration, the continuing crisis in the Arab municipalities and the reduction in fund transfers to Palestinian public institutions (e.g. the Waqf), mean there will be no early solution to this problem, with its attendant political consequences.

UNRWA

The United Nations Relief and Works Agency was founded in 1949 to provide relief for Palestinian refugees, and began its operations in 1950, headed by a general representative appointed by the secretary-general of the United Nations. UNRWA headquarters previously in Beirut, were transferred to Vienna as a result of the civil war in Lebanon. It is composed of six departments: administration, welfare, health, education, financial, and legal. The agency works through field offices composed of two branches: services and refugee camps.

The service branch comprises four departments: welfare, health, education, and supply and transportation. The welfare department registers the refugees and distributes food and personal relief; the health department deals with preventive medicine, sanitation, water supply, the training of nurses; the education department deals with all areas of education and teacher training (See EDUCATION (ARAB)); the supply and transportation department is responsible for bringing monthly supplies to the storage areas.

Until 1967 the refugee camps department was responsible for about 25 camps (See REFUGEE CAMPS), which were administered from five district offices. At the head of each local office was an administrator directly responsible to the field office, and under his command were the directors of the refugee camps in his district. In 1967 the number of camps in Trans-Jordan doubled because of the mass flight after the war.

UNRWA defines a Palestinian refugee as anyone whose permanent residence had been Palestine for at least two years before the 1948 war and who lost both his home and means of livelihood (not just one of the two) as a result of that war.

In recent years UNRWA has reduced the services it supplies to the refugees, claiming a shortage of resources. That step provoked protests among the refugees, who accuse UNRWA of joining in the conspiracy to make the Palestinian question disappear by stamping out the Palestinian national movement and settling the refugees permanently in their place of exile.

According to a census of June 1983, the Palestinian refugees are distributed as follows:

Jordan	799,724
West Bank	357,704
Gaza Strip	427,892
Lebanon	263,599
Syria	244,626
Total:	2,093,545

Of those refugees, 35 percent live in about 50 camps established after 1948 and about 10 more established after 1967 (See REFUGEES).

Institutions of Higher Education Belonging to UNRWA (See also EDUCATION)

UNRWA runs eight institutions of higher education for professional training. The first institution was established in 1953, and by 1982 the number of graduates of those institutions reached 25,000. They found work in a number of countries, including Saudi Arabia and the Gulf states.

The institutions, called "centers," are as follows:

Lebanon – one center – Siblin, near Sidon.

Syria – one center – in Damascus.

Jordan – two centers – in Amman and Wadi al-Asim.

West Bank – three centers.

Gaza Strip – one center.

The al-Tira Training Center for Girls, Ramallah

This center is a combination of a number of centers for professional training in various fields such as sewing, secretarial skills, pre-school education, home economics, laboratory techniques, cosmetics, and teaching. The studies at the center last two years for all subjects. In the 1982-83 academic year about 670 girls studied there, about 300 in the teacher training program and the rest in the other courses. The center accepts students from the West Bank and the Gaza Strip whose parents are registered with UNRWA as refugees. According to UNRWA procedures, any student at one of the UNRWA institutions of higher education or anyone who receives a job is automatically removed from the roster of refugees receiving welfare assistance.

The Professional Training Center in Kalandiya

The center offers vocational training to students on two levels: the first is for those who have finished ninth grade and the second is for high school graduates. Among the subjects studied are: mechanics, surveying, ironwork and welding. In 1982-83 there were 504 students. The center is known to the media because it is located on the highway to Ramallah next to the Kalandiya refugee camp. The students frequently take part in demonstrations and in stoning passing cars, and the authorities close the center for a number of weeks after each incident.

The Centers for Youth Activities

After UNRWA began providing services to the Palestinian refugees on the West Bank and in the Gaza Strip, centers for youth activities were set up in the refugee camps, one in each camp. Coordination among the various centers, the planning of their activities, including sports and cultural competitions among the various clubs, is carried out by an official in the head office of UNRWA.

The main activity of the centers is in the area of sports and culture, but since 1967 there has been increased nationalist momentum, particularly through Palestinian book and folklore exhibitions. A number of centers encourage voluntary activities such as providing aid to the needy or the improvement of services and sanitation in the camps. As a result of this nationalist activity and the increase in opposition to the occupation, the Israeli authorities have closed many of the youth centers in the refugee camps for unlimited periods. Some of the centers have been closed for years.

List of the centers:

Name	Number of Members
Shabab Balata	335
Shabab Askar	120
Camp No. 1	92
Camp al-Fara'a	120
Shabab Jenin	175
Shabab Tulkarm	270
Shabab Nur Shams Camp	169
Shabab Shuafat	120
Shabab Deir Amar	75

VENICE DECLARATION

Declaration concerning the Middle East by the European Economic Community, issued in Venice, June 13, 1981. Excerpts:

1. The time has come to promote the recognition and implementation of the two principles:

The right to existence and to security of all the states in the region, including Israel, and justice for all people, which implies the recognition of the legitimate rights of the Palestinian people.

2. A just solution must finally be found to the Palestinian problem, which

216

is not simply one of refugees. The Palestinian people must be placed in a "position... to exercise fully its right to self-determination."

3. The achievement of these objectives requires the involvement and support of all the parties concerned... and thus, the Palestinian people, and the Palestine Liberation Organization, (which) will have to be associated with the negotiations.

4. The Nine (EEC countries) stress that they will not accept any unilateral initiative designed to change the status of Jerusalem.

5. Israel should put an end to the territorial occupation – settlements are illegal under international law.

The declaration was welcomed by the Arab states and vehemently rejected by Israel. During 1983-84 some changes in style occurred in the position of EEC members and no further attempts to formulate a unified policy have been initiated.

VILLAGE COUNCILS

Established by declaration of the Jordanian minister of the interior, whose authority has devolved on a staff officer in the civilian administration by virtue of the Village Management Law (No. 5, 1954). Their powers include the establishment and management of schools, markets, slaughterhouses, water systems, electricity and roads. In addition, they have the authority to arbitrate disputes between residents. The village council numbers from three to 12 members, in addition to the MUKHTARS. The council serves for three years.

Immediately preceding the 1967 war there were 96 village councils in the region. After the war, the military government gradually reactivated them, wishing to show the occupation as enlightened and also to create a centralized medium for controlling the West Bank's rural sector. At the beginning of the 1970s, 64 councils were operating. The establishment of the joint Jordanian-PLO fund created an additional incentive for activating the village councils, as Jordan distributed aid to villages with functioning councils. The Israeli administration and American voluntary aid organizations (See FOREIGN AID) also tended to approve development budgets for villages with organized administrative bodies. In the early 1980s the number of village councils rose to over 85.

When the VILLAGE LEAGUES were established and village administrative authority transferred to them, the power and performance of the village councils waned. Some ceased functioning in protest against the preference shown to the village leagues, and as part of the boycott against the CIVILIAN ADMINISTRATION. However, when the village leagues were no longer in favor, the village councils once again became the Israeli means of controlling the rural sector (See PUBLIC CONSUMPTION AND INVESTMENT).

Village Councils 1981:

1. — Name
2. — District
3. — No. of Residents
4. — Homes connected to water supply
5. — Homes connected to electric supply
6. — Schools (post-elementary)
7. — Students — boys
8. — Students — girls
9. — No. of mosques

1.	2.	3.	4.	5.	6.	7.	8.	9.
'Azariyah	Bethlehem	11,000	1,000	1000	prep (boys) high (girls)	598	600	3
Za'atarah	Bethlehem	5,000	300	300	prep	550	300	1
Beit Fajar	Bethlehem	5,000	400	400	prep	750	480	2
Dahariya	Hebron	13,000	1,000	—	high	700	400	2
Tarqumiya	Hebron	6,000	450	—	high	1,200	800	1
Tafuh	Hebron	3,000	—	—	prep	470	290	1
Bani Naim	Hebron	8,000	500	—	high	1,000	750	1
Beit 'Umar	Hebron	6,000	700	850	high	1,100	700	2
Surif	Hebron	5,000	550	600	high	900	650	2
Kharis	Hebron	2,500	220	220	high	400	250	1
Nuba	Hebron	2,000	150	160	prep	300	200	2
Sinjil	Ramallah	2,500	—	—	high	500	360	1
Turmus-Aya	Ramallah	2,300	—	350	el. prep	400	300	2
Beit Suriq	Ramallah	1,500	—	160	el.	140	70	1
Dir Qadis	Ramallah	800	120	—	el.	100	40	1
Atarah	Ramallah	1,700	140	150	el.	130	115	1
Jifnah	Ramallah	650	110	110	el.	100	—	2
Ramun	Ramallah	2,200	175	180	prep	200	165	1
'Arurah	Ramallah	1,400	—	—	high w/ Qubani	450	230	1
Mazr'at Sharqiya	Ramallah	3,000	320	380	prep	300	300	1
Bani Hareth	Ramallah	1,000	120	—	prep	150	60	1
Taibah	Ramallah	1,200	300		jt. prep.	450		3 churches
Na'alin	Ramallah	3,000	240	—	High	450	320	2
Beit Inan	Ramallah	3,000	—	280	prep	300	150	2

1.	2.	3.	4.	5.	6.	7.	8.	9.
Azun	Tulkarm	5,000	400	400	high	800	600	2
Juyus	Tulkarm	1,600	—	210	high	300	220	1
Baqah a-Sharqiya	Tulkarm	3,000	—	260	high	400	400	2
Kafr Labad	Tulkarm	2,200	—	250	—	—	—	—
Bidiya	Tulkarm	4,500	connected		high	650	500	1
Bala	Tulkarm	3,000	—	400	high	450	375	2
Beit-Lid	Tulkarm	4,000	—	370	high	300	—	1
Bruqin	Tulkarm	1,600	—	—	prep	250	200	1
Jama'in	Tulkarm	5,000	—	500	high	500	300	1
Deir Istiya	Tulkarm	3,700	—	260	high	350	220	2
Deir Ballut	Tulkarm	1,600	—	200	prep	220	170	1
Zeita	Tulkarm	2,300	—	300	high	330	220	2
Habla	Tulkarm	2,000	300	310	prep	500	315	1
Kafr Sur	Tulkarm	,100	—	80	high	160	50	1
Kafr Dik	Tulkarm	3,000	—	250	prep	380	210	1
Kafr Jamal	Tulkarm	1,500	—	—	el. high	200	85	1
Kafr Zibad	Tulkarm	700	—	100	prep	100	—	1
Kafr Thulth	Tulkarm	2,000	—	200	prep	270	230	2
Kafr Haris	Tulkarm	1,600	connected		high	300	300	1
Siniriah	Tulkarm	1,400	—	150	prep	140	110	1
Atar	Tulkarm	3,500	—	—	high	560	500	1
Farun	Tulkarm	1,500	300	230	prep	200	150	1
Kafin	Tulkarm	4,000	connected		high	—	—	2
Ramin	Tulkarm	1,500	—	180	prep	200	80	2
Sida	Tulkarm	1,500	—	90	prep	180	90	1
Deir al-Ghusun	Tulkarm	4,500	conn.	500	high	650	550	2
Jinsafut	Tulkarm	1,000	—	—	prep	240	110	1
Zababda	Jenin	2,200	180	300	high	300	200	1
						4 churches		
Jalama	Jenin	1,300	110	150	prep	200	80	1
al-Yamun	Jenin	10,000	—	650	high	1,180	820	2
Tamun	Jenin	6,000	300	450	priv. pr	720	480	1
Ajja	Jenin	2,500	—	280	prep	415	320	2
Silat Hartiya	Jenin	5,000	—	500	high	1000	600	1
Silat Dahar	Jenin	2,800	400	270	high	770	320	1
Kafr Ra'i	Jenin	5,000	—	600	high	700	450	2
Maythalun	Jenin	4,000	—	260	high	600	480	2
Tal	Nablus	2,300	—	200	high	300	220	1
Burqa	Nablus	3,000	700	500	priv. hi	460	280	2

1.	2.	3.	4.	5.	6.	7.	8.	9.
Beita	Nablus	5,500	—	conn.	high	550	360	3
Kafr Qalil	Nablus	1,500	—	200	prep	150	130	1
Akrabah	Nablus	4,500	—	400	high	500	400	1
Sabastiya	Nablus	1,900	360	350	high	400	220	1
Taluza	Nablus	5,000	150	170	high	355	260	2
Burin	Nablus	2,000	—	250	high	250	250	1
Beit Amrin	Nablus	1,500	250	150	prep	230	165	1
Qablan	Nablus	3,800	370	400	high	550	480	3
Asirah Shamaliya	Nablus	6,000	500	615	high	800	720	3

VILLAGE LEAGUES

An organization of the rural population of the West Bank, sponsored by the CIVILIAN ADMINISTRATION (1981-84) as a counterweight to the Palestinian mayors and the urban population, who were viewed as PLO sympathizers. According to the promoters of the village leagues, they were to "represent 70 percent of the residents of the West Bank, the silent, moderate, and cooperative majority," as opposed to the radical city dwellers. The village leagues were the cornerstone of the civilian administration's policies. The leaders of the village leagues were given broad authority, both statutory and other, funds for development were placed at their disposal, and they were permitted to raise armed militias. The residents were directed to approach the league leaders for recommendations for the release of detainees, family, reunification, etc.

In August 1978, there was one league in the Hebron mountains. In 1982 the leagues were active in five districts, Hebron, Bethlehem, Ramallah, Tulkarm, Nablus, and two sub-districts, Qabatiya and Silat a-Dahar. In 1981-82 the village leagues received financial aid amounting to $8.8 million, and in 1982-83 the sum was $12.0 million.

The village leagues attracted marginal elements in the Palestinian community, and in general their members were viewed as collaborators and their leaders as corrupt. The decision of the Jordanian government (March 1982) to treat membership in the village leagues as treason dealt them a death blow. Some of their leaders were arrested, tried, and found guilty of murder and corruption; the Israeli administration changed its attitude towards them in view of its failure, and from 1984 on they ceased to be a factor in the territories. At the same time a political movement was formed in Israel – HA'DEREKH LE'SHALOM – with the aim of fostering the village leagues.

VIOLENT INCIDENTS

Between 1977 and 1984 some 932 violent incidents (gunfire, throwing grenades or Molotov cocktails, setting explosive devices and laying mines) occurred on the West Bank. During the same period there were 10,871 "disturbances of the peace" – demonstrations and rock-throwing at Israeli vehicles. In the years 1968-1977, 495 violent acts were committed on the West Bank. If the number of such acts can serve as an indicator of the degree of confrontation between Israel and the Palestinians, there is no doubt that this has increased in intensity since the signing of the Camp David Accords, and in particular since the outbreak of the Lebanon War. In 1983/84 the number of violent acts reached a record level – 354 in a single year. During the period 1968-1983, 22 soldiers were killed on the West Bank and 97 wounded; 14 Israeli civilians were killed and 125 wounded. During the same period 92 Palestinian civilians were killed and 516 wounded.

The number of Israeli civilians killed and injured in Israel and the occupied territories between 1967-1985 (September) is:

Year	Civilians	
	Killed	Injured
1968	44	273
1969	23	228
1970	42	186
1971	10	52
1972	33	121
1973	4	41
1974	62	196
1975	33	185
1976	3	77
1977	5	155
1978	56	276
1979	21	303
1980	9	74
1981	11	131
1982	3	29
1983	9	63
1984	6	112
1985	9	35

Since the outbreak of the Lebanon War, the number of "disturbances of the peace," i.e., demonstrations and stone-throwing, has risen considerably. In the period 1977-1980 the number of incidents was between 400-500 per year. In 1981/82 this figure jumped to 1,506, and in 1982-83 to 4,417. In 1983/84 the number of disturbances and incidents of rock-throwing fell to 3,037. The growth in the number of incidents of stone-throwing at Israeli vehicles represents a new phase in Palestinian resistance. These are not carried out by organized groups but by youths undeterred by the consequences of their actions. As the number of Israeli settlers grows and the number of private Israeli vehicles on the West Bank roads increases, there is a greater supply of targets for attack. In the spring and summer of 1985 a new wave of violence erupted, involving the stabbing and killing of Jewish civilians. According to Palestinian sources, the "armed struggle" was deliberately stepped up at the beginning of the Mideast mission of American envoy Richard Murphy. It was directed at warning the parties concerned (U.S, Israel and Jordan) of the price of ignoring the Palestinians. Palestinian rejectionist groups stepped up their terrorist activities in order to sabotage Jordanian – PLO rapprochement. Sabotage and violent acts included naval operations (which were in every case preempted by the IDF), and a series of terrorist acts in Israel and the occupied territories. However according to an estimate, more than 50 percent of Palestinian violent actions in 1984-85 originated in the territories, with no direct orders from PLO leaders abroad: this highlights the grass-roots nature of violent actions and points to a new phase in the conflict.

With the increase in attacks on Israeli vehicles and persons, probably carried out on local initiative, the number of retaliatory attacks by Jewish settlers has also risen, involving gunfire, smashing windshields of parked Arab vehicles, burning houses and beating up passers-by. Settler violence reached a peak with the attack on the Arab mayors and the murderous attack on the Hebron University campus (See JEWISH TERRORISM). While the perpetrators of these attacks were caught and tried, violent, retaliatory attacks on the part of settlers were not punished or even curtailed. In September 1985, following the firing on an Israeli bus, settlers burned houses, shops and cars in an Arab town. The army did not intervene.

The increase in violence perpetrated by civilians on both sides points to a new stage in the Israeli-Palestinian confrontation on the West Bank, one which may be defined as violent communal conflict, as opposed to clashes of an army of occupation with a local populace.

WAQF (MUSLIM RELIGIOUS ENDOWMENT)

A Muslim religious body. Property is donated to the Waqf in perpetuity and cannot be sold or inherited. Waqf income is devoted to advancing its specific concerns, such as public prayer, education, social assistance, etc. (waqf khairi), or else for the benefit of the heirs of the donor (waqf therri). The Waqf is run by an administrator or as prescribed by the donor with the authorization of the Shari court (See COURTS (MUSLIM RELIGIOUS)). The main purpose of the Waqf is similar to a trust fund, to prevent the dispersal of family property through inheritance, or its misuse by the heirs, to prevent the arbitrary seizure of the property by the authorities, and concern for community needs. The Islamic Waqf owns considerable real estate on the West Bank, including buildings and land. The Waqf is administered by offices responsible to the SUPREME MUSLIM COUNCIL and the Ministry of Wawf in Amman.

WATER

Most of the West Bank area is part of the Israeli hydrological system. About a quarter of Israel's annual water potential has its source beyond the green line (some 475 million cubic meters per year out of 1,900 million cubic meters). This is the basis for the Israeli claim that control over West Bank water potential must remain in Israel's hands in all circumstances. Otherwise, Israel argues, the entire Israeli system, already overpumping water, will collapse.

The total water potential of the West Bank is estimated at 600 million cubic meters per year. About 125 million cubic meters of this are situated east of the watershed and therefore do not affect Israeli potential. The western water table (Yarkon-Taninim), with a capacity of 335 million cubic meters per year, and the northeastern water table (Gilboa-Beit She'an), which collects some 140 million cubic meters per year, directly affect Israeli potential.

Of this joint potential, Israel uses the vast majority of the water and the West Bank, only about 20 million cubic meters per year (1982). According to estimates, Israel is overpumping these water tables, so that the main water potential of the West Bank, shared with Israel, is exploited to its limit, in a ratio of 4.5 percent to the West Bank and 95.5 percent to Israel. In the eastern water tables (Samaria, Nablus-Jenin, Wadi Fari'ah, Wadi Baydun, Petsael, and Fasha) some 80 million cubic meters are used by the Palestinians, including 20 million cubic meters on the mountain plateau and about 50-60 million cubic meters in the Jordan Valley and its eastern slopes. Some 30 million cubic meters from the same water table are used by the Israeli agricultural settlements in the Jordan Valley, part of which is supplied by sources outside the region. There is a water surplus in the eastern tables, but the authorities have not permitted the residents of the West Bank to expand the utilization of their water sources. Total water consumption of the Palestinian sector on the West Bank reached some 115 million cubic meters per year at the beginning of the 1980s, of which some 100 million cubic meters go for irrigation and the rest for domestic and industrial use.

The water sources are boreholes (some 230), springs (some 300), reservoirs and cisterns. Some 50-60 million cubic meters are pumped from springs, 55 million from boreholes, nine million from the Jordan River and five million from reservoirs and cisterns. The quantity of water available annually to Palestinian residents is about 20 percent higher than in 1967. The irrigated area came to approximately 100,000 dunams at the beginning of the 1980s. The water available for agriculture was frozen at a level of 90-100 million cubic meters, and according to the official development plans, the Palestinian water consumption will not expand even by the year 2010. The freeze results from water rationing and high prices for water for agricultural purposes.

By contrast, the amount of water available for Israeli agriculture (mostly in the Jordan Valley, but also in the Etzion bloc and southern Mt. Hebron) will increase by more than 100 percent during the 1980s. In 1990, 60 million cubic meters of water will be available to some 30 Israeli agricultural settlements, only one-third less than the amount available for 400 Palestinian villages. The planned supplement to the Arab sector is intended for domestic use only, reflecting population growth and increased demand for water per capita. In 1982, the consumption per capita in Arab settlements was estimated at 35 cubic meters (per annum) in towns and 15 cubic meters (per annum) in villages. According to forecasts, the consumption per capita (per annum) will increase gradually to 50 cubic meters per person in towns and 25 cubic meters per capita in villages, by 1990; and by 2010, to 60 cubic meters and 35 cubic meters respectively.

The planned level of consumption per capita in the Jewish settlements has been fixed at 90 cubic meters. The estimated rate in western Europe is 83 cubic meters (per annum). The price of water in the two sectors is also different, with Jewish consumers benefiting from a high subsidy. The total amount of water planned for allocation to the Arab sector (agriculture and domestic consumption) at the end of the decade is 137 million cubic meters per year (for about one million people) and for the Jewish population, approximately 100 million cubic meters, for about 100,000 persons. The water available to the Palestinian population amounts to 6.3 percent of the total water resources of western Palestine, or 23 percent of the water potential of the West Bank (some 600 million cubic meters). According to the water development plan, the relative quantity of water available for Palestinian use will not be altered.

The Israeli water authority is working on the integration of the West Bank system into large regional plants linked up with the Israeli network. The separate West Bank water system, which was under military government management since 1967, was handed over to the Israeli national water company, Mekorot, in 1982.

WOMEN'S ASSOCIATIONS

1. The Arab Women's Association of Nablus
Founded 1945. Today runs the "al-Itihad" hospital in Nablus, an orphan girls' home (housing some 100 girls), three-day centers for blind girls, an athletic club, and a vocational training center for girls (sewing and embroidery).

2. The Arab Women's Organization of Jerusalem (Al-Itihad An-Nisai Al-Arabi)
An independent association with no connection with other organizations. Founded in 1929, it has about 60 members. Its goal is to raise the educational, cultural, and social level of women.

The association runs a school (Grades 1 through 12), a medical center, a mother-and-child-care center, an old age home in Jericho, and a center for girls and single women.

3. The Women's Action Committee (Lajnat Al-Amal An-Nisai)
A women's movement founded at the beginning of the 1980s, which has established branches in most of the cities and villages on the West Bank. Its goal is to raise economic, social, cultural, and health standards, as well as the national consciousness of Arab women under occupation.

The committee's activity centers on the improvement of working conditions for women in employment, offering courses in basic education and handicrafts, and running kindergartens and day-care centers to serve working women.

WORLD ZIONIST ORGANIZATION

The body formally responsible for the development of settlement on the West Bank and in the Gaza Strip, the settlement department of the World Zionist Organization (WZO) is none other than the settlement department of the Jewish Agency. To prevent political and legal complications arising over investments in occupied territory "over the green line,"activities ruled out by the tax exemption on United Jewish Appeal funds and by the articles of the Jewish Agency institutions in

America, it functions in the territories in the guise of the World Zionist Organization. WZO activities are limited to the establishment of "pioneering" settlements (See COMMUNITY SETTLEMENTS).

Settlement activities are coordinated in theory by the MINISTERIAL COMMITTEE FOR SETTLEMENT but in reality, competition and lack of coordination prevail between the WZO, the MINISTRY OF HOUSING AND CONSTRUCTION and the MINISTRY OF AGRICULTURE. Even within the settlement department itself two philosophies are in competition – the Likud's as represented by Matityahu Drobless (See DROBLESS PLAN), and the second, the Alignment's ALLON PLAN. Other departments of the WZO, the youth aliyah, youth and pioneering, and public affairs departments, deal with various aspects of West Bank and Gaza Strip settlements.

For the budget of the settlements department, see DROBLESS PLAN.

YESHA (ASSOCIATION OF ISRAELI SETTLERS)

A voluntary organization working in the framework of The Association for the Advancement of Settlement in Judea, Samaria, Gaza, and the Jordan Valley, it was founded in 1979, and acts as the lobby of the settlements in the territories.

Goals
1. To work towards the establishment of Israeli sovereignty in the entire area of Judea, Samaria and the Gaza Strip, and to develop settlement in these territories.
2. To ensure, through the Israeli government, the security of the population of Judea, Samaria and Gaza.
3. To encourage and develop the economic infrastructure in the territories.
4. To promote cooperation between the various settlements in the region.
5. To enhance awareness of the necessity of settling Eretz Israel through public relations activity in Israel and abroad.

Institutions
The Council – A limited forum representing all the settlements. Its function is to elect committees – legal, organizational, financial, security, propaganda, and special operations. It meets every three months, or on demand of one-third of the representatives.

Administration – The executive arm of the council is composed of its chairman, the secretary-general, the heads of the regional councils and local councils in Judea, Samaria, and Gaza.

The activities of the Yesha council are financed by the regional and local councils, taxes from residents of the territories, contributions from Israel and other countries, and from the settlement movements and government ministries.

With the founding of the Yesha council, the settlement movement became institutionalized, forming a single political unit. It formed an effective pressure group influencing policy regarding the territories, the establishment of new settlements, and securing budget allocations for the consolidation of existing ones.

Due to increasing tensions between Palestinians and settlers in the last few years, the council has focused its activity on lobbying the government to take harsh measures against all signs of Palestinian resistance. Yesha has organized independent vigilante activity and staged violent demonstrations against the security forces. Its members have access to firearms through their participation in TERRITORIAL DEFENSE. When the Jewish underground (See JEWISH TERRORISM) operating in the area was uncovered, the Yesha council published a position paper (May 4, 1984) objecting to illegal actions by residents of the West Bank and Gaza. Nonetheless the Yesha Council established a fund to aid the prisoners and their families.

Since the end of 1984, when the population of the urban townships in the Tel Aviv and Jerusalem metropolitan areas (Ariel, Ma'aleh Adumim, etc.) began to increase swiftly (See DEMOGRAPHY), there have been signs of tension between the ideologically motivated settlers and those in the open suburban settlements. The latter do not necessarily identify with the political views associated with Yesha. Some ISRAELI LOCAL COUNCIL chairmen have suspended their participation in Yesha and established their own organization of council chairmen.

The Yesha council has worked towards the establishment of an economic and logistic base which will allow it to act in the territories with organizational and budgetary independence, if necessary even contrary to government decisions (See DEVELOPMENT CORPORATIONS).

YOUNG MEN'S CHRISTIAN ASSOCIATION (YMCA)

The East Jerusalem branch of the YMCA was established in 1948, and today there are also branches in Ramallah, Beit Sahur and Jericho. There are about 1,500 members, both Christians and Muslims. Most of its activities are in sports.

YOUNG MEN'S MUSLIM ASSOCIATION

Founded in 1972, with about 1,500 members in 1984, its purpose is to educate young men in the spirit of the Islamic religion. The members participate in educational, athletic and social activities. The association also has a scouting movement. It provides material assistance to needy families. To help the indigent sick it established two clinics, in al-Ram and a-Sawahira a-Sharaqiya.

YOUNG WOMEN'S CHRISTIAN ASSOCIATION (YWCA)

Founded in Jerusalem in 1893, a branch was opened in Ramallah after prolonged contacts with the civilian administration, which demanded that membership in the branch be limited to residents of the Ramallah district. In 1983 about 200 young women were members of the Ramallah branch. The goal of the association is the advancement of women to enable them to play an active role in society. The association offers courses in language, secretarial skills, sewing, home economics, etc.

YOUNG WOMEN'S MUSLIM ASSOCIATION

Founded in 1979 by a committee of 13 women from Jerusalem, this organization provides an Islamic education to young women. It is similar to the YOUNG MEN'S MUSLIM ASSOCIATION, and runs an elementary school which it plans to expand.

MAPS

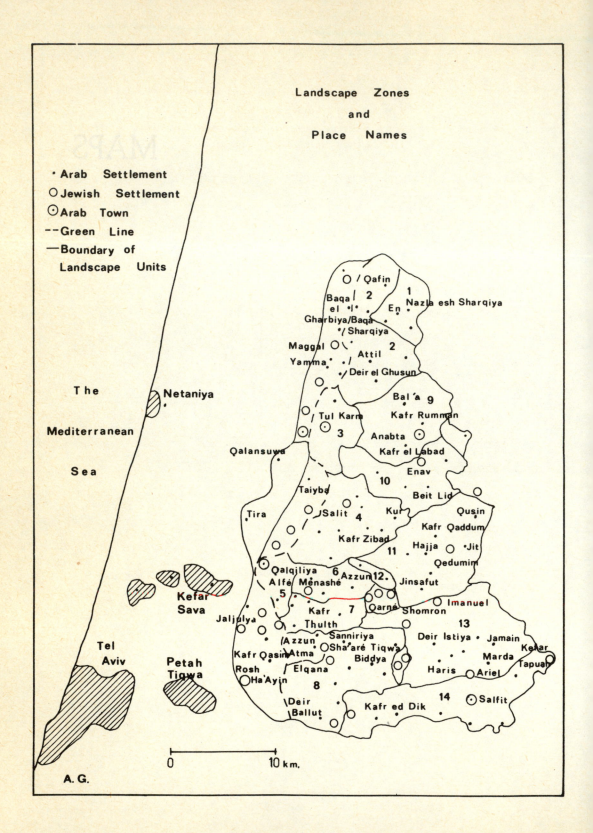

Landscape Zones

and

Place Names

- • Arab Settlement
- ○ Jewish Settlement
- ⊙ Arab Town
- -- Green Line
- — Boundary of Landscape Units

The

Mediterranean

Sea

Netaniya

Qafin

Baqa el
Gharbiya/Baqa / Sharqiya

En

Nazla esh Sharqiya

1

2

Maggal

Yamma

Attil

2

Deir el Ghusun

Bal'a 9

Kafr Rumman

Tul Karm

3

Anabta ⊙

Qalansuwa

Kafr el Labad

Enav

10

Taiyba

Beit Lid

Tira

Salit

4

Kur

Qusin

Kafr Qaddum

Kafr Zibad

Hajja

Jit

11

Qedumim

Qalqiliya

6

Azzun 12.

Jinsafut

Alfé Menashe

5

Qarné

Kefar
Sava

Shomron

Imanuel

Kafr

7

13

Jaljulya

Thulth

Deir Istiya

Jamain

Sanniriya

Azzun

Atma

Sha'aré Tiqwa

Kefar
Tapuah

Tel
Aviv

Kafr Qasim

Biddya

Marda

Petah
Tiqwa

Rosh

Elqana

Haris

Ariel

Ha'Ayin

8

14

Salfit ⊙

Deir
Ballut

Kafr ed Dik

0   10 km.

A. G.

Arab and Jewish population
in the landscape zones of the
Tulkarm Sub-District and adjacent
areas in Israel (1984).

Numbers indicate landscape zones
(see text for explanation).

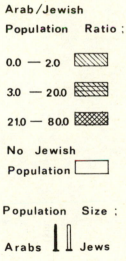

Arab/Jewish
Population Ratio:

0.0 — 2.0

3.0 — 20.0

21.0 — 80.0

No Jewish
Population

Population Size:

Arabs   Jews

(1 cm. = 10,000 people)

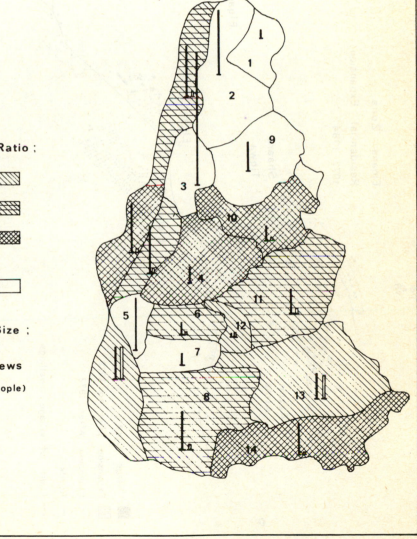

A. G.

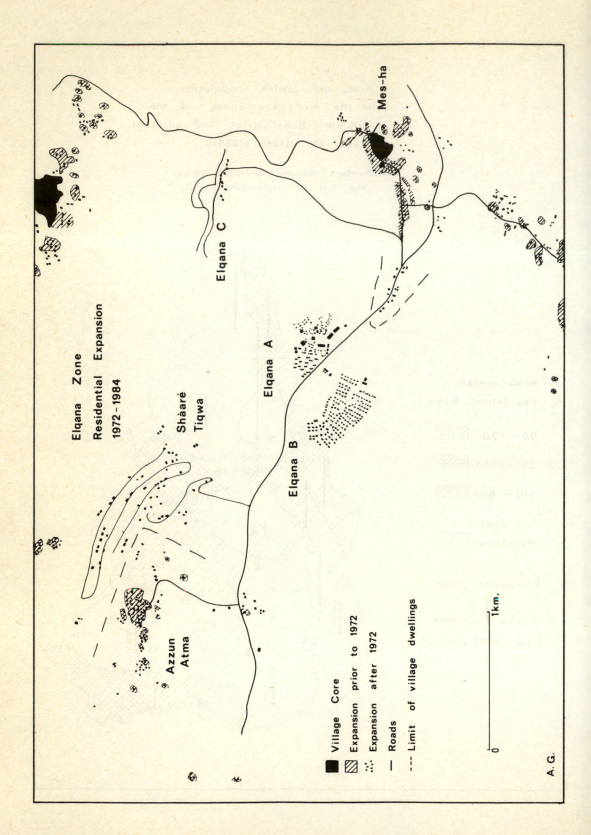

Elqana Zone
Residential Expansion
1972-1984

Mes-ha

Elqana C

Elqana A

Elqana B

Shàaré
Tiqwa

Azzun
Atma

■ Village Core
▨ Expansion prior to 1972
⠿ Expansion after 1972
— Roads
--- Limit of village dwellings

0   1km.

A. G.

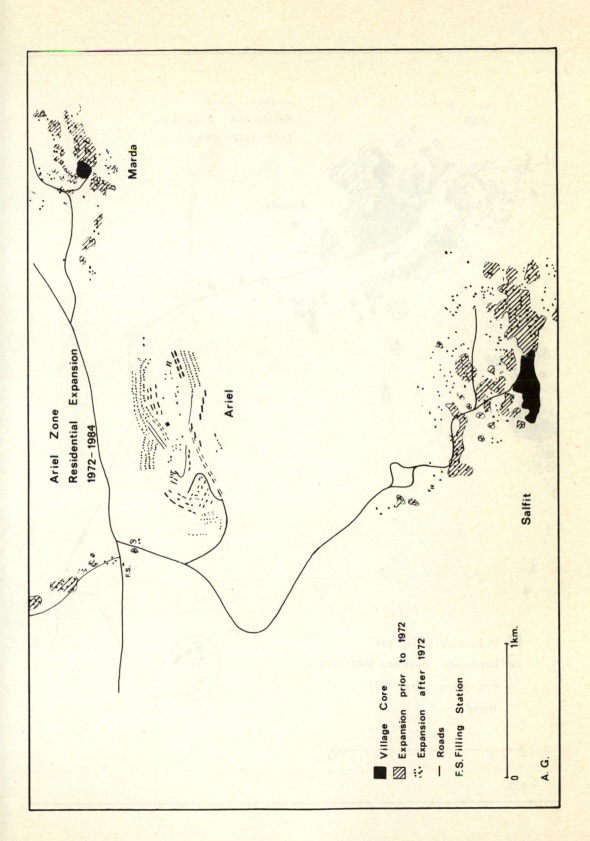

Ariel Zone
Residential Expansion
1972–1984

Marda

Ariel

Salfit

F.S.

■ Village Core
▨ Expansion prior to 1972
⠂ Expansion after 1972
— Roads
F.S. Filling Station

A.G.

0 _____ 1km.

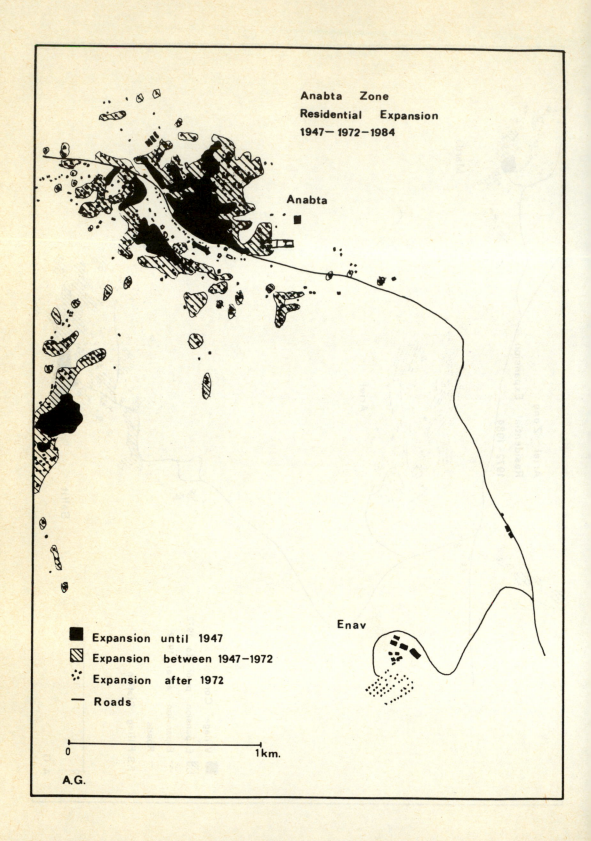

Anabta Zone
Residential Expansion
1947— 1972—1984

Anabta

Enav

■ Expansion until 1947
▨ Expansion between 1947—1972
⁖ Expansion after 1972
— Roads

0   1km.

A.G.

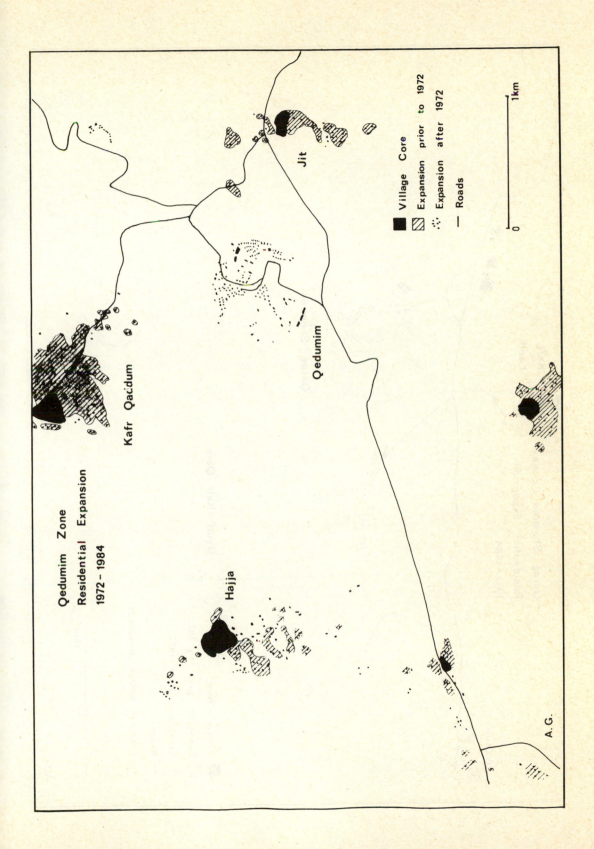

Qedumim Zone
Residential Expansion
1972 – 1984

Kafr Qaddum

Hajja

Qedumim

Jit

Village Core
Expansion prior to 1972
Expansion after 1972
Roads

0   1km

A.G.

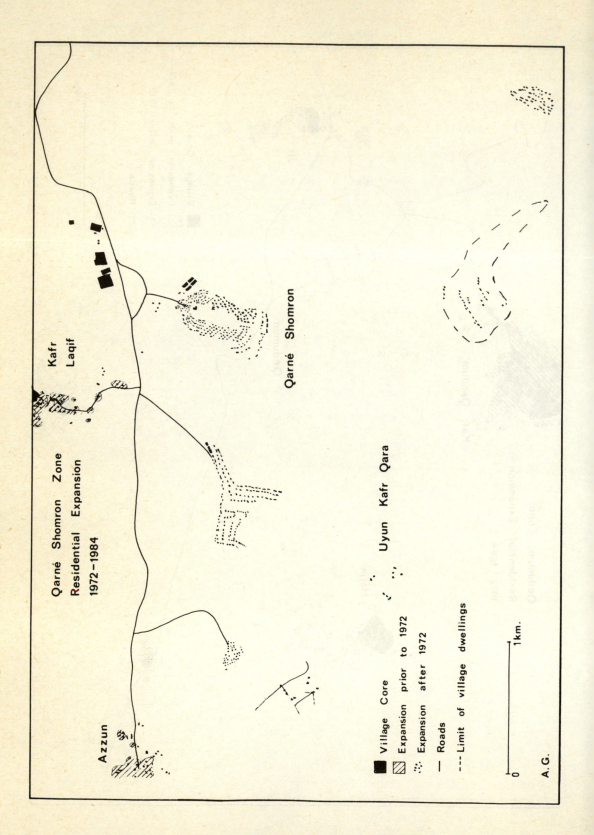

Qarné Shomron Zone
Residential Expansion
1972–1984

Kafr Laqif

Qarné Shomron

Azzun

Uyun Kafr Qara

■ Village Core

▨ Expansion prior to 1972

∴ Expansion after 1972

— Roads

--- Limit of village dwellings

0 ———— 1 km.

A. G.

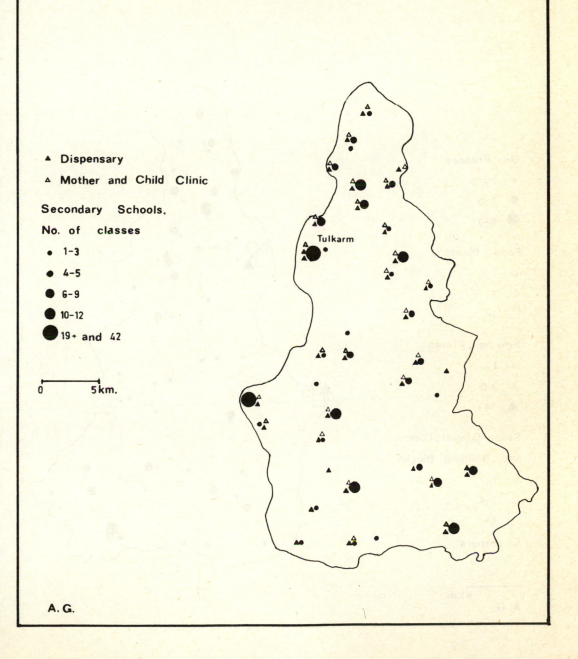

Distribution of services
Arab Sector
Tulkarm Sub-District, 1985

▲ Dispensary

△ Mother and Child Clinic

Secondary Schools,
No. of classes

• 1-3

• 4-5

● 6-9

● 10-12

● 19+ and 42

0   5 km.

Tulkarm

A.G.

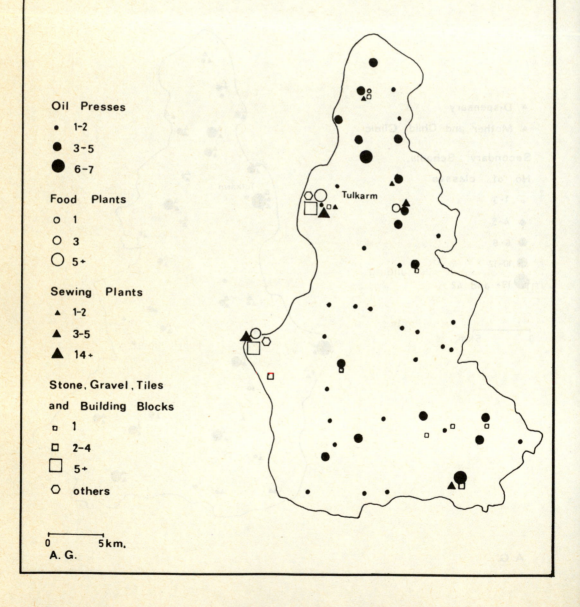

Distribution of industries
Arab Sector
Tulkarm Sub-District, 1985

Oil Presses
• 1-2
● 3-5
⬤ 6-7

Food Plants
○ 1
○ 3
◯ 5+

Sewing Plants
▲ 1-2
▲ 3-5
▲ 14+

Stone, Gravel, Tiles
and Building Blocks
▫ 1
□ 2-4
▢ 5+
⬡ others

Tulkarm

0   5km.

A. G.

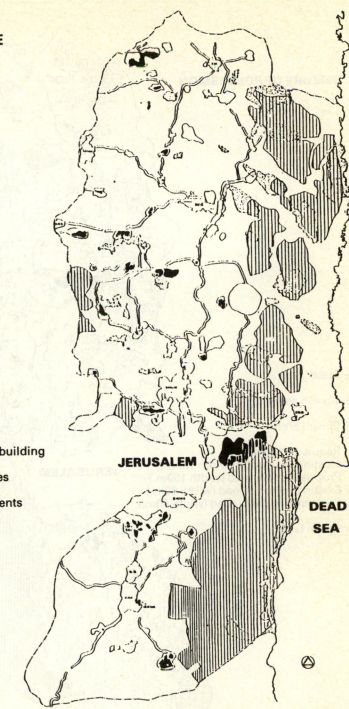

**RESTRICTIONS
ON LAND USE**

Green Line
Prohibition of building
Combat zones
Nature reserves
Arab towns
Israeli settlements

JERUSALEM

DEAD

SEA

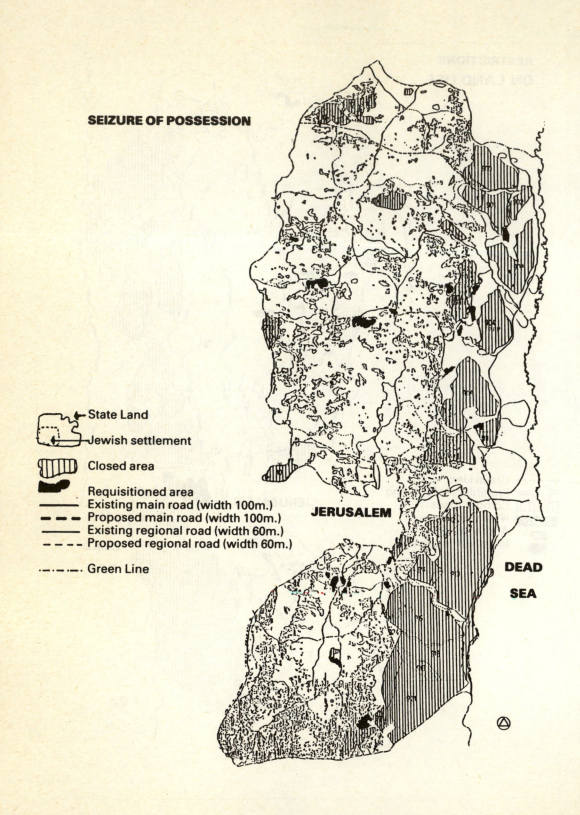

SEIZURE OF POSSESSION

State Land

Jewish settlement

Closed area

Requisitioned area

Existing main road (width 100m.)

Proposed main road (width 100m.)

Existing regional road (width 60m.)

Proposed regional road (width 60m.)

Green Line

JERUSALEM

DEAD

SEA

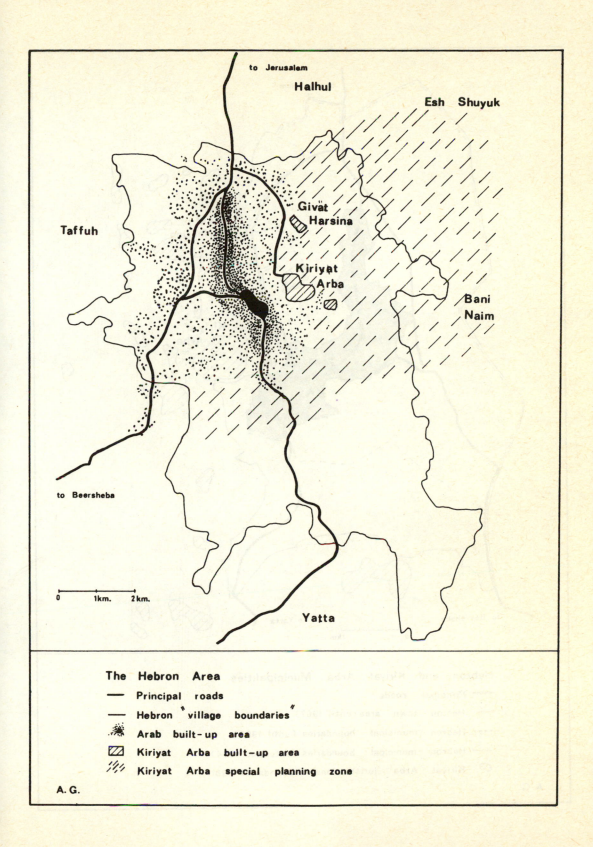

to Jerusalem

Halhul

Esh Shuyuk

Givat
Harsina

Kiriyat
Arba

Taffuh

Bani
Naim

to Beersheba

0   1km.   2km.

Yatta

The Hebron Area

— Principal roads

— Hebron "village boundaries"

Arab built-up area

Kiriyat Arba built-up area

Kiriyat Arba special planning zone

A. G.

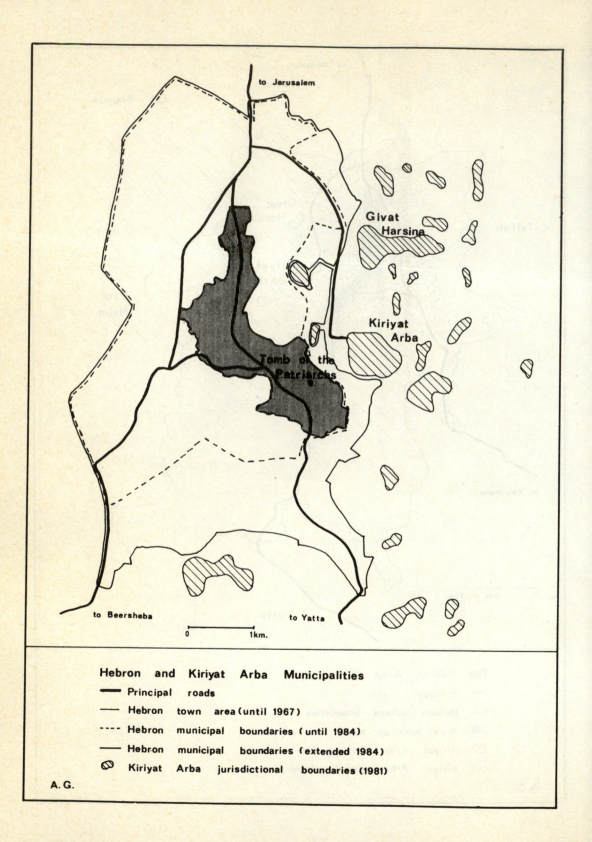

to Jerusalem

Givat
Harsina

Kiriyat
Arba

Tomb of the
Patriarchs

to Beersheba

0   1km.

to Yatta

Hebron and Kiriyat Arba Municipalities

━━━ Principal   roads

───── Hebron   town   area (until 1967)

- - - - - Hebron   municipal   boundaries (until 1984)

───── Hebron   municipal   boundaries (extended 1984)

◎ Kiriyat Arba jurisdictional boundaries (1981)

A.G.

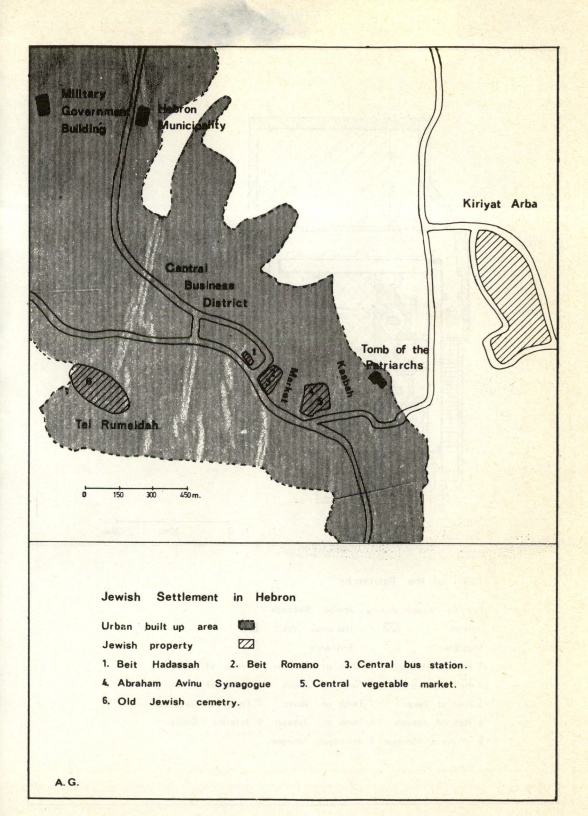

Military
Government
Building

Hebron
Municipality

Kiriyat Arba

Central
Business
District

Tomb of the
Patriarchs

Tel Rumeidah

Market

Kasbah

0   150   300   450 m.

Jewish   Settlement   in   Hebron

Urban built up area

Jewish property

1. Beit Hadassah   2. Beit Romano   3. Central bus station.

4. Abraham Avinu Synagogue   5. Central vegetable market.

6. Old Jewish cemetry.

A. G.

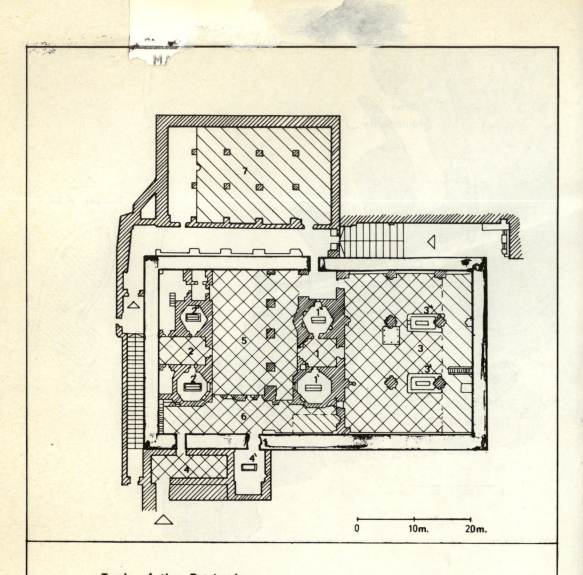

Tomb of the Patriarchs

Praying space during Jewish Sabbath

Jewish ⊠	Herodian Wall ▨	
Moslem ⧄	Entrance ▷	

1 Hall of Abraham	1ˈ Tomb of Abraham	1ˈˈ Tomb of Sarah
2 Hall of Jacob	2ˈ Tomb of Jacob	2ˈˈ Tomb of Leah
3 Hall of Isaac	3ˈ Tomb of Isaac	3ˈˈ Tomb of Rebecca
4 Hall of Joseph	4ˈ Tomb of Joseph	5 Interior Court
6 Womens Mosque	7 Jawaliyah Mosque	

A.G.